Lecture Notes of the Institute for Computer Sciences, Social Informatics and Telecommunications Engineering 242

More information about this series at http://www.springer.com/series/8197

Giancarlo Fortino · Carlos E. Palau
Antonio Guerrieri · Nora Cuppens
Frédéric Cuppens · Hakima Chaouchi
Alban Gabillon (Eds.)

Interoperability, Safety and Security in IoT

Third International Conference, InterIoT 2017
and Fourth International Conference, SaSeIot 2017
Valencia, Spain, November 6–7, 2017
Proceedings

 Springer

Editors
Giancarlo Fortino
Universita della Calabria
Rende, Cosenza
Italy

Carlos E. Palau
School of Telecommunications Engineering
Universitat Politècnica de València
Valencia, Valencia
Spain

Antonio Guerrieri
ICAR-CNR
Rende
Italy

Nora Cuppens
IMT Atlantique Bretagne-Pays de la Loire
Rennes
France

Frédéric Cuppens
IMT Atlantique Bretagne-Pays de la Loire
Rennes
France

Hakima Chaouchi
Telecom Sud Paris, Institut Mines Telecom
Evry
France

Alban Gabillon
Université de la Polynésie Française
Faaa
French Polynesia

ISSN 1867-8211   ISSN 1867-822X   (electronic)
Lecture Notes of the Institute for Computer Sciences, Social Informatics
and Telecommunications Engineering
ISBN 978-3-319-93796-0   ISBN 978-3-319-93797-7   (eBook)
https://doi.org/10.1007/978-3-319-93797-7

Library of Congress Control Number: 2018948125

This Springer imprint is published by the registered company Springer Nature Switzerland AG
The registered company address is: Gewerbestrasse 11, 6330 Cham, Switzerland

Preface

Welcome to the proceedings of the third edition of the EAI International Conference on Interoperability in IoT (InterIoT2017). We are delighted to introduce the proceedings of this conference that has brought together researchers, developers, and practitioners around the world.

While still in its infancy, the IoT domain already includes a number of implemented solutions, ranging from networked smart devices to even large-scale distributed platforms. However, the heterogeneity at all levels of these solutions is preventing different systems from interoperating effectively, despite significant efforts in the development of a unique reference standard for IoT systems technology. The situation is likely to worsen in the near future, as a lack of interoperability causes major technological and business-oriented issues such as impossibility to plug non-interoperable IoT devices into heterogeneous IoT platforms, inability to develop IoT applications exploiting multiple platforms in homogeneous and/or cross domains, slowness of IoT technology introduction at large-scale, discouragement in adopting IoT technology, increase of costs, scarce reusability of technical solutions, and user dissatisfaction.

This conference was created with the aim of investigating such lack of interoperability in the IoT realm by welcoming papers providing innovative research-oriented as well as industry-oriented contributions focusing on interoperability, integration, and interconnection of heterogeneous IoT systems, at any level. It is worth highlighting that Prof. Fortino and Prof. Palau are also partners in the H2020 ICT-30 Call INTER-IoT project having "IoT Interoperability" as the main goal.

Ten papers were selected that cover some of the main topics related to IoT development, interoperability, integration, and interconnection, from several viewpoints: device, networking, middleware, application services, semantics, and overall IoT platform.

We hope you enjoy our program and contribute to future editions of this conference. We would like to thank the Technical Program Committee for working hard in selecting the best papers that represent the intended scope of the conference.

Last but not least, we thank the authors and attendees for making this conference an interesting reality. With your help, we hope to further promote the growth of our conference series.

May 2018

Giancarlo Fortino
Carlos E. Palau
Athanasios V. Vasilakos
Antonio Liotta
Raffaele Gravina
Antonio Guerrieri

Preface

We are delighted to introduce the proceedings of the fourth edition of the 2017 European Alliance for Innovation (EAI) International Conference on Safety and Security in Internet of Things (SaSeIoT). This conference has brought together technology experts, researchers, designers, practitioners in academia, authorities, and industry experts from around the world who are leveraging and developing IoT technologies in the context of safety and security. The Fourth EAI International Conference on Safety and Security in Internet of Things (SaSeIoT 2017) was held in Valencia, Spain, on November 6, 2017, in conjunction with InterIoT 2017 conference.

This international conference attracted submissions from various countries. Each paper went through a rigorous peer-review process, with each submission receiving multiple reviews from the members of the Technical Program Committee. We could only select a few of the highest-quality papers for inclusion in the final program. Thus the technical program of SaSeIoT 2017 consisted of seven full papers in oral presentation sessions at the main conference themes. The conference themes were: Theme 1, "Ensuring the Resilience and Security of IoT-Dependent Infrastructures"; Theme 2, "Using IoT for Crisis and Emergency Management"; Theme 3, "Privacy in IoT"; and Theme 4, "Security and IoT Cloudification." The accepted papers, which focus on security, safety, and privacy issues, provided great insight into the latest research findings in the area of the Internet of Things. Aside from the high-quality technical paper presentations, the technical program also featured two excellent invited talks. The invited talks were presented by Prof. Antonio F. Skarmeta from the University of Murcia, Spain, and Prof. Juan Tapiador from Universidad Carlos III de Madrid, Spain.

We strongly believe that the SaSeIoT conference provides a good platform for all researchers, experts, developers, authorities, and professionals to discuss all safety and security technology aspects that are relevant to IoT. We would like to thank all the people who worked hard to make this conference a real success. First and foremost, we thank all authors who submitted their papers for consideration as well as all Technical Program Committee members for providing rigorous, timely reviews. We would also like to thank the European Alliance for Innovation (EAI) for its sponsorship.

November 2017

Hakima Chaouchi
Alban Gabillon
Frederic Cuppens
Nora Cuppens
Khan Ferdous Wahid

InterIoT Conference Organization

Steering Committee

Steering Committee Chair

Imrich Chlamtac   EAI/CREATE-NET, Italy

General Chairs

Nathalie Mitton   Inria, France
Thomas Noel   University of Strasbourg, France

Organizing Committee

General Chair

Giancarlo Fortino   Università della Calabria, Italy

General Co-chair

Carlos E. Palau   Universitat Politecnica de Valencia, Spain

Technical Program Committee Co-chairs

Raffaele Gravina   University of Calabria, Italy
Antonio Liotta   Eindhoven University of Technology, The Netherlands
Athanasios V. Vasilakos Lulea University of Technology, Sweden

Special Track Chairs

Nathalie Mitton   Inria, France
Thomas Noel   Université de Strasbourg, France

Web Chair

Raffaele Gravina   University of Calabria, Italy

Publicity and Social Media Chair

Marcin Paprzycki   SRIPAS, Poland

Publications Chair

Maria Ganzha   SRIPAS, Poland

Local Chair

Carlos E. Palau   Universitat Politecnica de Valencia, Spain

Conference Manager

Alžbeta Macková   European Alliance for Innovation

Technical Program Committee

Cedric Adjih   Inria, France
Stefano Basagni   Northeastern University, USA
Tengfei Chang   Inria, France
Simon Duquennoy   SICS, Sweden
Silvia Giordano   SUPSI, Switzerland
Pedro Henrique Gomes   University of Southern California, USA
Segio Ilarri   University of Zaragoza, Spain
Valerie Issarny   Inria, France
Srdjan Krco   DunavNET, Serbia
Ivan Mezei   University of Novi Sad, Serbia
Maria Ines Robles   Ericsson, Finland
Gregor Schiele   Universität Duisburg-Essen, Germany
Pere Tuset   Universitat Oberta de Catalunya, Spain
Peter van der Stok   Vanderstok Consultancy, The Netherlands
César Viho   IRISA/Université de Rennes 1, France
Qin Wang   University of Science and Technology Beijing, China

SaSeIoT Conference Organization

Steering Committee

Steering Committee Chair

Imrich Chlamtac   President of European Alliance for Innovation (EAI)

Steering Committee Members

Hakima Chaouchi   Telecom Sud Paris, Institut Mines Telecom, Evry, France
Alban Gabillon   University of French Polynesia

General Co-chairs

Hakima Chaouchi   Telecom Sud Paris, Institut Mines Telecom, Evry, France
Alban Gabillon   University of French Polynesia

Technical Program Committee Co-chairs

Frederic Cuppens   IMT Atlantic, France
Noral Cuppens   IMT Atlantic, France

Publication Chair

Wahid Khan Ferdous   Airbus, Munich, Germany

Sponsorship and Exhibits Chair

Hakima Chaouchi   Telecom Sud Paris, Institut Mines Telecom, Evry, France

Web Chair

Thomas Bourgeau   Blumenlab, France

Tutorials and Publicity Chair

Firas Al-Khalil   University College Cork

Conference Manager

Alžbeta Macková   European Alliance for Innovation

Technical Program Committee

Esma Aimeur	University of Montreal
Firas Al Khalil	University College Cork, Ireland
Ioannis Anagnostopoulos	University of Thessaly, Greece
Sergey Andreev	Tampere University of Technology, Finland
Samiha Ayed	Devoteam
Zorica Bogdanović	University of Belgrade, Serbia
Alexis Bonnecaze	Aix Marseille University, France
Daniela Cancila	CEA, Commissariat à l'énergie atomique et aux énergies alternatives
Patrick Capolsini	University of French Polynesia
Hakima Chaouchi	Telecom Sud Paris, Institut Mines Telecom, Evry, France
Richard Chbeir	Univ. Pau & Pays Adour
Frederic Cuppens	IMT Atlantique
Ernesto Damiani	Universita' degli Studi di Milano
Sabrina De Capitani Di Vimercati	Università degli Studi di Milano, Italy
Ernesto Exposito	Università de Pau et des Pays de l'Adour
Alban Gabillon	University of French Polynesia
Debiao He	Wuhan University, China
Dossi Kamal	International University of Business Agriculture and Technology, Bangladesh
Dong-Seong Kim	University of Maryland College Park, USA
Nathalie Mitton	Inria Lille - Nord Europe
Manuel Munier	University of Pau and Pays de l'Adour
Giovanni Russello	University of Auckland
Nicolas Sklavos	University of Patras, Greece
Diego Suarez	Touceda

Contents

SaSeIoT Track

InterIoT Track

A Bayesian Approach for an Efficient Data Reduction in IoT

Cristanel Razafimandimby[1(✉)], Valeria Loscrí[1], Anna Maria Vegni[2],
Driss Aourir[1], and Alessandro Neri[2]

[1] Inria Lille - Nord Europe, Lille, France
{jean.razafimandimby_anjalalaina,valeria.loscri,driss.aourir}@inria.fr
[2] Department of Engineering, Roma Tre University COMLAB
Telecommunication Laboratory, Rome, Italy
{annamaria.vegni,alessandro.neri}@uniroma3.it

Abstract. Todays, Internet of Things (IoT) is starting to occupy a major place in our everyday lives. It has already achieved a huge success in several sectors and continues to bring us a range of new capabilities and services. However, despite the apparent success, one of issues which must be tackle is the big quantity of data produced and transmitted by the objects. Transmitting these big quantity of data not only increases the energy consumption of objects but can also cause network congestion.

To meet this issue, a Bayesian Inference Approach (BIA) that can avoid the transmission of highly correlated data is proposed. An hierarchical architecture with smart devices and data centers is adopted. We evaluate our BIA approach using the data obtained from the M3 sensors deployed in the FIT IoT-LAB platform and three distinct scenarios. The obtained results prove the effectiveness of our BIA approach. The number of transmitted data and energy consumption are significantly reduced, and the information accuracy is maintained at a good level.

Keywords: Markov random fields · IoT · Belief propagation
Bayesian · Smart node

1 Introduction

Despite of the large success of IoT, there still remain a lot of problems to be solved and the management of huge amount of data produced by sensing devices is one of them. Probably, it will be difficult to store this huge amount of data locally. Therefore, exploiting the capacity of Cloud is necessary [3], but regrettably that will not be sufficient. However, it has been observed that, increasing sensor density results in a highly strong redundancy of data produced by IoT devices. In this case, uploading sensing data to the cloud can become inefficient due to memory wastage and network overhead.

To solve this problem, we proposed in [6,7] an effective and efficient Bayesian Inference Approach (BIA) for indoor and outdoor environments in the IoT context. For this aim, we used real data collected from sensor nodes deployed in

© ICST Institute for Computer Sciences, Social Informatics and Telecommunications Engineering 2018
G. Fortino et al. (Eds.): InterIoT 2017/SaSeIoT 2017, LNICST 242, pp. 3–10, 2018.
https://doi.org/10.1007/978-3-319-93797-7_1

the Intel Berkeley lab [5] and in the PEACH project [9]. Although these data allowed simulating the efficiency of our proposed approach, the lack of access to the deployed sensors did not allow us to experiment our Bayesian approach directly on the sensors. In this paper, in order to validate the scalability of our BIA approach and filter the raw data directly in the sensing nodes, we run experimentation on our FIT IoT-LAB platform [1].

One can sum up our main contributions in a few points:

- Design of a Bayesian Inference scheme that can avoid sending highly correlated data is proposed in heterogeneous IoT networks. We use Pearl's Belief Propagation (BP) algorithm [10] to predict the missing data;
- Use of smart devices (i.e., node and gateway) to decrease the prediction error and extend the lifetime of the network. Smart in the sense that the node and gateway know exactly when to send or not the data;
- Assessment of the performance using data obtained from the M3 sensors deployed in the FIT IoT-LAB platform.

The rest of this paper is organized as follows. Section 2 presents the network model for the IoT scenario. Section 3 describes our Bayesian Inference Approach which uses the BP algorithm for the data prediction. Section 4 is intended for experiments and evaluations of the proposed BIA scheme in different real scenarios. Section 5 is dedicated to the conclusion.

2   Network Model

As illustrated in Fig. 1, a BIA scheme in a cloud-based architecture with M3 sensors, smart gateways and data centers is adopted. Each entity present in our architecture has a different role according to their capabilities (e.g. communication, computation, storage). Multiple subnets associated with different

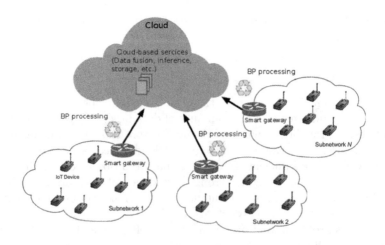

Fig. 1. A cloud-based IoT network model.

applications can be included on our network model. In our case, each subnet corresponds to one site of the FIT IoT-Lab testbed and contains interconnected IoT devices, and an intelligent gateway which forwards the raw data to the cloud. The cloud in turn is responsible for storing data and all the cloud-based services.

3   Bayesian Inference Approach

As previously reported, our first target is to cease sending highly correlated data, while maintaining a good information accuracy level. For this purpose, we propose a Bayesian Inference Approach (BIA) which is built with Pearl's Belief propagation algorithm that we will describe below.

First of all, the choice and design of the model is necessary before performing the inference procedure. In this paper, we use Probabilistic Graphical Models (PGM). PGMs are a mix of graph and probability theories where each node represents a random variable and the edges illustrate the probabilistic relationships among variables. One talks about *Bayesian networks* when the graph is directed, and *Markov Random Fields* (MRF) when the graph is undirected [8]. MRF model coupled with factor graph was chosen to perform the data inference in this paper. Hence, the main goal is to infer the state X of the sensed environment using the data sets obtained by each sensor node. Applying the Hammersley-Clifford theorem, the joint distribution $P_X(x)$ of an MRF model can be calculated as the product of all the potential functions *i.e.*,

$$P_X(x) = \frac{1}{Z} \prod_i \psi_i(x_i) \prod_{i,j \in E} \psi_{ij}(x_i, x_j), \tag{1}$$

where Z is the normalization factor, $\psi_i(x_i)$ represents the evidence function, E is the set of edges encoding the statistical dependencies between nodes i and j, and $\psi_{ij}(\cdot)$ is the potential function. It is important to highlight that the PGMs parameters (*i.e.*, ψ_i and ψ_{ij}) can be learned from the collected data by applying a learning algorithm like in [2,4].

For simplicity, in our proposed model, we have used pairwise MRF, *i.e.*, MRF with the maximum clique[1] of two nodes.

The main purpose when working with PGMs is the computation of certain marginal distributions (i.e., the inference), as as illustrated in Eq. (2). Hence, PGMs are used to infer the most likely assignment for a variable node. For the convenience of the notation, let us assume that X and Y are two different random variables with assignments $x \in \mathcal{X}^m$ and $y \in \mathcal{Y}^n$. We call hidden nodes all the nodes in Y and observed nodes those in X. So, given the i-th node in our model, the known data we intend to share (*e.g.*, pressure) will be noted as x_i and the data we want to infer, (*e.g.*, temperature) will be associated to y_i

$$p(y_v|x) = \sum_{y_1} \sum_{y_2} \cdots \sum_{y_n} p(y_1, y_2, y_3, \dots, y_n|x). \tag{2}$$

---

[1] A clique is defined as a fully connected subset of nodes in the graph.

Clearly, using (2), a direct computation of marginal probabilities would take exponential time i.e. $O(|\mathcal{Y}|^{n-1})$, which is intractable for most choices of n. Therefore, a faster algorithm like Belief Propagation (BP)[2] [10] is needed for computing the marginal probability. BP is a well known algorithm for performing inference on PGMs [10].

For the following, let note $p(y_i)$ the marginal distribution of i-th node. Then, BP algorithm is used to compute $p(y_i)$ at each node i using a message passing algorithm. The message from the i-th to the j-th node related to the local information y_i is defined as:

$$m_{ji}(y_i) \propto \int \psi_{ji}(y_j, y_i)\psi_j(y_j) \prod_{u \in \Gamma(j), u \neq i} m_{uj}(y_j)dy_j, \qquad (3)$$

where $\Gamma(j)$ represents the neighbors of node j and m_{uj} denotes the incoming messages from previous iteration. The message passing (3) will always be carried out between all nodes in the model until the convergence or if a maximum number of iterations I_{max} will be reached. Thus, the belief at the i-th node, *i.e.* the prediction, can be computed using all the incoming messages from the neighboring nodes and the local belief, *i.e.*:

$$\hat{y}_i = belief(y_i) = k \cdot \psi_i(y_i) \prod_{u \in \Gamma(i)} m_{ui}(y_i), \qquad (4)$$

where k represents a normalization constant. Finally, it is worth to highlight that the Belief propagation algorithm can compute the exact marginal probability on a tree-structured PGMs.

4   Experimental Results

In this part, the experimental results of our proposed approach with the FIT IoT-LAB testbed [1] is provided. Ten nodes from Lille site and ten nodes from Grenoble site were used for the data collection. Nodes were of the M3 type [1], which are equipped with an 32-bit ARM Cortex-M3 MCU, 64 kB of RAM, 256 kB of ROM, an IEEE 802.15.4 2.4 GHz radio transceiver and four different sensors (light, accelerometer, gyroscope, pressure & temperature). Data collected from all the M3 nodes has been used to build the BIA model. Each collection of data was done every 15 min and the collected data includes 2.5 days of readings.

During the 2.5 days of reading, we observed a good correlation between pressure and temperature (it is about -0.7720841). So, we can easily infer the temperature value from the pressure and conversely, we can also infer the pressure from temperature. In this work, we decide to infer temperature from pressure. The temperature is expressed in degrees Celsius, whilst the pressure is in mbar.

Our assessment is based on four different metrics: (*i*) the total number of transmitted data, (*ii*) average value of the estimation error (ER), (*iii*) average

---

[2] Only take linear time.

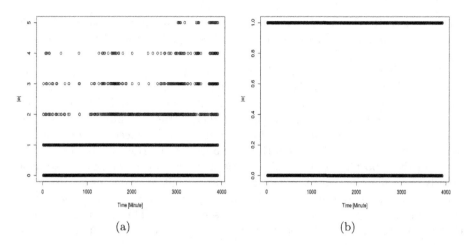

(a)   (b)

Fig. 2. Variation of $|e|$ in scenario s_2 (a), and s_3 (b) versus 2.5 days collection time.

value of the distortion level as a Mean squared Error (MSE), and (*iv*) the energy consumption (EC).

Regarding the assessments of the energy consumption, we assume that the energy cost for sending one temperature and one pressure value is 14 mW.

Furthermore, we use three different scenarios (*i.e.*, s_1, s_2, and s_3) to well assess the proposed approach.

In the first scenario s_1, the M3 node transmits to the gateway all the pressure and the temperature data it receives. In this case, no inference is performed on the gateway. In scenario s_2, the M3 nodes transmits the pressure only to the gateway, and the corresponding temperature will be inferred on the gateway using the Belief propagation algorithm. Finally, in the third scenario s_3, we set the M3 nodes as a "smart" nodes, meaning that before transmitting their data in the gateway, they first calculate the probability $\Pr(e_r|T, P)$ of doing an error of inference (e_r) on the gateway given the temperature data T, and the pressure data P. In the case where the error magnitude *i.e.*, $|e_r|$ is greater than a predefined threshold *i.e.*, $|e|_{Max}$, the M3 node transmits both pressure and temperature data to the gateway, else the M3 node only transmits the pressure, and the temperature value will be inferred in the gateway using the BP algorithm. We can model this mathematically as the probability of inference error greater than a maximum allowed value $|e|_{Max}$, and conditioned to the temperature and pressure values *i.e.*, T and h, is lower or at least equal to a given threshold P_e^{Max}, that is:

$$\Pr\{|e_r| > |e|_{Max}|T, P\} \leq P_e^{Max}, \tag{5}$$

where BP algorithm was used to compute $\Pr(e_r|T, P)$. It is important to highlight that this computation needs the knowledge of the a priori probability of inference error *i.e.*, $\Pr(e_r)$. Also, the choice of the threshold $|e|_{Max}$ value strictly depends on the application context. In our case, this value was set equal to 1 but later we will see how the choice of this value may influence our results. We can apply a similar consideration to the probability threshold P_e^{Max}, which was set to 0.5.

Table 1 illustrates the obtained results during 2.5 days of readings, for different simulated scenarios. We can observed that our proposed approach considerably decreases the total number of transmitted data and the energy consumption, while keeping a good level of inference error and information quality. We can observed also that the estimation error was reduced considerably by using the fird scenario s_3. Indeed, the M3 nodes are smarter in this case *i.e.*, by knowing the a posteriori probability of the inference error, the M3 nodes know exactly the right time and the data type to transmit in the gateway. However, this increases the total number of transmitted data (and obviously the energy consumption), as compared to the second scenario s_2. This is due to the fact that in s_2, the M3 node transmits only the pressure data without taking into account the risk of inference error in the gateway. It is important to say that we have a good quality of information in the scenario s_3 despite the fact that we have an inference error of 43%. This is due to the fact that we allow only a maximum error of one unit (i.e. $|e|_{Max} = 1$)

Table 1. Results obtained during the two days and half of readings.

Scenario	#Transmitted data	EC (kJ)	MSE	ER
s1	10440	1716.64	-	-
s2	5220	858.32	1.43	0.55
s3	5829	958.46	0.43	0.43

Figure 2 shows the variation of $|e|$ during the 2.5 days of reading using s_2 and s_3, where $|e|$ is the gap between the true and inferred values of temperature *i.e.*, $|e| = |\hat{y}_i - y_i|$. This metric represents therefore the inference error of our approach during the 2.5 days of readings. There is no inference error when $|e| = 0$, i.e., for $\hat{y}_i = y_i$. In s_2, we notice no inference error for most of time *i.e.*, the probability of having a null inference error is $Pr(|e| = 0) = 45.13\%$, while we have $Pr(|e| = 1) = 41.83\%$, $Pr(|e| = 2) = 6.91\%$, $Pr(|e| = 3) = 4.04\%$, $Pr(|e| = 4) = 1.60\%$, $Pr(|e| = 5) = 0.45\%$, and $Pr(|e| = 6) = 0\%$. Best performances are for scenario s_3, where we observe no error for the 57.32% of time, while we have $Pr(|e| = 1) = 42.68\%$ for the remaining time.

As we stated before, the choice of the threshold $|e|_{Max}$ value strictly depends on the criticality of the used system. For example we can use a bigger threshold for a tolerant system, but conversely, have to use a small value of threshold for non tolerant system. Its choice has therefore a non-negligible impact on the final results. From Fig. 3, for example, we can say that the more we use a higher threshold, the less we send data but also the more we get an inference error and the more we lose in information quality.

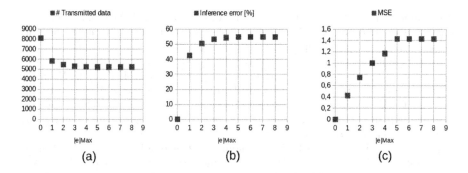

Fig. 3. Variation of (a) the transmitted data, (b) the estimation error and (c) MSE according the value of the threshold $|e|_{Max}$.

5 Conclusions

In this paper, a Bayesian Inference scheme which can avoid the transmission of highly correlated data was proposed. A good data correlation was necessary for this study. Indeed, It is important to have a good data correlation to avoid a very high error rate. Through experimentation on FIT IoT-LAB platform using the M3 nodes, we have showed that our proposed approach is scalable and decreases drastically the total number of transmitted data and the energy consumption, while maintaining a good inference error level and information quality. We have also shown that the use of smart node reduces the inference error.

Acknowledgment. This work was partially supported by a grant from CPER Nord-Pas-de-Calais/FEDER Campus Intelligence Ambiante.

References

1. Adjih, C., Baccelli, E., Fleury, E., Harter, G., Mitton, N., Noel, T., Pissard-Gibollet, R., Saint-Marcel, F., Schreiner, G., Vandaele, J., et al.: FIT IoT-LAB: a large scale open experimental IoT testbed. In: IEEE 2nd World Forum on Internet of Things (WF-IoT), 2015, pp. 459–464. IEEE (2015)
2. Dempster, A.P., Laird, N.M., Rubin, D.B.: Maximum likelihood from incomplete data via the EM algorithm. J. Roy. Stat. Soc. Ser. B (Methodological) **39**, 1–38 (1977)
3. Fortino, G., Guerrieri, A., Russo, W., Savaglio, C.: Integration of agent-based and cloud computing for the smart objects-oriented IoT. In: Proceedings of the 2014 IEEE 18th International Conference on Computer Supported Cooperative Work in Design (CSCWD), pp. 493–498. IEEE (2014)
4. Ghahramani, Z.: Graphical models: parameter learning. Handb. Brain Theory Neural Networks **2**, 486–490 (2002)
5. Hong, W., Madden, S., Paskin, M., Bodik, P., Guestrin, C., Thibaux, R.: Intel lab data. http://www.select.cs.cmu.edu/data/labapp3/index.html. Accessed 20 July 2016

6. Razafimandimby, C., Loscri, V., Vegni, A.M., Neri, A.: A Bayesian and smart gateway based communication for noisy IoT scenario. In: International Conference on Computing, Networking and Communications (2017)
7. Razafimandimby, C., Loscri, V., Vegni, A.M., Neri, A.: Efficient Bayesian communication approach for smart agriculture applications. In: IEEE 86th Vehicular Technology Conference, Toronto, Canada, p. 2017, September 2017
8. Wang, C., Komodakis, N., Paragios, N.: Markov random field modeling, inference & learning in computer vision & image understanding: a survey. Comput. Vis. Image Underst. **117**(11), 1610–1627 (2013)
9. Watteyne, T., Diedrichs, A.L., Brun-Laguna, K., Chaar, J.E., Dujovne, D., Taffernaberry, J.C., Mercado, G.: PEACH: predicting frost events in peach orchards using IoT technology. In: EAI Endorsed Transactions on the Internet of Things (2016)
10. Yedidia, J.S., Freeman, W.T., Weiss, Y.: Understanding belief propagation and its generalizations. Exploring Artif. Intell. New Millennium **8**, 236–239 (2003)

Battery Friendly Internet of Medical Media Things Networks

Sandeep Pirbhulal[1], Ali Hassan Sodhro[2,3], Aicha Sekhari[3],
Yacine Ouzrout[3], and Wanqing Wu[1(✉)]

[1] Shenzhen Institutes of Advanced Technology,
Chinese Academy of Sciences, Shenzhen, China
{sandeep,wq.wu}@siat.ac.cn
[2] Sukkur IBA University, Sukkur, Sindh, Pakistan
ali.hassan@iba-suk.edu.pk
[3] DISP LAB, University Lumiere Lyon 2, Lyon, France
{aicha.sekhari,yacine.ouzrout}@univ-lyon2.fr

Abstract. Rapid proliferation in the medical wearable device market has become the center of attention and changed the every corner of the medical world for the effective and economical information transmission, but because of the tiny size and high power drain more battery charge is consumed, so to remedy that problem this paper proposes ON-OFF Battery Friendly Algorithm (OBFA) to minimize the energy drain and hence to enhance the battery lifetime of these portable devices. Patient's bio-signals such as, electrocardiogram (ECG) data from World's larger database, i.e., PhysioNet is taken and examined with our proposed OBFA for further transmission over joint IoT and Wireless Body Sensor Networks (WBSNs). Experimental platform reveals that battery charge consumption is reduced and lifetime is improved in comparison with traditional baseline scheme.

Keywords: Battery friendly · OBFA · ON-OFF medical media
WBSNs

1 Introduction

Recently, Internet of Things (IoT) has become one of the most powerful communication paradigms of the 21st century. In the IoT paradigm, all objects in our daily life have connected to the internet because of their communication and computing capabilities including micro controllers, transceivers for digital communication. IoT encompasses the concept of the Internet and sorts it more widespread by allowing seamless interactions among different types of devices such as a medical sensor, monitoring cameras, so on. Therefore, IoT has become more productive in several areas such as healthcare system [1, 2]. The WBSNs technology is one of the most important techniques used in IoT-based current healthcare system [3]. It is an association of low-

---

First Co-Author—S. Pirbhulal and A. H. Sodhro.

© ICST Institute for Computer Sciences, Social Informatics and Telecommunications Engineering 2018
G. Fortino et al. (Eds.): InterIoT 2017/SaSeIoT 2017, LNICST 242, pp. 11–18, 2018.
https://doi.org/10.1007/978-3-319-93797-7_2

power and lightweight wireless sensor devices that are applied to observe the individuals functions and the surrounding environment. A crucial challenge in all of these wireless technologies is battery's charge consumption and short lifetime during media (i.e., ECG) streaming over joint IoT and WBSNs. The main contribution of this paper is twofold. First, we design ON-OFF Battery Friendly Algorithm (OBFA) to minimize battery charge consumption and extend the lifetime of battery-operated devices for medical health, besides OFBA is tested with ECG data sets from PhysioNet. Second, a joint IoT and WBSN framework is proposed. The rest of the paper is organized as follows. Section 2, gives related work in detail. Section 3, discusses joint IoT and WBSNs Architecture. Proposed OBFA is presented in Sect. 4. Experimental results are revealed in Sect. 5, and paper is concluded in Sect. 6.

2   Related Work

This section has two parts, first joint IoT and WBSNs, and second, battery model with recovery effect.

2.1   Joint IoT and WBSN

The advancement of WBSN in healthcare applications has made patient monitoring more feasible. Recently, several wireless healthcare types of research and projects have been proposed, which can aim to provide continuous patient monitoring, in-ambulatory, in-clinic, etc. Some of the traditional research projects about healthcare system using body sensor networks are, CodeBlue [3] a modern healthcare research project based on BSN developed at Harvard Sensor Network Lab. In this architecture, several bio-sensors are placed on patient's body. But until now battery charge consumption and its lifetime extension is still pending and is very imperative for critical healthcare applications [4].

2.2   Battery Model and Recovery Effect

Due to the emerging need of the wearable devices there is a highly demand of the battery models so this research proposes the impact of the recovery effect and the battery model by introducing the concept of the idle time (δ) between tasks during medical media transmission over joint IoT and WBSNs, as revealed by Fig. 2.

2.2.1   Battery Model

To develop the battery-efficient techniques it is very vital to clearly understand the features of the battery, because it impacts a lot on the entire platform of the medical health from diagnosis to examination. So, analytical battery model is designed by following the [5]

$$\alpha(t) = \sum_{k=1}^{N} I_k \Delta_k + \sum_{k=1}^{N} 2I_k \sum_{m=1}^{\infty} \frac{e^{-\beta^2 m^2 (L - t_k - \Delta_k)} - e^{-\beta^2 m^2 (L - t_k)}}{\beta^2 m^2} \tag{1}$$

$$\sigma(t) = \underbrace{\sum_{k=1}^{M} I_k \Delta_k}_{C(t)} + \underbrace{\sum_{k=1}^{M} 2I_k \sum_{m=1}^{\infty} \frac{e^{-\beta^2 m^2 (T-t_k-\Delta_k)} - e^{-\beta^2 m^2 (T-t_k)}}{\beta^2 m^2}}_{U(t)} \qquad (2)$$

Parameter α presents the fully charged status of battery, and the β depicts it's the non-linearity and provides information about rapid dispersal rate of the battery. The battery accomplishment will be appeared and un-available charge converts into charged ones with increased value of β. To find the battery charge depletion $\sigma(t)$ after the processing of M ($M < N$) at time T ($T < L$), then by changing N with M and L with T in Eq. (1), which gives Eq. (2). m reveals the number of tasks and T is the deadline time for finishing tasks. The battery's cost function $\sigma(t)$ in Eq. (2), includes two parts one is consumed charge $C(t)$, and other is unavailable charge $U(t)$ over time t. The $C(t)$ is the original charge value linearly connected to current I_k and time between the two packets Δ_k.

2.2.2 Recovery Effect

In Eq. (2) the empty level or unavailable charge $U(t)$ vanishes over time t when charge is drained in a non-stop manner. Figure 1, reveals that a random charge drain enhances the lifetime of a battery because of ineffective schedule and charge recovery time. For an uninterrupted charge recovery, the slant is fixed according the need. For a regular discharge nevertheless, battery regains little depleted charge, leads to piecewise-regular discharge deviation. High residual charge will be kept at top most priority than the nodes with less charge capacity with backoff time. Battery charge will be increased by one unit with probability R_{x_i, y_i} at unit i, as represented in Eq. (3).

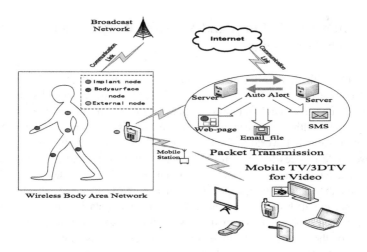

Fig. 1. Limited battery lifetime problem during medical media streaming over joint IoT and WBSNs

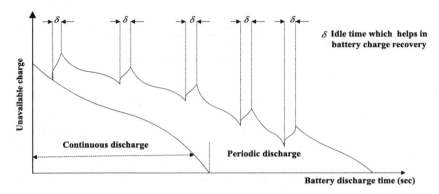

Fig. 2. Battery recovery effect during ECG data transmission over joint IoT and WBSN

$$R_{x_i, y_i} = \begin{cases} e^{-g \times (x - x_i) - \phi(y_i)} & x_i \in [1, x] \\ & y_i \in [1, y] \\ 0 & otherwise \end{cases} \tag{3}$$

Whereas, g and $\phi(y_i)$ reveals the fixed value entities and function which is helping units transferred according to battery properties, respectively. Ordinarily, the value of $\phi(y_i)$ badly encounters the battery recovery. The x and y reveals the apparent and analytical storage of the battery, subsequently. IoT platform is very powerful in which various nodes communicate with and interlinked with the wireless link, by MAC protocol's mechanism [2, 6].

3 Joint Internet of Things and Wireless Body Sensor Networks Architecture

In the recent health monitoring environment, the selection of the IoT technologies creates the convenience and ease to the hospital staff with the extended support to the other inter-related services including patient information management, real-time monitoring, and healthcare management. The WBSN is the building block to establish the path towards IoT world to facilitate the common citizen with the emergence of the tiny wearable devices [4]. So, in this paper we have proposed an architecture for ECG data packet transmission from the human body to the base station (BS) or receiver, then that data is transmitted through a wireless link (i.e., channel) to the central internet cloud. From central internet cloud, ECG data is further disseminated and observed in the wearable sensor devices. In this regard for a long time watching and analysis of the data at handheld wearable devices such as mobile, PDAs, LCDs, etc. there must be longer lifetime and less charge consumption (Fig. 3).

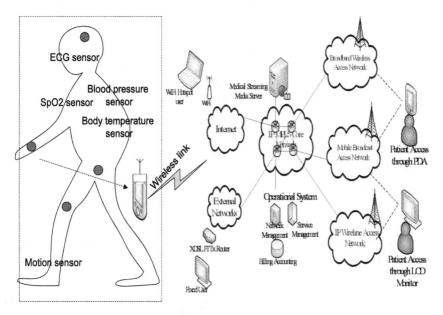

Fig. 3. Proposed joint IoT and WBSNs architecture

4 ON-OFF Battery Friendly Algorithm (OBFA)

We design OBFA which takes longer time in ECG data packet transmission in an ON and OFF manner and arranges Current values higher to lower order. Besides, OFBA avoids from increasing Current value, by dynamically adjusting the average ECG packet transmission time according to the remaining idle time and size of the backlog (i.e., buffer). The interarrival time and arrival times of ECG data packets are denoted by Δ_k, t_k, respectively, as shown in the Figs. 4 and 5. Suppose, there are M ECG data packets which are processed in the time interval $[0, T]$.

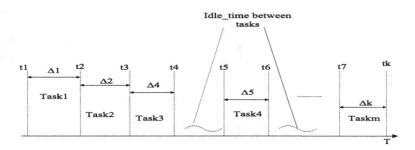

Fig. 4. ECG data packet arrival [0,T] in OBFA

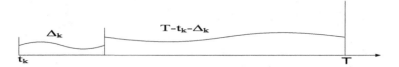

Fig. 5. Idle time of ECG data packets

$$d_M = T - t_M \tag{3}$$

$$\sum_{i=1}^{M} d_i = T \tag{4}$$

Assume the transmission period of the M deadline constraint data received by the transmission schedule is, $\vec{\tau} = [\tau_1, \tau_2, \ldots \ldots \ldots \tau_M]$. The transmission of the jth packets will be started at a time $t(0 < t < T)$.

$$\tau(j, b_j, t) = \frac{1}{M - j + 1 + b_j} \sum_{i=j}^{M} d_i \tag{5}$$

Whereby, d_i is the inter-arrival time of $(M - j + 1)$ ECG packets arrive in period (t, T) (Figs. 6 and 7).

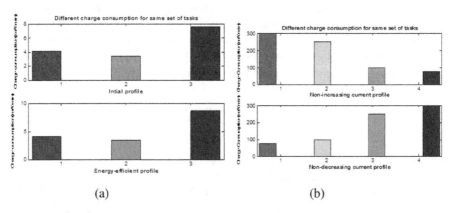

(a)   (b)

Fig. 6. (a) Charge consumption with different current profile, (b) Charge consumption with same energy

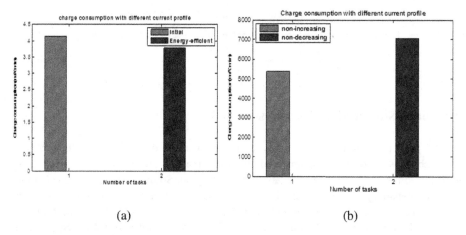

Fig. 7. (a) Charge consumption with decreasing current profile. (b) Charge consumption with increasing current profile

Table 1. Initial task specification

Task	Duration (min)	Deadline (min)	Current (mA)
1	10	25	300
2	10	25	200
3	20	25	150
4	40	25	75

5 Results and Discussion

Particular analysis in MATLAB, we used ECG data sets (average size 200 bytes) from PhysioNet, the maximum Current value I of 200 mA and packet transmission time of 7 min to minimize battery charge consumption during medical media streaming in over joint IoT and WBSN. Assume that there are four communication tasks with arrival time $t = 0$. For each transmission task, the duration, load current, and deadline are described in Table 1. It is also evident that non-increasing Current profile does significantly better, which is 9.5% improvement in the residual charge for same data set duration of only 40 min. Therefore, proposed OBFA generates load profiles that enhance battery performance, with decreasing Current value (Table 2).

Table 2. Charge consumption of OBFA and Baseline

Charge drain (σ) [mA.mint]	Supplent charge = (α − σ) [mA.mint]
1068.70	34163.3
1051.07	34180.93

6 Conclusion and Future Research Work

Battery properties are the key to analyze the performance of the entire system then to made changes accordingly in terms of lifetime enhancement during vital sign signal transmission is not equivalent to extending its life time. So the best way to broaden the lifetime of battery-driven devices is to design Battery Friendly Algorithm. We first develop a battery model according to the behavior of the IoT and WBSNs, second, we developed OFBA and tested with selected ECG data over joint IoT and WBSNs, third, due to the battery recovery effect, rate capacity, charge minimization is minimized as compared to the conventional baseline scheme. In near future IoMT and the Tele-medicine will be focused.

Acknowledgements. We gratefully acknowledge the volunteers who participated in our study. This work was supported in part by the science technology and innovation committee of Shenzhen for research projects (Grant JCYJ20160429174426094, JCYJ20170413170901569, JCYJ20151030151431727, JCYJ20150529164154046), Science and the Technology Planning Project of Guangdong Province (No. 2016A030310129 and 2014A020212257), the Guangzhou Science and Technology Planning Project (No. 201704020079), the National Key Research and Development Program of China (2016YFC1300300) and CAS President's International Fellowship for Visiting Scientists (2017VTA0011).

References

1. Sodhro, A.H., Li, Y., Shah, M.A.: Energy-efficient adaptive transmission power control in wireless body area networks. IET Commun. **10**(1), 81–90 (2016)
2. Sodhro, A.H., Li, Y., Shah, M.A.: Green and friendly media transmission algorithms for wireless body sensor networks. J. Multimed. Tools Appl. **76**, 1–25 (2017)
3. Sandeep, P., et al.: An efficient biometric-based algorithm using heart rate variability for securing body sensor networks. Sensors **15**, 15067–15089 (2015)
4. Sodhro, A.H., Fortino, G.: Energy management during video transmission in WBSNs. In: 14th IEEE International Conference on Networking, Sensing, and Control (ICNSC), pp. 16–18 (2017)
5. Rakhmatov, D., Vrudhula, S., Wallach, D.A.: A model for battery lifetime analysis for organizing applications on a pocket computer. IEEE Trans. VLSI Syst. **11**(6), 1019–1030 (2003)
6. Sandeep, P.: A comparative study of fuzzy vault based security methods for wireless body sensor networks. In: IEEE 10th International Conference on Sensing Technology (ICST), pp. 1–6 (2016)

Semantically Enriched Hypermedia APIs for Next Generation IoT

Andriy Mazayev$^{(\boxtimes)}$, Jaime A. Martins, and Noélia Correia

Centre of Electronics, Optoelectronics and Telecommunications (CEOT),
University of Algarve, Faro, Portugal
{amazayev,jamartins,ncorreia}@ualg.pt

Abstract. As the Internet of Things is gaining momentum, the number of Internet connected devices is growing exponentially, as well as the data generated by them. This raises several issues to solve in this field, most notably the ones regarding interoperability between various devices. To ease Machine-to-Machine communication, new data models must be created to explicitly describe devices and their capabilities in a standardized way. This paper discusses the IETF's *Media Types for Hypertext Sensor Markup* data model that is currently in the design process. First, we present an overview of how semantic Web technologies can be used create self-describing APIs, and then present a smart home use case that relies on these technologies.

Keywords: Web of Things · Semantic Web · Internet of Things
REST APIs · Media Types for Hypertext Sensor Markup
Machine to machine

1 Introduction

According to Cisco Systems, there are currently about 25 billion devices connected to the internet, and by the year 2020 it is expected that this number will double and reach 50 billion [1]. Cisco also estimates that Internet of Things (IoT) devices will generate around 500 zettabytes of data per year, by 2019 [2]. To deal with the massive amount of simultaneously connected devices and data produced, new infrastructure, protocols and data models, to properly annotate device data, must be created.

5G is seen as a backbone of upcoming IoT revolution as it will have staggering characteristics. According to an International Telecommunication Union draft report [3] it is expected that 5G will have at least 20 Gbps downlink and 10Gbps uplink per base station, and the connection density per square kilometre is expected to be of at least one million devices. The latency for Ultra-Reliable and Low-Latency Communications (URLLC) is expected to be as low as 1 ms. Although we are still a couple of years from seeing 5G in action, it is expected to be a perfect fit to cover the massive requirements of IoT. While the infrastructure

© ICST Institute for Computer Sciences, Social Informatics and Telecommunications Engineering 2018
G. Fortino et al. (Eds.): InterIoT 2017/SaSeIoT 2017, LNICST 242, pp. 19–26, 2018.
https://doi.org/10.1007/978-3-319-93797-7_3

issues related to IoT's growth seem to be covered by 5G, there is another and probably more important issue that still needs to be solved – the data model.

IoT technologies, so far, have focused on solving network issues, such as discovery of nearby devices, ensuring the delivery of data from a source to a destination and other Quality of Service aspects. While the delivery of the data has been solved, which data model should be used when exchanging data between devices is not. At this moment, device manufacturers have a lot of freedom to design their proprietary data models. As a result of this freedom, we have a completely fragmented IoT environment. Figure 1 is a good representation of current state of IoT. There is little to none integration between devices.

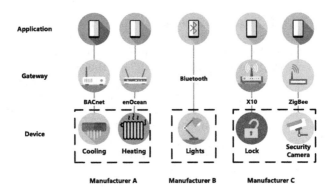

Fig. 1. The current fragmented state of IoT. One-app to one-device relationship (adapted from [4]).

The current approach to overcome these incompatibility issues is to create a proxy service, at a gateway or cloud level, that will do the translation between data models. This approach is time and money consuming, and infeasible for the enormous amount of IoT devices and data that will appear in the near future. To solve the interoperability issue and to promote ubiquitous computation, the latest research has promoted the design of specific data models that could describe explicitly devices and their capabilities. The goal is to design open source models that could be used by any manufacturer and any device. These data models are combined with standard web protocols, which have already proven to be very successful, to create something called the Web of Things (WoT). WoT is focused on data and application logic while leaving the networking problems to IoT. In this new paradigm, devices are accessed and controlled by web protocols, just as regular web pages.

This paper makes an overview of the IETF's *Media Types for Hypertext Sensor Markup* (HSML) model [5], and discusses its use for the WoT. We believe that this discussion can help foster future improvements of this model.

This paper is organized as follows: Sect. 2 introduces the HSML data model and describes its core features; Sect. 3 introduces Semantic Web technologies and discusses how their usage could improve the design of Application Programming

Interfaces (APIs) for IoT; Sect. 4 describes a Smart Home use case, with its multiple devices, that uses a semantically annotated API to create rich interactions on-the-fly; Finally, Sect. 5 has the final remarks.

2   Media Types for Hypertext Sensor Markup

HSML [5] is a reusable data model based on the REST design style for machine-to-machine interactions. It is built upon the CoRE Link-format standard specified in [6] and the SenML Internet Draft specified in [7]. It borrows some of their data structures and key identifiers to expose links and items (web resources) in a collection pattern. HSML has five core concepts:

Collection: A collection is a "document" resource that may contain: (1) a set of links that point to resources, and (2) a set of items.

Item: The items are resources that contain data (e.g., sensor readings). Items may be referenced by one or more links in one or more collections.

Link: A link exposes metadata about resources and provides hypermedia controls. Through Actions and Monitors link-extensions, it can also allow interactions with devices.

Action: An action is a hypermedia control form that informs a client about how to change (e.g., through the HTTP/COAP POST method) the state of a device. For example, an Action may represent a task of opening or closing a gate.

Monitor: A monitor is a hypermedia control, similar to CoRE Dynamic Linking [8] that observes a context resource (source) and, if the source's data satisfies some defined constraint parameters, notifies the target resource (destination). Figure 2 is a representation of a Monitor internal structure and it also shows the data flow. This is a generic service that enables the fine grained filtering of data, and allows the creation of rich interactions between resources and/or devices.

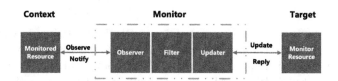

Fig. 2. Monitor internal structure and data flow (Adapted from [9])

With these simple concepts it is possible to describe virtually any device and interactions that can be done with it. Figure 3 shows a response to a GET method performed on a device that uses the HSML data model. The /sensors/ collection contains a Base Element, Links and Items. The *Base Element* is an object that specifies the context under which to interpret subsequent resources in a collection. This element contains the base URI of a collection, and optionally a time stamp indicating the encapsulated state of the collection. *Links*, as said previously, are pointers to other resources and contain metadata about those resources. The first *Link* is a self-link, as it points to the /sensors/ collection and exposes the metadata about it: a "rel" key that describes the relationship of the /sensors/ collections with itself – in this case it says that it is equal to "self" and "index". The other two *Links* describe two resources ("temp" and "humid") and their relationship with the /sensors/ collection, in this case it indicates that these resources are *Items* and it also specifies their resource type "rt". This key is an application-specific semantic noun describing the type of resource. Usually, this key is filled with a value of an ontology that explicitly describes the type of "what" is being exposed. Semantics and ontologies are discussed in more detail in Sect. 3. Finally, the two remaining elements, the *Items*, hold the data about the actual sensor readings.

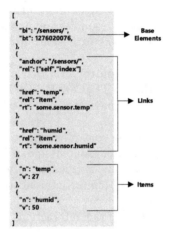

Fig. 3. Discovery of resources at /sensors/ collection

HSML content can be represented in CoRE Link [10] and SenML formats just by changing the media type (application/link-format+json or application/senml+json) of the request. This adaptability allows CoRE Link and SenML clients to interact with HSML API even without being fully compatible with it.

HSML, just as the well-known HTML, is highly flexible, as there is no fixed structure to expose resources and hypermedia controls. The developer has complete freedom in exposing device resources. The task of exploring each device (i.e., by following links), falls upon the client, in the same way as it happens with HTML.

An HSML collection is a very powerful data structure as it allows to create any combination of resources, through links that may point to any resource, and it also allows collective operations over the whole collection. For example, in a smart house scenario, it is possible to aggregate all lights of a house into a single collection or create separate collections for lights of each floor. Then, an operation over a collection containing the light's links would be performed over all resources that this collection contains; in this case it would turn on or off all the lights represented in the collection.

As HSML is based on standard web protocols, it is also easy to add authentication and permissions to access only a certain collection or resources. For example, a child may have restricted access to home appliances such as an oven or any other that may be harmful or dangerous.

3   Semantic Enrichment

Semantic Web technologies are a set of tools that enable the encoding of data and its meaning, through ontologies, in a structured way that machines are able to read, explore and comprehend. In other words, semantic tools are a standardized way to create and share metadata about data.

An ontology is an extensible representation of a knowledge model that defines a common vocabulary for classes, subclasses and properties. It can also represent complex relations and knowledge about Things or sets of Things [11]. For example, ontologies can be stored in a graph database and can be queried with SPARQL [12].

Currently, there are several initiatives to create ontologies that describe devices and their capabilities. DogOnt [13] was one of the first attempts to describe domotic systems. This ontology allows describing a device, its functionalities, location and much more.

Schema.org [14] is a collaborative and community driven organization, which is funded by Google, Microsoft, Yandex and Yahoo. Its goal it to create ontologies that explicitly describe the content of web pages and their meaning. A schema.org ontology offers a means to describe common things in everyday life, such as a person, place, company, event and much more. Given the success of Schema.org, used in over 10 million web sites, and due to the imminent arrival of the IoT revolution, the group has decided to work on an ontology to describe devices and their capabilities. The development (see [15]) is still on its initial stage, but given the popularity and large user-base, there is no doubts that this ontology will play and important role in solving the interoperability issues of devices.

Another interesting effort is being done by the W3C that created the Thing Description [16] ontology to describe devices capabilities. The core concepts of TD are very similar to the ones defined by HSML. TD defines the concept of *Property, Action, Event* and *Association* that are similar to HSML's *Item, Action, Monitor* and *Collection*. TD's concepts could be used in HSML's Links, more precisely in a Link's "rt" tag, to indicate the type of the resource being exposed. In this way a client that understands the TD could also interact, even without being fully compatible, with the HSML API.

WoT APIs, and in this case in particular the HSML API, combined with semantic Web technologies can be enriched with semantic meaning and thus create self-describing APIs, which will facilitate data integration and can ease ubiquitous computation.

SPARQL, just as the SQL in relational databases, is a language to query knowledge graphs. SPARQL contains capabilities for querying required and optional graph patterns along with their conjunctions and disjunctions [12]. This is a very powerful and expressive language that allows to discover complex relations between concepts.

The combination of ontologies, semantic APIs, the ability to store the APIs' descriptions in a single database, together with the ability to make queries (to discover devices, their capabilities, measurements and interactions) offers a unique possibility to create applications that integrate several devices, from different manufacturers, into a single application almost effortlessly.

4   Smart Home Use Case

The combination of the HSML data model with semantic annotation allows to easily build smart and adaptable systems. A Smart Home is an obvious use case where this data model can be applied. Figure 4 is an example of an architecture for such use case. This architecture has three main elements: the interface (smartphone), the gateway, and the devices.

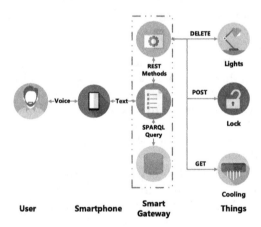

Fig. 4. Smart gateway architecture

The smartphone acts as an interface between the user and the devices. Current technologies that are available on our smartphones are able to convert (with a high degree of accuracy) human voice to text and, as such, voice commands can be easily translated into operations over the devices. Although a browser can also be used as an interface layer, we think that voice commands are more intuitive and easy to use.

The deticated gateway or the smarthpone itself [17,18] acts as a middleware between the user and the devices. When a new device is connected to the Local Area Network (LAN), the gateway will explore the device's API and store the semantically annotated data in a local database. After the completion of the exploration process, the newly connected device will be ready to use. The gateway is responsible for translation of the text commands into queries (in the case of device exploration) or REST commands (in the case of interaction with a physical device). By storing device's data at the gateway, we reduce the number of accesses that are made to the device. For example, if a client wants to know what *Actions* can be done on a certain device, the gateway can provide the answer without querying the device itself.

Finally, at the lowest level, the devices are physical objects that are digitally augmented and offer semantically enriched APIs, allowing remote interaction with them.

5   Conclusion

In this article, we discussed *Media Types for Hypertext Sensor Markup* and also exemplified how semantic Web technologies can be used to enrich this (or other) hypermedia APIs to ease interoperability and Machine-to-Machine communication. We also presented a Smart Home use case and its architecture to demonstrate how WoT APIs and semantic Web could create rich interactions between devices.

We hope that this paper may raise the awareness about some of the current limitations of IoT, and can foster community discussion about new standards, such as HSML, that try to overcome these limitations and ease ubiquitous computation.

Acknowledgment. This work was developed within the Centre for Electronic, Optoelectronic and Telecommunications (CEOT), and supported by the UID/MULTI/00631/2013 project of the Portuguese Foundation for Science and Technology (FCT).

References

1. Evans, D.: The internet of things: how the next evolution of the internet is changing everything. CISCO White Paper **1**(2011), 1–11 (2011)
2. C. V. Networking: Cisco global cloud index: Forecast and methodology, 2012–2017 (white paper) (2013)
3. I. T. U. R. S. Groups: Minimum requirements related to technical performance for IMT-2020 radio interface(s), February 2017. https://www.itu.int/md/R15-SG05-C-0040/en
4. Guinard, D., Trifa, V.: Building the Web of Things: With Examples in Node.Js and Raspberry Pi. Manning Publications Co. (2016)
5. Koster, M.: Media types for hypertext sensor markup. IETF, Internet-Draft draft-koster-t2trg-hsml-01, March 2017. https://datatracker.ietf.org/doc/html/draft-koster-t2trg-hsml-01. Work in Progress

6. Shelby, Z.: Constrained RESTful Environments (CoRE) Link Format. RFC 6690, August 2012. https://rfc-editor.org/rfc/rfc6690.txt

7. Jennings, C., Shelby, Z., Arkko, J., Keränen, A., Bormann, C.: Media Types for Sensor Measurement Lists (SenML). IETF, Internet-Draft draft-ietf-core-senml-10, July 2017. https://datatracker.ietf.org/doc/html/draft-ietf-core-senml-10. Work in Progress

8. Shelby, Z., Vial, M., Koster, M., Groves, C.: Dynamic Resource Linking for Constrained RESTful Environments. IETF, Internet-Draft draft-ietf-core-dynlink-03, March 2017. https://datatracker.ietf.org/doc/html/draft-ietf-core-dynlink-03. Work in Progress

9. Rest design patterns for robust asynchronous notification. https://github.com/hyperstate/hyperstate-docs/blob/master/RESTfulNotification.pdf. Accessed 25 July 2017

10. Li, K., Rahman, A., Bormann, C.: Representing Constrained RESTful Environments (CoRE) Link Format in JSON and CBOR. IETF, Internet-Draft draft-ietf-core-links-json-09, July 2017. https://datatracker.ietf.org/doc/html/draft-ietf-core-links-json-09. Work in Progress

11. Yu, L.: A Developer's Guide to the Semantic Web. Springer, Heidelberg (2014). https://doi.org/10.1007/978-3-662-43796-4

12. SPARQL query language for RDF. https://www.w3.org/TR/rdf-sparql-query/. Accessed 25 July 2017

13. Bonino, D., Corno, F.: DogOnt - ontology modeling for intelligent domotic environments. In: Sheth, A., Staab, S., Dean, M., Paolucci, M., Maynard, D., Finin, T., Thirunarayan, K. (eds.) ISWC 2008. LNCS, vol. 5318, pp. 790–803. Springer, Heidelberg (2008). https://doi.org/10.1007/978-3-540-88564-1_51

14. Schema.org. http://schema.org/. Accessed 25 July 2017

15. Iot and schema.org: Getting started. http://iot.webschemas.org/docs/iot-gettingstarted.html. Accessed 25 July 2017

16. Web of things (wot) thing description. https://w3c.github.io/wot-thing-description/. Accessed 25 July 2017

17. Aloi, G., Caliciuri, G., Fortino, G., Gravina, R., Pace, P., Russo, W., Savaglio, C.: A mobile multi-technology gateway to enable IoT interoperability. In: IEEE Internet-of-Things Design and Implementation, pp. 259–264 (2016)

18. Aloi, G., Caliciuri, G., Fortino, G., Gravina, R., Pace, P., Russo, W., Savaglio, C.: Enabling IoT interoperability through opportunistic smartphone-based mobile gateways. J. Netw. Comput. Appl. **81**, 74–84 (2017)

Smart Devices for Automated Emergency Calls

Mihai Buf[1], Barbara Guerra[2], and Marco Manso[2(✉)] (iD)

[1] Orange Romania, Bucharest, Romania
[2] Rinicom, Lancaster, UK
marco@rinicom.com

Abstract. The Internet-of-Things (IoT) promises to transform our society into smart environments, incorporating smart objects that cooperate to fulfil specific goals. Amongst its many applications, emergencies can also benefit from IoT principles and use of automation for a better emergency response and reducing the number of fatalities. Smart devices can be used to detect emergency events (e.g., fire, presence of hazardous gases) and automatically trigger alerts to emergency services. However, emergency services today mostly rely on circuit-switch networks and audio-based calls. Therefore, in this paper, we describe our concept to apply the IoT paradigm to the concept of automated calls, in which audio calls are generated from preformatted messages and a text-to-speech engine. Supported by an implemented prototype, our approach brings the benefits of automated calls without requiring significant investments to the infrastructure and systems of emergency services.

Keywords: Internet of Things · Text-to-speech · Emergency services

1 Introduction

The Internet-of-Things (IoT) promises to transform our society into smart environments, environmentally aware and well informed about its wellbeing, interests and security. IoT refers to the extension of the Internet paradigm to the world of objects and places, each able to communicate their own data and access aggregated information from other objects and places. Building blocks of the future IoT, smart objects cooperate to fulfil specific goals [1] finding applications across many societal domains - including agriculture, energy, environment, health and security - providing "live" capabilities such as monitoring, processing and actuation. Their presence is becoming ubiquitous and global: Gartner forecasted that 8.4 billion connected things will be in use worldwide by 2017 and will reach 20.4 billion by 2020 [2].

The emergency services sector is not immune to the penetration of IoT concepts and applications.

Emergency Services (ES) deal with urgent life threatening situations that require a swift response. While they mainly rely on voice calls (via the 112 number for most of Europe), initiatives like eCall, part of the eSafety initiative of the European Commission [3], represents a most notable and successful effort in bringing automated calls and data exchange with ES into reality. The eCall is applied to the specific event of a car accident: if the car's sensors detect a crash, the car automatically calls the nearest

© ICST Institute for Computer Sciences, Social Informatics and Telecommunications Engineering 2018
G. Fortino et al. (Eds.): InterIoT 2017/SaSeIoT 2017, LNICST 242, pp. 27–37, 2018.
https://doi.org/10.1007/978-3-319-93797-7_4

emergency centre. Even if no passenger is able to speak, e.g. due to injuries, a 'Minimum Set of Data' is sent, which includes the exact location of the crash site[1], the time of incident, the accurate position of the crashed vehicle and the direction of travel. The eCall concept was designed having in mind circuit switched emergency calls, specifically working in 2G and 3G networks using an in-band modem [4]. Despite, it is expected that eCall cuts emergency services response time by up to 50% in the countryside and 40% in urban areas. It is estimated that eCall can reduce the number of fatalities by at least 4% and the number of severe injuries by 6% [5].

Further applications can be deployed to the benefit of citizens. As proposed in [6], these include eHealth, Smart Building applications and the next generation eCall that fully exploit IoT concepts, IP and packet switched networks.

Despite novel approaches for ES, such as those taken by the EU funded action NEXES (Next Generation Emergency Systems) [7], which embrace IP technologies and data exchange, ES worldwide mainly rely on circuit switched voice calls.

This paper presents a concept supported by a prototype implementation that applies smart devices and IoT concepts to the ES context. It brings the benefits of automated features, sensor data and data processing while supporting legacy voice emergency calls thus able to operate with any ES deployed nowadays.

The remainder of this paper is structured as follows. It starts by presenting a fictional but representative use-case of a smart plant that had a chemical leak incident causing harm to humans. It then presents the overall concept to generate automated calls (from sensors to ES), followed by describing the system high-level architecture, including interfaces, protocols and components. The system workflow is then described, presenting the sequencing between the relevant steps, followed by the structure of the emergency messages. This paper finalises with the conclusions.

2   Emergency Use Case: Smart Chemical Plant

This section describes the use-case of a chemical plant that uses smart sensors and automated alerts to generate automatic emergency calls in a situation where human intervention is not possible. It is based on a use-case described in [8].

In the early hours of the morning, a tank at a small chemical plant develops a breach and hazardous materials begin leaking out. The security guard investigates the incident but fails to follow the appropriate security precautions and is quickly taken ill upon inhalation of noxious fumes. The guard attempts to call for assistance using his mobile device. Before being able to initiate the call, the guard loses consciousness.

Because the NEXES System has been adopted at the chemical plant, an automated emergency call via the NEXES telematics function is triggered following the detection of unusual and dangerous levels of chemicals in the air by installed sensors. Text-to-speech (TTS) is generated to convert a pre-defined message - describing the emergency type and, if relevant, incorporating sensor data - into audio in a form that can be understood by call takers operating in legacy ES. Upon receiving this automatic call,

---

[1] https://ec.europa.eu/digital-single-market/en/ecall-time-saved-lives-saved.

the emergency call taker develops awareness of the emergency situation and dispatches relevant personnel and resources, including specialist containment and decontamination crews and personal protective equipment.

This *futuristic* scenario highlights the potentially vital role of telematics in specific emergency scenarios. The use of telematics and automated calling means that in situations in which citizens are incapacitated, emergency services can still be timely contacted and properly informed about the incident, thus enhance the emergency response in terms of response time, the safety of the citizen and, in this situation, the safety of first responders as well.

3   Automated Emergency Calls for Legacy ES

The concept described in this paper consist in deploying IoT systems to perform sensing and incident detection together with components capable to trigger specific actions - specifically initiate an emergency call - and convert digital messages into audio in a form that can be received and understood by any ES nowadays.

The system concept overview is presented in Fig. 1. It comprises one or more connected sensors (i.e., smart devices) responsible for measuring specific physical quantities of interest and detecting key events (e.g., heart rate monitoring, seismic activity, gas concentration and smoke detection). The sensors communicate with a Gateway/Hub that collects sensor data and can further run data fusion and processing capabilities that may contribute to increase detection reliability (e.g., both fire and smoke sensor detect a relevant event). The Hub also has the capability to generate event messages into audio (using its TTS engine) and, for our specific use-case, initiate emergency calls[2] using the public network.

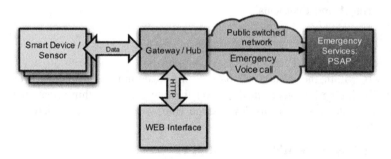

Fig. 1. System concept overview

Additionally, a web interface is devised allowing the user to perform management functions such as system configuration, reporting, alert recipient configuration, etc.

---

[2] Other approaches could instead opt for calling the owner phone or a service operator.

The chosen configuration allocates eventual "heavy" computational tasks, such as data processing and TTS, to the Hub. The sensors are often resource constrained devices[3] thus their requirements are "lightweight".

4 System Architecture, Interfaces and Protocols

Our proposed setup for automated emergency calls considers smart devices in a cluster configuration connected to a Hub (within a LAN or via a router). The Hub manages the sensor clusters and performs functions such as sensor data processing and initiation of emergency calls. Note that in our setting, sensors are installed in fixed locations. Next, we present the high level architecture of the system (focusing on the Hub components) and describe its main interfaces. The high level architecture is depicted in Fig. 2.

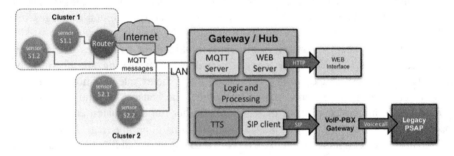

Fig. 2. High level architecture

4.1 Interfaces and Protocols

All-Over-IP.
The Internet Protocol (IP) is chosen as common protocol between all devices and components within the system. IP has become a dominant technology worldwide successfully linking billions of devices over the Internet and within private networks. IP is used to interconnect smart devices, the Hub, web-clients and initiation of calls (using SIP).

Sensor Data Exchange Middleware: MQTT.
The Message Queue Telemetry Transport (MQTT) is a message broker middleware based on the publish-subscribe paradigm standardised as ISO/IEC PRF 20922 (ISO/IEC 20922:2016). It has become very popular in the IoT community given its lightweight Client Server publish-subscribe messaging transport protocol, making it fit for resource-constrained devices.

---

[3] The resource constraints can be related to low processing power, low memory and low power, as well as network constraints.

Smart devices share information using MQTT, by publishing information to specific topics. The Hub receives data from sensors by subscribing to those topics.

Management Interface: HTTP.
The HUB system management is performed over the Hypertext Transfer Protocol (HTTP) supported by most web browsers.

Emergency Calls: SIP, TTS and PBX Gateway.
Our concept involves the automated establishment of an emergency call to emergency services (specifically, a Public Answering Safety Point (PSAP)) in case of an emergency. For this purpose, the Hub supports the SIP protocol, which is widely used for IP telephony all over the world. Additionally, to "reach" the legacy public switched telephone network (PSTN), a VoIP-PBX gateway is added to convert SIP signalling and VoIP to a form supported by PSTN. To generate audio, the Hub uses its TTS engine.

4.2   Hub System Architecture

The Hub architecture is designed taking in consideration the following main requirements:

- The Hub shall connect multiple sensors and smart devices via MQTT protocol;
- The Hub shall be able to process sensors' data and reliably determine the occurrence of an emergency situation;
- The Hub shall be able to establish SIP calls;
- The Hub shall generate TTS to generate audio to be streamed as part of a SIP call (the audio message should contain caller information and type of incident, including "live" sensor data if relevant);
- The Hub shall store information about caller - such as name, address, location - and make it available for the PSAP in case of emergency.

The Hub main components allowing to realise the above requirements are described next.

MQTT Server.
The MQTT Server manages publishers, subscribers and data exchange. It is responsible for message management, based on the publish/subscribe paradigm, disseminating messages to subscribers when these are published.

In our configuration, each sensor (i.e., publisher) has a specific topic to which it publishes messages (i.e., sensor data or alert). Via MQTT, the Hub allows authorised users to subscribe to sensor messages to e.g., monitor the area and be notified in case of emergencies. Internally, the "Logic and Processing", described later, also subscribes to sensor messages.

SIP Client.
The Hub includes a SIP client in order to be able to initiate SIP calls in case emergencies are detected. The SIP Client performs all required steps for setup (e.g., registration) and manage calls (e.g., initiation, establishment and termination).

TTS.

The TTS engine allows to convert text messages to audio. It requires significant processing and storage capabilities (typically above 1 GHz processor and several Mbytes of storage for audio voice files) typically not present in sensor devices.

Web-Server.

The Web-server allows the remote configuration and management of the Hub (and the system). It allows the user or administrator perform functions like system configuration (e.g., security, setup users, setup sensors), generate reports, configure recipients of alerts, "live" monitor the system, etc. It also allows to setup emergency events (e.g., fire), workflows and associated messages (see Sect. 5).

Logic and Processing.

The "Logic and Processing" is a central element of the Hub. It receives sensor data (via MQTT) and processes it to determine the occurrence of an emergency event and, if so, triggers related actions such the automatic initiation of an emergency call. In order to ensure high levels of reliability (even a small number of false positive or false negative detections are not acceptable in ES) techniques such as Complex Event Processing (CEP), which combine and correlate data from multiple sources to identify events, might be explored, as proposed in [10].

5   Workflow

The workflow related with our implementation of automated calls based on smart devices is depicted in Fig. 3 and described next.

The process starts with the **initialisation** procedure where the system setup and configuration is performed, including establishment of MQTT topics (to where sensors publish messages), SIP client registration, and the fulfilment of required authentication steps. After initialisation, the system enters a continuous loop. In it, each smart device **measures** their parameters of interest (for example, temperature, gas concentration or smoke detection) and publish the **value** using **MQTT** according to the defined criteria (e.g., raw measurement, measurement when above a certain threshold value or event) and to the appropriate topic.

The Hub **reads the sensors' values**, by receiving MQTT messages published in topics it subscribed.

The Hub then processes received messages to determine if there is an emergency situation (when out of **"value safe side"**), which can be based on direct sensor data (e.g., a smoke sensor produces a message with value "true" for fire indication), a threshold value for sensor data (e.g., the sensor temperature is above 60 °C) or the result from correlating data between multiple sensors (e.g., temperature sensor report values above 60 °C and smoke sensor indicates presence of fire). It is critical that this step is highly reliable otherwise, in case of false positives, false emergencies are reported (resulting in unnecessary deployment of resources) or, in case of true negatives, emergencies are missed (resulting in loss of material and possibly lives).

In case an emergency is detected, an emergency call is automatically initiated. In addition, a **local alarm** can be triggered as well to pre-defined recipients.

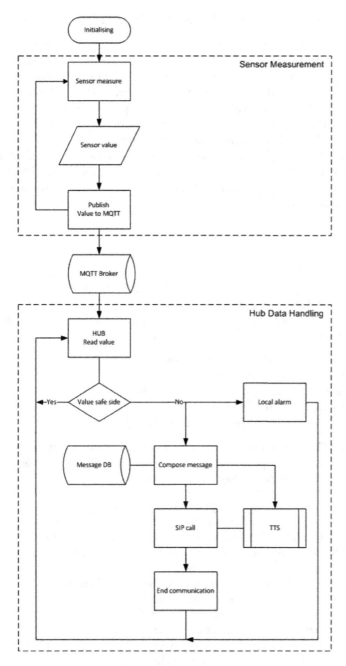

Fig. 3. Automated call workflow

The following steps are taken when **establishing an emergency call**:

- Based on the emergency type and using a database of predefined messages (**message DB**), **a text message is composed** containing pertinent information about the emergency, which includes type of incident, date&time and sensor information (where relevant), but also caller information (name, address and location);
- Initiate a **SIP outgoing call** to the emergency services (which will use the VoIP/PBX Gateway to reach the PSTN and subsequently the PSAP);
- Once the call is initiated, activate the **TTS engine** to convert the text message to audio (and thus automatically report the emergency in a human understandable form). To ensure the message is received and understood by the PSAP (human) operator, it can be replayed a number of times (in our case, we set to 3 times);
- Terminate the call.

6   Messages

During an emergency call, audio is generated from a text message that is built based on the type of event. Given the context of our application, the generated message needs to be simple, easy to understand and contain all relevant information for emergency services to react. As such, the text message should contain:

- The indication that it is an automatic message;
- Information about the type of emergency;
- Information about the subscriber/user (subscriber name);
- Location information (civic address);
- Optionally, associated sensor information when useful.

Example of pre-formatted messages, for situations of fire detection and abnormal temperature detection, are presented next. Note that dynamic fields inside brackets are filled based on configuration values or sensor data.

Fire emergency predefined message:
sipspeakfire: linphonecsh generic "speak default This is an automated emergency call from {{subscriber name}} home, address is {{civic address}}. Fire detected inside home. Please help."
High abnormal temperature predefined message:
sipspeakfire: linphonecsh generic "speak default Environment alarm at {{subscriber name}} home, address is {{civic address}}. The temperature is {{tdata}} degree. The humidity is {{hdata}}%. Please help."

7   Prototype Results

We implemented a simple prototype consisting of several deployed sensors (e.g., temperature, humidity, smoke, fire) and one Hub. For management, configuration and remote access the "Home Assistant" automation platform[4] was used.

For test purposes, a simulated PSAP supporting SIP was used (thus no VoIP-PBX Gateway was deployed). All data was exchanged within a local network.

Figure 4 presents collected sensor data in graphical form pertaining to smoke, temperature and humidity sensors. On top, it is shown the moment an event is triggered caused by the temperature sensor being above a predefined threshold (in our example, set to 35 °C, bar changing from blue to orange). The event initiated a SIP call with the simulated PSAP. The conveyed message was a "High abnormal temperature", containing temperature data, in audio form.

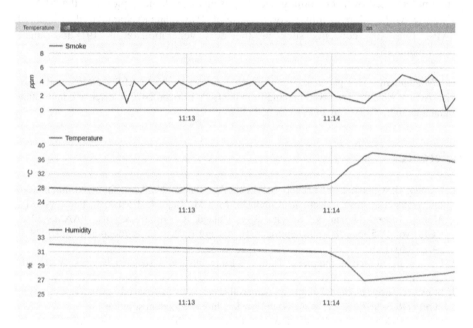

Fig. 4. Example of sensor data visualisation and event triggering (Color figure online)

8   Conclusion

The IoT paradigm and increasing presence of smart devices across all sectors of society continues to find new applications including in emergencies. The eCall initiative brought the concept of automated calls in situations of serious car accidents, aiming to improve emergency response time and reduce the number of fatalities. It is reasonable

---

[4] https://home-assistant.io.

to expect that other types of emergencies may benefit from this concept as well. In this paper, we presented the application the IoT paradigm to the concept of automated calls, specifically addressing smart buildings, where information provided by smart devices can be used to detect emergency events, such as fire and chemical gas contamination. Leveraged by widely used technologies and protocols in IoT (e.g., IP, MQTT), our application considers the legacy nature of ES and PSAP specifically, which mainly operates with audio-based calls. As such, we proposed a (simple) concept in which audio calls are generated from preformatted messages and TTS engine. In this way, IoT and the concept of automated calls can be implemented without requiring significant changes (and investments) to the ES infrastructure and systems.

Future work will include the application of CEP for improved reliability and security recommendations to protect the system from potential misuse and/or malicious exploitation. Furthermore, considering the forecasted evolution for next generation ES to be implemented over the coming decades, as envisaged and explored in the NEXES Action, we will explore in future work the use of IP and data exchange to data-enabled PSAPs, following concepts such as the next generation eCall [9] and smart environments [6].

Acknowledgment. This paper has been prepared as part of the NEXES Research and Innovation Action, which has received funding from the EU's Horizon 2020 research and innovation programme under Grant Agreement No. 653337.

References

1. Fortino, G., Guerrieri, A., Lacopo, M., Lucia, M., Russo, W.: An agent-based middleware for cooperating smart objects. In: Corchado, Juan M., Bajo, J., Kozlak, J., Pawlewski, P., Molina, Jose M., Julian, V., Silveira, R.A., Unland, R., Giroux, S. (eds.) PAAMS 2013. CCIS, vol. 365, pp. 387–398. Springer, Heidelberg (2013). https://doi.org/10.1007/978-3-642-38061-7_36
2. Gartner, Inc.: Forecast: Internet of Things — Endpoints and Associated Services, Worldwide (2016)
3. https://ec.europa.eu/digital-single-market/ecall-time-saved-lives-saved
4. 3GPP TR 26.967 V8.0.1: eCall Data Transfer; In-band modem solution
5. European Commission: Road safety statistics: what is behind the figures? La Valette, 28 March 2017. http://europa.eu/rapid/press-release_MEMO-17-675_en.htm
6. Manso, M., Guerra, B., Carjan, C., Sdongos, E., Bolovinou, A., Amditis, A., Donaldson, D.: The application of telematics and smart devices in emergencies. In: Gravina, R., Palau, Carlos E., Manso, M., Liotta, A., Fortino, G. (eds.) Integration, Interconnection, and Interoperability of IoT Systems. IT, pp. 169–197. Springer, Cham (2018). https://doi.org/10.1007/978-3-319-61300-0_9
7. NEXES. http://nexes.eu
8. Manso, M., Amditis, A., Carjan, C., Donaldson, D., Guerra, B., Jigman, A., Sdongos, E.: The application of telematics and smart devices in emergencies. In: Proceedings of 2016 IEEE First International Conference on Internet-of-Things Design and Implementation (IoTDI), Berlin, Germany, 4–8 April 2016

9. Gellens, R., Tschofenig, H.: Next-Generation Pan-European eCall, draft-ietf-ecrit-ecall-07. txt, The Internet Engineering Task Force, 19 February 2016. https://tools.ietf.org/html/draft-ietf-ecrit-ecall-07

10. Chen, C.Y., et al.: Complex event processing for the Internet of Things and its applications. In: 2014 IEEE International Conference on Automation Science and Engineering (CASE), pp. 18–22, August 2014

A Standardizable Network Architecture Supporting Interoperability in the Smart City Internet of Things

Cathryn Peoples[✉]

Ulster University, Cromore Road, Coleraine BT52 1SA, UK
c.peoples@ulster.ac.uk

Abstract. An increase of 2.5 billion people is expected in urban areas by 2050, when 66% of the world population will reside here. It is therefore reasonable to assume a parallel growth in the smart city Internet of Things (IoT). A challenge, however, is presented in the interoperability between the devices deployed, limited due to the ad hoc and proprietary ways which systems have been rolled out to date. A standardized network infrastructure specific to the IoT can work towards resolving the challenges. This approach to operation, however, raises questions with regard to how an architecture may support different devices and applications simultaneously, and additionally be extensible to accommodate applications and devices not available at the time of the framework's development. In this paper, these questions are explored, and an IoT infrastructure which accommodates the interoperability communication constraints and challenges today is proposed.

Keywords: Internet of Things (IoT) interoperability · Context data
Network protocols · Quality of Service (QoS) · Smart city · Standardization

1 Introduction

An increase of 2.5 billion people is expected in urban areas by 2050, when 66% of the world population will reside here. Parallel growth in the smart city Internet of Things (IoT) may subsequently also be anticipated. A challenge is presented, however, in the limited interoperability between solutions currently deployed, which is restricted due to the ad hoc and proprietary ways which systems have been rolled out to date. This is a well-recognized problem and different solutions have previously been proposed to support interoperability, as in [1, 2], for example; the work in these papers explores the use of gateways to facilitate interoperability. In this paper, on the other hand, a contrasting approach is presented with the argument that a standardized network infrastructure for the IoT can work towards resolving interoperability challenges by facilitating a common approach to communication between devices and data repositories. This builds on the promise of the INTER-IoT concept, which is working on the principle that, *"Open interoperability delivers on the promise of enabling vendors and developers to interact and interoperate, ..., the INTER-IoT voluntary approach will support and make it easy for any IoT stakeholder to design open IoT devices, smart*

© ICST Institute for Computer Sciences, Social Informatics and Telecommunications Engineering 2018
G. Fortino et al. (Eds.): InterIoT 2017/SaSeIoT 2017, LNICST 242, pp. 38–45, 2018.
https://doi.org/10.1007/978-3-319-93797-7_5

objects, services, and complex systems and get them to be operative and interconnected quickly, ..." [3]. While recognized by a body of researchers as necessary, the interoperable approach to operation raises questions with regard to how an architecture can simultaneously meet the requirements of different devices and applications: Can a 'one-size-fits-all' architecture support all operations anticipated in a smart city IoT? Can a common protocol support data transfer from all devices to a centralized cloud repository? To what extent will operation of the smart city be application-agnostic and therefore encourage interoperability? In this paper, these questions are explored, and a future smart city IoT network infrastructure which will overcome interoperability communication constraints and challenges is proposed.

2 Smart City IoT: The Need for a Standardizable Architecture

The need to develop a smart city IoT infrastructure is dependent on the scope with which we consider smart cities to exist: The term 'smart city' has recently evolved and, due to the fact that a single standardized architecture has not been made available by the Internet Engineering Task Force (IETF), the term is open to variation in its interpretation. A smart city is considered, for example, by the European Smart Cities to be one, "*performing in 6 characteristics built on the 'smart' combination of endowments and activities of self-decisive, independent and aware citizens*" [4]. This takes into account smart economy, mobility, governance, environment, people and living. Their concept agrees with a definition from the Department for Business Innovation & Skills (BIS), which defines a smart city as, "*an environment in which the citizen is a more active and participative member of the community, providing feedback on the quality of services*" [5]. These definitions agree in that the smart city focus is on the empowerment of its citizens. The BIS take this concept further, with the idea that the smart city, as a result of empowering the human population, becomes a dynamic environment in which the city becomes more livable and resilient, and therefore more able to respond quickly to challenges [5].

Other parties consider the smart city from a technical perspective: For the European Commission, for example, "*A smart city is a place where the traditional networks and services are made more efficient with the use of digital and telecommunication technologies for the benefit of its inhabitants and businesses*" [6]. The Innovation Cities Program also considers the technical perspective, with 'smart city' being a, "*term commonly used to refer to the creation of a knowledge infrastructure*" [7], where it is the data collected from the network and connected devices that drives intelligent operation as opposed to any role played by humans. In this view, the technology influences the role played by people in smart cities, and is provisioned with an assumption that users desire specific capabilities.

While these definitions each focus on a distinct perspective (i.e., from the technology or human viewpoint), other perceptions of smart cities recognize the role to be played simultaneously by both humans and technology. One definition which includes both contributors comes from Smart City Networks, for which a smart city, "*provides technologies that make our destinations smarter places to visit, live, and play*" [8].

This definition accommodates the idea that, as the ease with which solutions can be made available improves through more supportive technology, the extent to which smart technologies meet the desires of citizens grows in parallel. Both citizens and technology are therefore seen as essential in facilitating a successful infrastructure: "*Without Smart, Connected People, There are No Smart Cities*" [9].

It is interesting that, as technologies within the IoT become less focused on health, safety or government-oriented objectives (e.g., as in [10–12]) and move towards having more socially-aligned goals such as retail or leisure, it becomes more challenging to identify *show-case* deployments. Of course they exist, through the applications developed by individual users, but they are less likely to be advertised as *exemplar* solutions by city-wide working groups such as EuroCities [13] or Future Cities [14]. This confirms the early stage of evolution at which the smart city IoT is, through the fact that it is bodies with high levels of technical expertise who are developing solutions which are attractive to large user groups. To fulfil the visions of smart cities described above however, it will be necessary to develop an infrastructure that motivates the general public to engage, with the assumption that it will be them, and not industry, who will contribute solutions so that, "*the citizen is a more active ... member of the community*" and cities are "*smarter places to visit, live and play*".

Given that the technologies have, in general, been deployed by major technical players, IoT capability today requires that a city has a level of IT intelligence to use the data collected from connected devices, to integrate software solutions to meet smart city objectives, and to develop applications supported across a range of devices. As a result, we live within a smart city IoT where solutions are vendor and application-specific (e.g., as in [15–17]), and are not readily deployable by parties without a technical skillset. It can be assumed, however, that the majority of people who will want to use smart city technology have expertise beyond IT. There is therefore an opportunity that groups participating in the smart city can contribute their knowledge to facilitate wider goals of the IoT in solutions which meet the needs of users in an ad hoc manner. Current network architectures are missing capabilities which fulfil these expectations of the IoT, and as a result rapid application roll-out and intelligent data use is not possible by a user base with a wide range of expertise.

3   State-of-the-Art IoT Technology

In recognition of the limitations of technical solutions provided by industry in terms of their ability to achieve the envisaged perspective of the IoT, individual bodies are contributing solutions in an attempt to open the environment to allow implementation by a wider group than at present. The Smart Cities Council, for example, is working towards 2030 [18] with their vision of smart cities. Their framework consists of technology enablers (instrumentation and control, connectivity, interoperability, security and privacy, data management, and analytics) to facilitate perceived smart city responsibilities in the areas of the built environment, energy, telecommunications, transportation, water, health and human service, public safety, and payments. With partners which include Mastercard, IBM, Microsoft, Mercedes-Benz, Cisco, Verizon and Qualcomm, the Council is working on citizen engagement strategies and tools, financing and procurement tools, and policy frameworks and tools. Their concepts and ideas are far-reaching, but their solutions remain to be standalone.

As another example, AllSeen Alliance [19] is a consortium whose mission is, "*To enable widespread adoption and help accelerate the development and evolution of an interoperable peer connectivity and communications framework ... for devices and applications in the Internet of Everything*". The technology makes use of the *AllJoyn* open source project which enables devices in the IoT to work together. The peer-to-peer communication facility is defined as part of their base services, which include: Onboarding; Configuration; Notification; Control Panel; and Audio Streaming. The Configuration capability, for example, allows one to configure device attributes, such as a name, while the Notification functionality enables all devices to communicate.

As an exemplar system, its scope is also more limited than the novel applications anticipated in the IoT, as outlined in the previous section. The standard involves device discovery, device pairing, message routing, and user notifications. This does not suggest a solution significantly more novel than others available, nor does it suggest a particularly original use of IoT technology. Furthermore, while this architecture facilitates peer-to-peer communication between devices, it does not support the delivery of collected context or application data to a centralized repository. Instead, the functionality is limited to a restricted set of services. The envisaged perspective of the smart city is therefore unlikely to be achieved using such a technology alone, and a gap in the solutions available can consequently be considered to exist.

4   Research Proposal: A Standardizable Architecture for the IoT

In response to the limitations of state-of-the-art solutions to date, and the envisaged perspective of the future smart city, a proposal is made in this paper of a generic network architecture which supports interoperability in the future IoT, and which opens the technical environment to a wider set of participants than at present. The intention is that it will not be necessary for developers to create ad hoc protocols to integrate their technology within the IoT. The architecture is based around the potentially simultaneous support of multiple domains within any smart city IoT, such as the smart home, smart building, or smart vehicle, all of which may populate data fields in a supporting repository for use within or across the domain. The model, together with a selection of supporting comments which reveal how its specific mechanics will be designed in the near future, is shown in Fig. 1.

To explain the framework in more detail: It is assumed that context and application data will be collected from devices operating within the IoT, which enable citizens to become '*smart*' and '*connected*'. To support this technically requires that the devices generating data have functionality to enforce that this information is transported with each packet leaving IoT devices, functionality which belongs in the *Context Layer* proposed in this model. A *Data Repository* will therefore support operation within the IoT, within which data will be organized into one of two repository types, either one in which data can immediately be defined and organized, or one in which the data is not classifiable in relation to a specific device or application. In the latter, the data can be

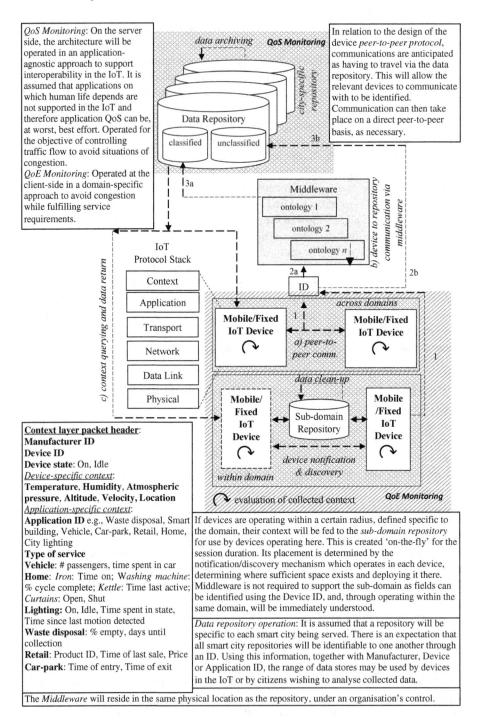

Fig. 1. End-to-end architecture facilitating Interoperation across the IoT

captured, but will be usable in a less autonomous way. The *Middleware* is crucial to facilitating organization and operation of the repository and, indeed, influencing the extent of interoperability achieved by the architecture overall: While the system's objective is to be generic, this being a core requirement to fulfil the IoT's diversity and desired interoperability, the middleware will have system-specific components, such as manufacturer, device and application ontologies. Using ontologies, context can be classified according to the device and manufacturer identifier, and then be passed for storage within the organized repository (Fig. 1, steps 2a, 3a). In the event that the device and manufacturer identifier is not represented (i.e., data is this field is not available or the ontology is not present), data will pass directly into the unclassified repository (Fig. 1, steps 2b, 3b). *Repository management* depends on the type of repository involved: In the organized repository, clean-up activities will involve data archiving, which will be important with a potentially large volume of data collected across the smart city IoT. In *sub-domain repositories*, on the other hand, it is less important that data is retained for long periods of time, it most likely being used on a short-term basis. A sub-domain in the context of this work refers to data relevant to an individual domain, and which is unlikely to have any purpose outside the domain. *Quality of Serivce (QoS)* and *Quality of Experience (QoE) monitoring* are also important within the IoT at both client and server sides of the network. The objective of QoS monitoring on the server side is to facilitate a solution which is scalable and ready to accept data when it arrives for storage, and to return the collected or processed context accurately when requested. The objective of QoE monitoring on the client side is to facilitate the operational requirements of clients.

5 Challenges of a 'One-Size-Fits-All' Approach in the IoT

It is a challenging proposal to develop a 'one-size-fits-all' architecture which supports all applications and devices in the IoT. The design of the framework proposed in this work demonstrates a system-specific approach, to a certain extent. This may not be expected, given the objective of supporting interoperability in the future IoT, where an awareness of any specific aspect may suggest limited ability to respond to new developments and therefore overall restricted interoperability. Attention has been given in the design however, to support extensibility and therefore interoperability for developments not existing at the time of the framework's creation through the provision of a middleware. This design choice depends on the participation of manufacturers and developers, and their provision of ontologies which may be uploaded to the middleware. While an end-to-end network infrastructure is proposed in this work, the protocols intended to operate in each section of the architecture are currently under development. Operational challenges are being taken into account in their design: For example, how will data be organized when an ontology has not been provided in order to achieve any utility from it? In relation to context data collection from the IoT network and devices operating within, how will the rate of packet generation vary depending on the application, device and real-time network state? Furthermore, how can operation across domains be supported, such that context generated in one is recognized and usable in another? Protocol designs which respond to these questions will be explored in future work.

6 Conclusion

It can be concluded that current network architectures are missing capabilities which fulfil expectations of smart cities, restricting the ease of rapid application roll-out and intelligent data use by a user base with a range of expertise. The infrastructure proposed in this paper involves a generic yet standardizable framework, with device and application-specific aspects which allow a greater level of utility to be exploited, and avoiding a situation where operation is restricted based on a vendor or application type. It is proposed in this paper that application- and device-specific aspects must exist in the IoT framework to achieve the full utility required, and manufacturers must take responsibility by make ontologies available for incorporation within the framework's middleware. There are challenges to overcome, and the evolution of a single smart city IoT technology which meets the requirements of all applications and devices is an ambitious goal. Future work involves development of the protocols which will support the IoT framework proposed in this paper.

References

1. Aloi, G., Caliciuri, G., Fortino, G., Gravina, R., Pace, P., Russo, W., Savaglio, C.: A mobile multi-technology gateway to enable IoT interoperability. In: IEEE 1st International Conference on Internet-of-Things Design and Implementation, IoTDI 2016, pp. 259–264 (2016)
2. Aloi, G., Caliciuri, G., Fortino, G., Gravina, R., Pace, P., Russo, W., Savaglio, C.: Enabling IoT interoperability through opportunistic smartphone-based mobile gateways. J. Netw. Comput. Appl. **81**, 74–84 (2017)
3. Fortino, G., Savaglio, C., Palau, C.E., de Puga, J.S., Ghanza, M., Paprzycki, M., Montesinos, M., Liotta, A., Llop, M.: Towards multi-layer interoperability of heterogeneous IoT platforms: the INTER-IoT approach. In: Gravina, R., Palau, C., Manso, M., Liotta, A., Fortino, G. (eds.) Integration, Interconnection, and Interoperability of IoT Systems. Internet of Things, pp. 199–232. Springer, Cham (2018). https://doi.org/10.1007/978-3-319-61300-0_10. ISBN 9783319612997
4. European Smart Cities: The Smart City Model. http://www.smart-cities.eu/model.html
5. Department for Business Innovation & Skills: Smart Cities: Background Paper, October 2013
6. European Commission: Smart Cities. http://ec.europa.eu/
7. Innovation Cities Program: Definition of a Smart City. http://www.innovation-cities.com/
8. Smart City Networks: Smart City Networks named Anaheim Convention Center's Exclusive Telecommunications Provider, September 2014. http://www.smartcitynetworks.com/
9. Vander Veen, C.: Without Smart, Connected People There Are No Smart Cities, February 2015. http://www.govtech.com/
10. Department for Business Innovation & Skills: The Smart City Market: Opportunities for the UK, October 2013
11. Government of India Ministry of Urban Development; Homepage. http://moud.gov.in/

12. Ministry of Urban Development Government of India; Homepage. http://indiansmartcities. in/
13. EUROCITIES: Smart Cities. http://www.eurocities.eu/
14. Future Cities: Smart Cities. https://futurecities.catapult.org.uk/
15. Hamaguchi, K., Ma, Y., Takada, M., Nishjima, T., Shimura, T.: Telecommunication systems in smart cities. Hitachi Rev. **61**(3), 152–158 (2012)
16. Cisco Systems: Smart City Framework a Systematic Process for Enabling Smart+Connected Communities, pp. 1–11, September 2012
17. IBM: Smarter Planet. http://www.ibm.com/smarterplanet/uk/en/
18. Smart Cities Council: Architecture 2030 Beta Testing Urban Planning Tool, May 2013. http://smartcitiescouncil.com/
19. AllSeen Alliance Homepage. https://allseenalliance.org/

AmI Open Source System for the Intelligent Control of Residences for the Elderly

Regel Gonzalez-Usach[1,2(✉)], Diana Yacchirema[1], Vicente Collado[2], and Carlos Palau[1]

[1] Universitat Politecnica de Valencia, Valencia, Spain
regonus@doctor.upv.es, diayacl@upv.es,
cpalau@dcom.upv.es
[2] ISECO S.L., Valencia, Spain
vcollado@iseco.es

Abstract. The IoT has an enormous potential to dramatically improve the quality of life and health of elderly population. In this sense, Ambient Intelligent (AmI) environments focused on the domains of Assisted Living (AAL) represent one of the most promising IoT areas to explore and exploit. We present an intelligent AmI open-source system that aims to monitor and control smart homes and residences for elderly people in order to enhance the safety, health and comfort of the elderly people. For achieving an interoperable interface for collecting, storing and retrieving data from very heterogeneous sensors it integrates a Sensor Observation Service of the Open Geospatial Consortium and follows open standards. Our system is validated from a practical perspective as it is implemented in a pilot residence in Spain.

Keywords: Interoperability · Ambient intelligence · Ambient assisted living
Open source system · Sensor observation service · Sensor web enablement

1 Introduction

The steep increase of elderly population in modern society [1] alongside with the special caring needs that they require, it has recently promoted a strong interest in the Ambient Assisted Living (AAL) domain of IoT [2]. AAL constitutes an area of Ambient Intelligence (AmI) [3], and comprises areas such as e-Health [4] and Elderly Smart Home [5]. These areas may be assisted and boosted through the utilization of IoT technologies. An instance of this is the use of Body Sensor Networks (BSN) in e-Health [6], which enable the remote monitoring of human bodily signals for medical purposes by means of IoT wireless sensors.

Ambient Intelligence involves the employment of sensor networks in order to collect information from the environment in a way that is transparent for the end user. However, underlying that final clearness there is inbuilt, occult, multilayered complexity. IoT Sensor networks usually feature a marked heterogeneity, as different sensors have different specifications, come from diverse providers and present distinct measurement patterns. Besides, those sensors may present mobility instead of being located in a fixed spot. The data that the sensors gather is transmitted by means of very

© ICST Institute for Computer Sciences, Social Informatics and Telecommunications Engineering 2018
G. Fortino et al. (Eds.): InterIoT 2017/SaSeIoT 2017, LNICST 242, pp. 46–52, 2018.
https://doi.org/10.1007/978-3-319-93797-7_6

diverse technologies and protocols. As a consequence of this heterogeneity, the integration of sensors and their data is not trivial, as well as the access and management of that data [6, 7].

Another interoperability issue posed in AAL and AmI is the need of addressing sensor mobility and geospatial data support. Even for fixed sensors, the position of a smart object may be relevant for the analysis of data. Many sensors are mobile, and this characteristic enables sorts of environment monitoring that could not be addressed otherwise. Mobile phones are a good example of the pervasive presence of mobile smart objects in IoT. The mobility aspects of smart objects should be addressed bearing in mind potential roaming across different networks and seeking to more thoroughly interpret monitoring information. In special environments, mobile sensor networks may even require the utilization of mobile gateways [8]; in such IoT systems, information about gateway and sensor position is evidently crucial for system operation and the analysis of monitoring data.

We present an innovative open source AAL system that solves this interoperability issues through the use of open standards and Sensor Web Enablement components from the Open Geospatial Consortium standardization initiative. Our system intends to improve the life quality of elderly people living in smart homes and nursing houses and has been validated through its implementation in a pilot residence.

This paper is laid out as follows. Section 2 expounds open OGC standards and the SWE framework. Section 3 explains our architecture proposal. Section 4 expounds a use case of our system in a pilot residence. Finally, Sect. 5 puts forth conclusions and outlook.

2 Sensor Web Enablement

There are few standardized initiatives that address the interoperability issues mentioned in the introduction section and put forth solutions. The most relevant initiative is probably the Sensor Web Enablement (SWE) [9] framework of the Open Geospatial Consortium (OGC), which permits the integration of sensors and their data. The Sensor Observation Service (SOS), as a component of the SWE specification, plays a major role in that integration by defining an interface for accessing sensor data and metadata [10]. The SOS offers a standardized web service interface that enables customers to interact with registered sensors and their measurement data [10] and also to register new sensors and types of observations or to erase them.

Mobility aspects may be especially relevant in AAL, given that information stemming from location and tracking can be critical for the proper functioning of many services in a nursing home or in the smart homes of the elderly. The employment of geospatial metadata can solve the aforementioned issues. In this sense OGC provides geospatial standards that support the geolocation of sensors and their measurements, allowing the use of sensor data and metadata.

We employ components of the Sensor Web Enablement framework in our system to solve the interoperability issues posed by the high heterogeneity of sensors in order to collect and manage their data, and by the need of addressing additional geospatial information for this data.

3   System Architecture

The architecture of our system is shown in Fig. 1 and it is explained in this section from a component perspective. Conjointly, it is also detailed the general software architecture of the central system, that only has open-source components.

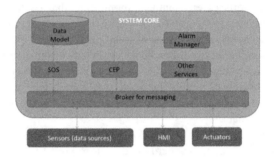

Fig. 1. System architecture of the AmI open source system

Our system is composed by a Human-Machine Interface a Central System, an Actuator Module and a Sensor Module. Their functionality and role within the system are described in the following paragraphs.

The Sensors Module is a set of sensors that are placed in a residence as a part of an Ambient Intelligence environment (together with the system intelligence and the actuators). They send monitoring data to the system through the local network to a Sensor Data Acquisition Module, that is responsible for collecting and sending the data to the central system.

The Actuator Module is composed by a set of actuators that are placed in the residence. They respond to the orders of the central system.

The Central system is the core of our system, and it is able to collect and store data from the sensors and analyze it. In case its intelligence considers that an action must take place in response to a specific situation, the system will create notifications visible through the HMI, send orders to the actuators and/or launch alarms. This system will handle alarms as events with the highest priority.

The Human-Machine Interface (HMI) can be accessed on-line through a web interface. It shows to authorized users relevant monitoring information, alarm notifications and provides access to real-time sensor information as well as records. Administrator users can configure the system and perform control actions.

The Central System is composed by a SOS, that enables standardized sensor data management, a Complex Event Processor (CEP) that provides analysis intelligence to the system, a Sensor Alarm Service, to handle alarms and events of high priority, and a broker that allows for the communication among the aforementioned components. These system core components are described in more detail in the following paragraphs.

The Sensor Observation Service collects and stores the data from the sensors following the Open Geospatial Consortium (OGC) standards, and provides a standard interface for managing and retrieving the meta-data and observations from the sensors system [11]. The OGC SOS accomplishes the specification O&M [12] for sensor observation modelling, the specification SensorML [13] for modelling sensor metadata, and follows the Sensor Web Enablement [9] framework. SOS is based on widely accept-ed web technologies like XML, JSON and SOAP. The OGC SOS has geospatial support for sensor observations. The SOS requires a database with geospatial support for storing the sensor data using a specific data model designed for registering SOS observations and sensors. Our system uses 52° North SOS implementation [14], and a PostGreSQL database with PosGis support.

The broker allows for the communication of the different elements of the Core system. It is as well the interface between the core system and the external sensor information sources. We use RabbitMQ broker, that employs AMQP protocol for messaging [15].

The Complex Event Processor (CEP) processes events that are registered and through the SOS. The CEP has several rules that define specific patterns of events, and the actions to be triggered if those patterns are detected. Auxiliary tables, such as schedules for performing specific actions, can be used in CEP rules. The set of rules is adapted to the specific needs of a residence. In this sense, an administrator of the system can add, change or remove CEP rules, and modify or create auxiliary tables, through the system HMI. Rule definitions can entail high complexity. The CEP engine used is ESPER, an Event Stream Processing (ESP) [16].

An Alarm Manager that handles alarms and certain incidences of high priority detected by the Complex Event Processor. The Alarm Manager used is Sensor Alert Service (SAS) [17], a component of the 52° North SOS and the SWE framework. Alarms are handled separately from other events due to its high priority.

4 Use Case

In this section we describe a use case of our system in a residence for the elderly.

A pilot of our system has been deployed in a nursing home in the area of Valencia (Spain). The main features of the pilot are the following: it has 136 residents, 42 caregivers that work on three daily shifts and 80 rooms (66 bedrooms for elderly people and 12 regular rooms). The services that are currently implemented within our system are Intruder detection, Fire alarm, Medical Emergency, Access Control, Air Conditioning and Lighting Intelligent Service.

It integrates the human actors (caregivers and residents) of the nursing home in our system through a set of sensors, actuators and the Human-Machine Interface (HMI).

For the residence monitoring, we use 1378 sensors (room alarm buttons, terminals, access control points, air conditioning sensors, smoke detectors). All the residence area offers internet connectivity to the sensors. Thus, sensors communicate with the central system using wired LAN connectivity, in the case of fixed sensors, and WiFi, in the case of mobile sensors.

Our system receives the data produced from the sensors, stores and analyzes it. As a result of the analysis performed by the intelligence of the system, some control actions may take place. Notifications are sent to caregivers, alarms are launched if their trigger conditions are accomplished, and actuators receive orders. These type of actions can also be performed as a result of a previous programming and configuration of the system. For example, the automatic activation of the intruder alarm at a specific hour at night.

Caregivers can interact with the system through the HMI. As a consequence of the awareness of relevant monitoring information, the Caregivers can be more effective, faster, efficient, and have a better coordination in the service that give to the elderly people.

The main services offered in the pilot residence are intruder detection, fire alarm, medical emergency, access control, air conditioning regulation and intelligent lighting system. Those services are described in more detail in the following paragraphs.

Intruder detection is a service that protects certain access points of the residence at specific hours from unauthorized access, launches alarms if there is any attempt of trespassing and maintains the doors remotely closed. It is programmed to be active at some specific hours (i.e. at night) in the central system.

The fire alarm service detects if a concentration of CO_2 or CO is higher than regular and launches a fire alarm, allowing for rapid dislodgment and or other measures for fire suffocation. As a matter of fact, to have a quick response is critical in fire situations. Smoke sensors are distributed in the whole area of the residence, including all rooms, and inform the central system of the existence of a potential fire in their specific location, and an alarm is automatically launched. This alarm can be deactivated manually, through the HMI of the central system, or after a timeout period if smoke sensors are not triggering it.

Medical Emergency is a service that aims to give the residents and caregivers a quick way to trigger an alarm in case of emergency, to immediately alert the system and the other caregivers in order to achieve the most rapid and efficient reaction possible. It is specially thought for medical emergencies. To this end, many rooms in the residence are provided of emergency buttons or handlers that can be easily pushed and activated by residents or caregivers in case of emergency. Then, the central system will receive information about the existence of an emergency and its location. The alarm will be active in the system until a caregiver informs the system that the emergency is being attended. The alarm will be then in a standby state until finally, a caregiver closes it when it is resolved. If it were necessary, health services will be called. Actually, each of the common rooms (i.e. a gym, a dining room, lounges and bathrooms), the bedrooms and private bathrooms contain at least one emergency button or handler in addition to a voice communicator. This service allows for a rapid response of caregivers and health services in case of accidents, medical emergencies or any other risk situations.

Access Control: this service restricts the entrance to different areas of the residence to only authorized people, for security and privacy reasons. The doors that limit certain areas of the residence have a card access control system that only allows the access of people with valid access permissions. The system has a registry of residents and caregivers, the access points that they are able to open with their access cards, and the end date of those permissions. If the access is authorized the door will be unlocked and opened. This system guarantees the privacy of residents in the rooms in which they live, that can only be accessed by them, caregivers or personnel of the cleaning service. As well, this service avoids the entrance of intruders in other residence areas.

Air Conditioning: Temperature is automatically regulated by the system to provide the most appropriate environmental conditions for the comfort of the ancient residents. It is critical to offer an appropriate temperature as a measure to prevent health problems in elderly people. Air conditioning devices have several sensors and actuators connected to the system. These sensors measure the current environmental temperature, the air velocity and the target temperature registered in the device, and send this information to the central system. Actuators can change the target temperature of the device and the velocity of the air. From the central system it is possible to set the target temperature of all the residence or to particularize it for specific devices (for example, some rooms could be empty and do not need to be warm). Also, it is possible to program times, air velocity and temperatures for a set of air conditioning devices, or specific ones, through the HMI as an administrator user.

Lighting Intelligent Service: this services allows luminaries of common rooms in the residence to be automatically switch on and switch off by the system. System administrators can program the start and end time of the lighting time. When the start time

5 Conclusions and Outlook

We have presented our system as an AAL open source solution with the goal of maximizing the comfort, safety and service effectiveness for aged people in smart homes and residences. For this aim, it utilizes a set of sensors and actuators to gather relevant information, applies intelligent data analysis to decide and perform the best course actions and it provides the caregivers a Human-Machine Interface to facilitate management and monitoring.

Our system aims to be adaptable to any type of sensors, services and building topology. The use of data from a very heterogeneous range of sensors poses an interoperability problem in IoT systems in other to collect, store and retrieve their monitoring data. Moreover, the mobility of sensors and the use of geospatial information, which is required in our system services, extends this interoperability problem. We solved both issues through the use of open standards (O&M and SensorML) for data management and the incorporation in our system of an OGC SOS that offers an interoperable interface for the collecting, storing and retrieving sensor data from heterogeneous sources.

The core of the system is composed by four main elements: the SOS that stores sensor observations in a database with geospatial support, a CEP that processes events and provides intelligence to the system, a Sensor Alarm Service that handles alarms from the CEP, and finally a broker that enables communication among the different elements. Our system is open source as it only uses open source components and its code will be released in the short future.

The main functionalities of our system have been validated not only from a theoretical scope, but in practice as it has been deployed in a pilot residence in Spain, covering a variety of services such as access control, medical emergency alarms and intruder detection.

In the short future, we will increment our system functionality, and integrate it into public emergency services, to increase the safety of residence and decrease the reaction time to any medical emergency.

Acknowledgments. This research was partially financed by SAFE-ECH, funded by the Spanish Ministerio de Industria, Economía y Competitividad (MINECO) under Grant Agreement RTC-2015-4502-1, and by the European Union's "Horizon 2020" research and innovation programme as part of the INTERIoT project under Grant Agreement 687283.

References

1. European Centre. http://www.euro.centre.org/search_index.php. Accessed Jan. 2017
2. Rashidi, P., Mihailidis, A.: A survey on ambient assisted living tools for older adults. IEEE J. Biomed. Health Inform. PP(99), 1 (2013)
3. José Bravo, V.V., Hervás, R.: Ambient assisted living. In: Third International Workshop, IWAAL 2011, p. 236 (2011)
4. Yang, G., et al.: A health-IoT platform based on the integration of intelligent packaging, unobtrusive bio-sensor, and intelligent medicine box. IEEE Trans. Industr. Inf. **10**(4), 2180–2191 (2014)
5. Cicirelli, F., Fortino, G., Giordano, A., Guerrieri, A., Spezzano, G., Vinci, A.: On the design of smart homes: a framework for activity recognition in home environment. J. Med. Syst. **40**(9), 200:1–200:17 (2016)
6. Gravina, R., Alinia, P., Ghasemzadeh, H., Fortino, G.: Multi-sensor fusion in body sensor networks: State-of-the-art and research challenges. Inf. Fusion **35**, 68–80 (2017)
7. Fortino, G., Giannantonio, R., Gravina, R., Kuryloski, P., Jafari, R.: Enabling Effective Programming and Flexible Management of Efficient Body Sensor Network Applications. IEEE Trans. Hum. Mach. Syst. **43**(1), 115–133 (2013)
8. Aloi, G., Caliciuri, G., Fortino, G., Gravina, R., Pace, P., Russo, W., Savaglio, C.: Enabling IoT interoperability through opportunistic smartphone-based mobile gateways. J. Netw. Comput. Appl. **81**, 74–84 (2017)
9. OGC SWE Project Website. http://www.open-geospatial.org/ogc/marketstechnologies/swe Accessed Jan 2017
10. Na, A., Priest, M.: OpenGIS sensor observation service implementation specification. In: Open Geospatial Consortium (OGC), Wayland, MA, OGC, pp. 1–104 (2006)
11. Bröring, A., Stasch, C.: OGC® Sensor Observation Service (2012)
12. Cox, S.: Observations and Measurements - Part 1 - Observation schema. in Open Geospatial Consortium (OGC), Wayland, MA, pp. 1–85 (2007). OGC Document, OGC 07-022r1
13. Botts, M., Robin, A.: OpenGIS Sensor Model Language (SensorML) implementation specification. In: Open Geospatial Consortium (OGC), Wayland, MA, pp. 1–180 (2007). OGC Document, OGC 07-000
14. 52 North: 52 North. Sensor Web Community. http://52north.org/communities/sensorweb/index.html. Accessed Jan 2017
15. RabbitMQ https://www.rabbitmq.com. Accessed Jan 2017
16. Esper: http://www.espertech.com/esper. Accessed Jan 2017
17. Simonis, I., Echterhoff, J.: OpenGIS sensor alert service implementation specification. In: Open Geospatial Consortium (OGC), Wayland, MA, pp. 1–144 (2006). OGC Document, OGC 06-028r5

A Scalable Agent-Based Smart Environment for Edge-Based Urban IoT Systems

Franco Cicirelli[1], Giancarlo Fortino[1,2], Antonio Guerrieri[1], Giandomenico Spezzano[1(✉)], and Andrea Vinci[1]

[1] CNR – National Research Council of Italy, Institute for High Performance Computing and Networking (ICAR), Via P. Bucci 7-11C, 87036 Rende (CS), Italy
{cicirelli,guerrieri,spezzano,vinci}@icar.cnr.it
[2] Department of Informatics, Modeling, Electronics, and Systems, University of Calabria, 87036 Rende, Italy
fortino@unical.it

Abstract. New Internet of Things (IoT) applications are encouraging Smart City and Smart Environments initiatives all over the world, by leveraging big data and ubiquitous connectivity. This new technology enables systems to monitor, manage and control devices, and to create new knowledge and actionable information, by the real-time analysis of data streams. In order to develop applications in the depicted scenario, the adoption of new paradigms is required. This paper suggests combining the emergent concept of edge/fog computing with the agent metaphor, so as to enable designing systems based on the decentralization of control functions over distributed autonomous and cooperative entities, which run at the edge of the network. Moreover, we suggest the adoption of the *iSapiens* platform as a reference, as it was designed specifically for the mentioned purposes. Multi-agent applications running on top of *iSapiens* can create smart services using adaptive and decentralized algorithms which exploit the principles of cognitive IoT.

Keywords: IoT · Urban computing · Smart environments
Intelligent agents · Edge computing

1 Introduction

The Internet of Things is realizing a scenario where interconnected objects or things can behave as autonomous entities and can cooperate among them for reaching some common goal, with minimum human intervention. Such smart things must have the ability to sense the environment where they are immersed, analyze the collected information, and take decisions and actions to achieve their objectives.

Many IoT applications are not yet developed because they require being capable of scaling to incorporate a huge number of objects [1]. Centralized solutions

© ICST Institute for Computer Sciences, Social Informatics and Telecommunications Engineering 2018
G. Fortino et al. (Eds.): InterIoT 2017/SaSeIoT 2017, LNICST 242, pp. 53–59, 2018.
https://doi.org/10.1007/978-3-319-93797-7_7

do not fit well with such requirement, and systems that have static configuration are not adequate for managing the complexity of environments which evolve continuously. Several IoT applications rely on a cloud-based architecture, where the main computation and storage is concentrated on remote servers. Such approach is not capable of realizing application having real-time requirements, high volume of data, or limited network bandwidth constraints. This raises the need for approaches relying on decentralized processing, where mission-critical processes can run locally even if communication with the operation centers is not adequate. An architecture capable of distributing computation in edge nodes is often the only exploitable solution. However, in order to exploit edge computing for realizing IoT applications, many challenges must be addressed.

This paper proposes an agent-oriented framework called *iSapiens* [2] for developing IoT smart environments based on a networks of smart objects, which can be exploited for the creation of services related to transportation, parking, lighting, traffic, waste and safety [3]. In the proposed framework, smart objects are modeled as agents, running on a multi-agent system, which cooperate for achieving specific goals. We propose to use agents, running close to the controlled objects, in order to mitigate the issues of lack of scalability and reliability, and to furnish reasoning and intelligence capabilities to the things part of an IoT system. The idea is to mirror every thing with an agent, having embedded reasoning, intelligence, and cooperation capabilities. The ability of objects to reason about the environments where they are immersed can contribute to useful outcomes for humans, using cognitive IoT techniques [4], and through the exploitation of self-organizing, decentralized control mechanisms.

This vision is made possible using the concept of *edge computing*. The term edge computing, also referred to as *fog computing*, essentially means that, instead of working from a remote cloud, systems operate on network ends [5]. Thus, data can be processed closer to smart devices rather than being sent to the cloud for elaboration. This approach well suits with IoT because it allows action in real time on the incoming data, without exceeding limits of available bandwidth. By using this distributed strategy, it is possible to both lower costs and improve efficiency.

The paper is structured as follows: Sect. 2 presents the cognitive model to develop a self-configuring agents. Section 3 describes the three-layer software architecture of the platform *iSapiens*. Section 4 presents the use of *iSapiens* platform for potential applications in the surveillance sector using video/audio analytics techniques. Finally, Sect. 5 concludes the paper.

2   Self-adaptive Embodied Agents

Networked objects with self-configuration mechanisms make it possible for distributed systems to adapt to dynamic environments by automatically bootstrapping and reconfiguring themselves which is part of the self-managed process of an automatic system. In this context, Neto et al. [6] implemented a platform that helps the realization of self-adaptive agents with the aim of realizing *autonomic computing*, as proposed by IBM.

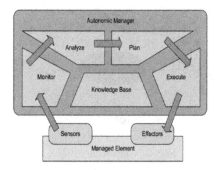

Fig. 1. Autonomic cycle.

Such adaptive agents rely on a loop of control (see Fig. 1) consisting in four activities, namely:

– **Collect**: realizes the collection of the application data;
– **Analyze**: realizes the analysis of the collected data to try in detecting if there are problems;
– **Plan**: realizes the decisions on what to do in the case in which problems are detected;
– **Execute**: realizes some changes in the run of the application, consequently to the executed actions.

The control loop coming from the proposal by IBM and that defines the behavior of the self-adaptive agents can be customized. Moreover, instead of running analysis and planning activities, the adaptive agents can realize decisions by exploiting *controllers* data. Such controllers could be defined as an intelligent entity able to adapt relationships with users and the environment. As the environment is constantly evolving in time and connecting to the network by using sensors and actuators. The autonomic computing approach can be considered as appropriate to design the controller enabling the adaptivity and reconfigurability of the system.

We have defined a controller as an intelligent agent that is capable of sensing the environment, infer knowledge from data and generalize what has already learned in the future situations. The common shared model useful for the description of the behavior of an intelligent (cognitive) agent is the so-called cognitive cycle (see Fig. 2) which is usually considered as composed by four phases:

– **Sensing**: when the system continuously acquires information and knowledge about the objects that interact in the system and about their internal statuses;
– **Analysis**: here the gathered knowledge is elaborated so to obtain a peculiar and concise awareness;
– **Decision**: here, the processed data from the analysis phase is elaborated and is selected a new system configuration according to the given objectives;
– **Action**: in this state, the system runs the configuration that have been provided by the Decision phase.

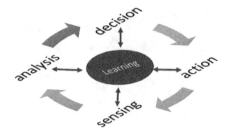

Fig. 2. Cognitive cycle.

In this schema, the learning phase involves all the stages (within certain limits) of the cognitive cycle, thus being continuously executed.

The cognitive cycle introduced above can be mapped straightforwardly to agents' behaviors.

In creating an intelligent agent, the sensing and actuation functions will be inherent in the object; for example, when constructing an intelligent lamp, the bulb (actuator) will be part of the lamp. However, the computational capabilities of the object may follow on of these patterns:

- **Embedded computation**, in which a processor, memory and storage are built into the object
- **Augmented computation**, in which a computational device is connected to an everyday object (e.g. an intelligent chair can be developed by adding pressure sensors and an Arduino controller to an existing office chair)
- **External computation**, in which the object perform computation by communicating via a network interface with an agent running in a edge node.

3   iSapiens Architecture

iSapiens is a Java-based platform for the development of a pervasive SE. A typical *iSapiens* application comprehends a set of physical devices (which can be sensors, actuators or even more complex smart objects) directly spread in a smart environment and connected to a network of *iSapiens* computing nodes (see Fig. 3).

The agent metaphor is used for designing and implementing the business logic of the application to develop. Software agents execute on the *iSapiens* computational nodes close to the physical devices they have to control, thus implementing edge computation (in-network computation). On behalf of the final users, agents can also exploit out-of-the-edge services (off-network computation) which can be purposely developed for a specific application, or which can be made directly available by third-party service providers. Off-network computation is useful when an application requires specific functions that cannot be executed on the edge nodes due, e.g., to computational limitations, or in the

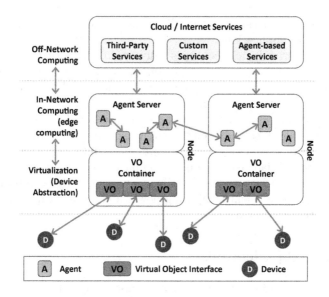

Fig. 3. iSapiens's architecture.

case that a centralized and global view of the system is required. Such functions include predictive analysis, data mining, off-line analytics, and so on.

The devices connected to an iSapiens node are abstracted as the union of Virtual Objects (VOs). All the VOs residing in a specific node are managed by a Virtual Objects Container. VOs offer a transparent access to the physical part due to a common and well-established interface exposed as API. The VO abstraction aims at hiding the low level heterogeneity in terms of communication protocols and specific hardware of all the connected physical devices.

Each *iSapiens* computing node also hosts an Agent Server that is responsible for the management, the execution, and for supporting communication among software agents. Communication is based on asynchronous exchange of messages. The platform offers a specific kind of messages, namely acquaintance messages, that can be used to dynamically establish asymmetric acquaintance relationships among agents. An agent can use the hardware devices abstracted through VOs, and it can access the social network of a controlled device through the SO representing the device from a social perspective. Social-based services are accessed by functionalities provides from the Yellow Pages Agents. The Yellow Pages agents, all-together, implement a distributed service which permits the search of previously registered applicative agents on the basis of attributes specified as <key, value> pairs. Agent Servers and VO Containers running on each networked *iSapiens* computing node, constitute a middleware allowing the exploitation of distributed in-network computation. All the components introduced so far, either a physical device, a virtual object, an agent, or a whole computing node, can be dynamically added, removed, or up-dated. Also the relationships among agents can be dynamically updated through yellow pages and acquaintance messages. All of this allows the development of scalable, extensible and pervasive applications.

The above described architecture is fully compliant with the paradigm of edge computing. A way to look at edge computing is to consider it as a virtualized platform that is typically located between end user devices and the cloud data centers hosted within the Internet. Thus edge computing can provide better quality of service in terms of delay, power consumption, reduced data traffic over the Internet. The main feature of edge computing is its ability to support applications that require low latency, location awareness and mobility. This ability is made possible by the fact that the edge computing systems are deployed very close to the end users in a widely distributed manner. Edge computing nodes hosted must possess sufficient computing power and storage capacity to handle the resource intensive user requests.

4   Potential Applications

The need of protecting infrastructures is an important task that sometimes goes beyond predictive maintenance.

iSapiens actually have been used in protecting infrastructures such as streets, school buildings, water supply, sewer through deployments of cameras and by combining video analytics with other devices like motion sensors, radar or acoustic/seismic sensors. In this way, probability of detection increases dramatically with a reciprocal decrease in false alarm rates [7].

In the context of video surveillance, detecting anomalies is of paramount importance. In this field, iSapiens detects anomalies by using a novel mechanism able to detect if normal or abnormal things happen over time. We have defined some anomaly indexes that, when overcome, represent an anomaly [8,9].

These technologies are very useful for security and safety purposes. Video analytics is also used to detect anomalies in the density of people at some events.

Nowadays, video surveillance systems can be deployed to store what happens in an area of interest. These systems take signals that are related to the security and to the safety. Video analytics systems enhance such video surveillance systems by adding real time detection on events together with analysis of what is already happened (the event). All of this is done to increase the effectiveness of the video surveillance system with respect to the traditional one. In this field, audio analytics is added to have more information about the controlled place. Moreover, not everything can be taken by some cameras. In this context, our audio analytics can be able to detect dangers.

Building a system capable of recognizing and reacting to the sounds around us means, at the best of our knowledge, doing things that have never been done before.

We envision a future where omnipresent, intelligent, context-aware computing is able to better help people by responding to the sounds around them, no matter where they are.

5 Conclusions

We have proposed a solution to support a new approach to mitigate the issues of lack of scalability, reliability, reasoning and intelligence in things in the IoT systems. *iSapiens* an agent-based framework has been presented to developing analytics for embedded systems in an environment of fog computing. In many case, the analytics run directly in embodied agents allocated in the sensors. Potential applications that we are developing through *iSapiens* are mentioned and discussed.

Acknowledgements. This work has been partially supported by *"Smart platform for monitoring and management of in-home security and safety of people and structures"* project that is part of the DOMUS District, funded by the Italian Government (PON03PE_00050_1).

References

1. Atzori, L., Iera, A., Morabito, G.: The Internet of Things: a survey. Comput. Netw. **54**, 2787–2805 (2010)
2. Cicirelli, F., Guerrieri, A., Spezzano, G., Vinci, A., Briante, O., Ruggeri, G.: iSapiens: a platform for social and pervasive smart environments. In: WF-IoT, pp. 365–370 (2016)
3. Roukounaki, A., Soldatos, J., Petrolo, R., Loscri, V., Mitton, N., Serrano, M.: Visual development environment for semantically interoperable smart cities applications. In: Mandler, B., et al. (eds.) IoT360 2015. LNICST, vol. 170, pp. 439–449. Springer, Cham (2016). https://doi.org/10.1007/978-3-319-47075-7_48
4. Liotta, A.: The cognitive net is coming. IEEE Spectr. **50**(8), 26–31 (2013)
5. Bonomi, F., Milito, R., Natarajan, P., Zhu, J.: Fog computing: a platform for Internet of Things and analytics. In: Bessis, N., Dobre, C. (eds.) Big Data and Internet of Things: A Roadmap for Smart Environments. SCI, vol. 546, pp. 169–186. Springer, Cham (2014). https://doi.org/10.1007/978-3-319-05029-4_7
6. Neto, B., Costa, A., Netto, M., Silva, V., Lucena, C.: JAAF: a framework to implement self-adaptive agents. In: International Conference on Software Engineering and Knowledge Engineering (2009)
7. Cicirelli, F., Guerrieri, A., Spezzano, G., Vinci, A.: An edge-based platform for dynamic Smart City applications. Future Gener. Comp. Syst. **76**, 106–118 (2017)
8. Bosman, H., Iacca, G., Tejada, A., Wortche, H., Liotta, A.: Spatial anomaly detection in sensor networks using neighborhood information. Inf. Fusion J. **33**, 41–56 (2017)
9. Bosman, H., Iacca, G., Tejada, A., Wortche, H., Liotta, A.: Ensembles of incremental learners to detect anomalies in ad-hoc sensor networks. Ad Hoc Netw. (Special Issue on Big Data Inspired Data Sensing, Processing and Networking Technologies) **35**, 14–36 (2015)

Observing Interoperability of IoT Systems Through Model-Based Testing

Koray Incki[(⊠)] and Ismail Ari

Department of Computer Science, Özyeğin University, Istanbul, Turkey
ben@korayincki.com

Abstract. Internet of Things (IoT) has drastically modified the industrial services provided through autonomous machine-to-machine interactions. Such systems comprise of devices manufactured by various suppliers. Verification is a challenge due to high heterogeneity of composing devices. In this paper, we present initial results of model-based interoperability testing for IoT systems to facilitate automatic test case generation. We utilize messaging model of Constrained Application Protocol so as to deduce complex relations between participating devices. We use Complex-Event Processing (CEP) techniques in order to streamline the verification process after generating proper runtime monitors from sequence diagrams. We demonstrate our solution on a fictitious healthcare system.

Keywords: Internet of Things · Model-based testing
Constrained-Application Protocol · Runtime verification
Complex-event processing

1 Introduction

IoT presents a new computing phenomenon for such devices that are smart yet resource-constrained devices. Those devices involve heterogeneous day-to-day smart objects [1], which aim to seamlessly construct new services and applications through untethered autonomous machine-to-machine (M2M) collaborations. Interoperability is a major challenge in achieving such a goal, as there might occur unprecedented interactions between those objects. It is an issue in such systems of systems that are composed of subsystems with various communication protocols, application interfaces. Such interoperability as in communication layers involves protocol specific interoperability; for example, CoAP-based devices must be interoperable with respect to the CoAP standard [4,14].

IETF task force CoRE (Constrained RESTful Environments) [3] has promoted adoption of service-oriented in IoT domain with the introduction of an application layer protocol. The Constrained-Application Protocol (CoAP) [4] presents a RESTful-like programming environment that not only helps to develop such systems, but also raises new challenges in providing for interoperability between endpoints. In this paper, we attack the interoperability problem of application layer interfaces in CoRE IoT domain.

© ICST Institute for Computer Sciences, Social Informatics and Telecommunications Engineering 2018
G. Fortino et al. (Eds.): InterIoT 2017/SaSeIoT 2017, LNICST 242, pp. 60–66, 2018.
https://doi.org/10.1007/978-3-319-93797-7_8

IoT systems are intrinsically hot swap systems, such that an endpoint can be exchanged with another endpoint providing (supposedly) the same services with the same address. But, endpoint configuration can have flaws before swapping. Thus, this might cause runtime failures even though the overall system design is verified in the development phase. Thus, we believe that a runtime solution for interoperability testing is a necessity in IoT domain.

IoT systems usually consist of commercial-off-the shelf (COTS) products with nearly no knowledge of internal implementation details, we promote a black-box testing approach for providing interoperability. We propose that a model-based testing approach that leverages the RESTful-like application layer interaction model of CoAP-based IoT systems should facilitate interoperability testing efforts. Model-based testing (MBT) has been utilized in several domains [8]. We demonstrate the applicability of MBT in IoT domain through implementation of a case study with Papyrus [5] modeling tool. Our previous work on runtime verification of IoT systems [6] has demonstrated that an IoT system can be described in terms of simple events occurring in the system. Thereby, we proposed a verification approach that utilized complex-event processing (CEP) technique. In this paper, we further that research with a MBT solution that allows automatically generating test cases from sequence diagrams in a UML model.

The paper is organized such that Sect. 2 discusses recent research on interoperability testing, Sect. 3 provides our solution framework, and Sect. 4 elaborates on the implementation. In Sect. 5 we conclude with a discussion and future work.

2   Related Work

A black-box testing approach for assuring interoperability assumes that the individual components are thoroughly tested by the manufacturer. But, when it comes to the complexities of the integrated heterogeneous system of systems, the runtime actions of the system might be overlooked with black-box testing. In [8] Wu et al. proposes using Unified Modeling Language (UML) [7] to express the expected behavior of a component-based software. They utilize interaction diagrams to capture functionality expected from the system. They explain how UML interaction diagrams can be used to extract the context-dependence and content-dependence relations so as to use in deciding if test cases are comprehensive or not. The research doesn't provide any guidance through implementation nor the automation of a model-based testing approach.

Internet community is majorly built around web services concept, thus interoperability of those distributed and heterogeneous services is an ongoing challenge. Bertolino et al. [10] proposed an audition framework for solving this problem. They extend the UDDI registries so that the services registered to a directory is audited before it is registered. Thereby, they validate the claimed behavior of the service before such services with the same UDDI registry can collaborate with proclaimed service contracts. This is a solid contribution in service registry coordination, however it lacks to observe the runtime behavior of services.

In [13], Smythe discusses that using a the modeling approach in development of a distributed service oriented system facilitates both implementation and testing efforts. The interoperability tests are automatically generated through a series of XML Metadata Interchange (XMI) transformations over a UML model of the system. Our approach also use XMI transformations in order to facilitate runtime EPL statements for interoperability testing.

In [14] authors proposes a new solution for certification of products, which involves conformance testing of IoT devices with respect to CoAP standards [4]. In their approach, they first record the live network traffic, and save them in files for post processing. When the system test run finishes, they collect those record files and apply post mortem tests on those logs so as to find any deviation in the CoAP communication primitives from the standard specification. The test cases are prerecorded according to the standard specification. Since, they operate on recorded log files, the approach does not scale well to runtime (online) interoperability testing. Moreover, they focus solely on protocol implementation interoperability, so the solution does not scale well for application specific interaction models.

3   Model-Based Testing for Interoperability

Software intensive systems has increasingly being developed with component-based architectures [9]. IoT systems are no exception to that adoption in the industry. Particularly, application layer protocols such as CoAP have made it possible to treat such systems purely as service-oriented systems. Monitoring of services in SOA systems has been valuable for post mortem analysis [12]. Thus, we will define how model-based testing approach can be used for describing the service interactions, and consequently facilitate interoperability testing at runtime.

Interoperability issue might be present at various levels of communication layers. Application level interoperability can be defined to occur between service calls, such that endpoint-A calls a service that exists in endpoint-B with the correct signature and parameters, and also data interoperability. In this research we address solely service call interoperability.

Figure 1 summarizes our solution framework. A system integrator first (Step-1) needs to model the interoperability scenarios in sequence diagrams. Each diagram captures expected behavior of an individual service of a particular endpoint in terms of CoAP interactions with other endpoints; thus, there must be as much sequence diagrams as the number of services provided by an endpoint in an IoT system, in order for fully covering all behaviors. The interactions are represented as asynchronous message exchanges in the sequence diagrams. In second step, a model-to-text transformation algorithm is exerted on each sequence diagram to transform event relations in it into EPL statements. EPL statements act as runtime monitors. EPL statement is an executable special purpose instruction written in Event Processing Language (EPL) of Esper CEP engine [15]. EPL statements are implemented as (see Sect. 4) Java classes that

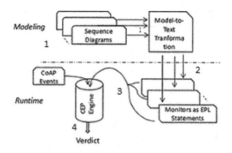

Fig. 1. MBT process for interoperability

can be run on any Java compatible platform. Those are registered (in Step-3) with an Esper engine running either on a stand-alone endpoint acting as an edge computing solution for interoperability testing, or it can be provided as a service over a cloud implementation. In step 4, the CoAP events that are captured from the running network by means of sniffing it passively are injected into the Esper engine for monitoring through complex-event processing. The *Verdict* can either be *SUCCESS* or *FAIL* depending on the result.

4   Implementation

The example implementation assumes a healthcare system based on research in [16]. They present a case study on interoperability testing for HL7 systems with a sample hardware reference implementation. The communication model is based on CoAP (Fig. 2).

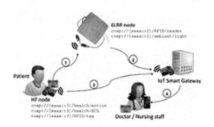

Fig. 2. Healthcare interoperability [16]

In [6] we showed that a CoAPsystem can be expressed in terms of *Send Events* in the system. Thus, we can represent a patient consent scenario with a sequence diagram as in Fig. 3. For ensuring privacy, a doctor must first request patient's consent for observing health data (e.g., ECG) (m_1). After the patient grants the consent (m_2), the doctor can ask to observe the patient data (m_3).

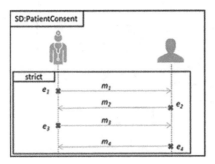

Fig. 3. Patient consent sequence diagram

After that, the sensor on patient can periodically sends the measured data (m_4). Each e_i represents a *send event* for corresponding message m_i.

$$Follows(e_i, t_i, e_j, t_j)$$
$$\equiv \exists e_i, t_i, e_j, t_j Happens(e_i, t_i) \wedge Happens(e_j, t_j) \wedge (t_i < t_j) \qquad (1)$$

The system in Fig. 3 can be represented in terms of events (Eq. 1) by using *Follows* relations as described in [6]. Equation 1 states that e_i must be followed by e_j if they appear sequentially on the sequence diagram (e.g., e_2 follows e_1). Thus, by observing if each sequential pair of (e_i, e_j) at runtime satisfies *Follows* relation we can conclude that interoperability patient consent requirement. In order to conclude with a *SUCCESS* verdict (Eq. 2), we must have $e_1 \prec e_2 \prec e_3 \prec e_4$, where $\prec$ denotes the precedence relation. For a *FAIL* result (Eq. 3), a $e_i \nprec e_j$ must hold for $(i, j) \in \{(1,2), (2,3), (3,4)\}$, where $\nprec$ represents doesn't precede relation. Equation 3 states that the CEP engine must select all the complex events that occur as a result of m_1 is followed by either m_3 or m_4 message before an m_2 event occurs in order to indicate a failure case. The same rule can be extended for other messages as well.

$$select\ 'SUCCESS'\ from\ HealthEvent\ match\_recognize($$
$$measures\ A.mId\ as\ a\_id, B.mId\ as\ b\_id, C.mId\ as\ c\_id, D.mId\ as\ d\_id$$
$$pattern\ (A\ B\ C\ D)\ define\ A\ as\ A.mId = m_1, B\ as\ B.mId = m_2,$$
$$C\ as\ C.mId = m_3, D'asD.mId = m_4); \qquad (2)$$

$$select\ 'FAIL', m1\ from\ pattern\ [everym1 = HealthEvent(mId = m1) - >$$
$$((m3 = HealthEvent(mId = m3)\ or\ m4 = HealthEvent(mId = m4))\ and$$
$$not\ m2 = HealthEvent(mId = m2))]; \qquad (3)$$

Figures 4 and 5 list algorithms for generating EPL statements for *Success* and *Fail* cases of interoperability testing in Acceleo. Acceleo runs over XMI definitions of sequence diagrams, and generates Java classes containing corresponding EPL statements (Eqs. 2 and 3). After executing M2T code in Papyrus [5], a Java class

```
1   for each CombinedFragment F in InteractionDiagram ID
2       if InteractionOperator equals 'strict'
3           Print EPL Statement of "SUCCESS" monitor by traversing
4           MATCH_RECOGNIZE PATTERN(M1 M2 M3 M4)
5           for each MessageOccurrenceSpecification M of ID
6               Print M
```

Fig. 4. Algorithm for generating epl statement of success verdict

```
1    for each CombinedFragment F in InteractionDiagram ID
2        if InteractionOperator equals 'strict'
3            Print EPL Statement of "FAIL" monitor
4            EVERY
5            for each MessageOccurrenceSpecification MI of ID
6                Print MI
7                for each MessageOccurrenceSpecification MJ of ID
8                    if (MJ - MI) > 1
9                        Print MJ or
10               else
11                       Print "and not" MJ
```

Fig. 5. Algorithm for generating EPL statement of fail verdict

containing a similar EPL statement as in Eq. 2 is generated. This EPL statement selects all the matching sequences of messages as described in Fig. 3.

The solution framework can be extended to other scenarios by following the procedure and implementation details described in Sects. 3 and 4. The event relations logic, how to sniff a network for CoAP packets through a CoAP sniffer, and how to run runtime monitors as EPL statements are explained in [6]. Note that, the solution framework would be applicable to both online and offline testing provided that raw CoAP packets are injected into the CoAP Sniffer. This solution enables for observing interoperability of IoT systems at runtime.

5   Conclusion

The paper presented a framework for facilitating interoperability testing of IoT systems. The framework promotes interoperability through model-based testing techniques. We utilized sequence diagrams in order to describe expected interactions between endpoints. Then, those are extracted from the diagram so as to compose a set of runtime monitors in terms of CEP EPL statements. We demonstrated the applicability of this approach with a case study on a healthcare system. Our future work will address a more comprehensive interoperability approach by involving structural and semantics testing; which will present a domain-specific metamodel for CoAP-based IoT systems, and the framework will be incorporated in a cloud service such that the solution can be used as a service. We believe that we can model the interactions between IoT systems with thorough event relations, which elaborates on the application layer protocol behavior.

References

1. Fortino, G., Trunfio, P.: Internet of Things Based on Smart Objects, Technology, Middleware and Applications. Springer, Cham (2014). https://doi.org/10.1007/978-3-319-00491-4
2. Spichkova, M., Schmidt, H., Peake, I.: From abstract modelling to remote cyber-physical integration/interoperability testing. CoRR Journal, abs/1403.1005 (2014)
3. IETF Constrained RESTful Environments (core) Working Group. https://datatracker.ietf.org/wg/core/about/
4. Shelby, Z., Hartke, K., Bormann, C.: The constrained application protocol (CoAP). IETF RFC-7252 (2014)
5. Papyrus Modeling Environment. https://eclipse.org/papyrus/
6. İnçki, K., Arı, İ., Sözer, H.: Runtime verification of IoT system using complex event processing. In: Proceedings of 14th IEEE International Conference on Networking, Sensing and Control, Italy. IEEE Press (2017)
7. Unified Modeling Language (UML) Version 2.5. http://www.omg.org/spec/UML/2.5/
8. Wu, Y., Chen, M.-H., Offutt, J.: UML-based integration testing for component-based software. In: Erdogmus, H., Weng, T. (eds.) ICCBSS 2003. LNCS, vol. 2580, pp. 251–260. Springer, Heidelberg (2003). https://doi.org/10.1007/3-540-36465-X_24
9. Allen, P.: Component-based Development for Enterprise Systems: Applying the SELECT Perspective. Cambridge University Press, Cambridge, UK, New York (1998)
10. Bertolino, A., Polini, C.: The audition framework for testing web services interoperability. In: 31st EUROMICRO Conference on Software Engineering and Advanced Applications (2005)
11. Vega, D.E., Schieferdecker, I., Din, G.: Design of a test framework for automated interoperability testing of healthcare information systems. In: 2010 Second International Conference on eHealth, Telemedicine, and Social Medicine (2010)
12. Canfora, G., Di Penta, M.: Testing services and service-centric systems: challenges and opportunities. IEEE IT Prof. 8(2), 10–17 (2005)
13. Smythe, C.: Initial investigations into interoperability testing of web services from their specification using the unified modelling language. In: Proceedings of International Workshop on Web Services Modeling and Testing (WS-MaTe 2006) (2006)
14. Chen, N., Viho, C., Baire, A., Huang, X., Zha, J.: Ensuring interoperability for the Internet of Things: experience with CoAP protocol testing. Automatika 54(4) (2013)
15. EsperTech Complex-Event Processing Tool. http://espertech.com/
16. Gebase, L., Snelick, R., Skall, M.: Conformance testing and interoperability: a case study in healthcare data exchange. In: Proceedings of the 2008 International Conference on Software Engineering Research and Practice, SERP 2008, Las Vegas (2008)
17. Acceleo Model to Text Language. https://www.eclipse.org/acceleo/

Towards High Throughput Semantic Translation

Maria Ganzha[1,4], Marcin Paprzycki[1,5], Wiesław Pawłowski[2(✉)],
Paweł Szmeja[1], Katarzyna Wasielewska[1], Bartłomiej Solarz-Niesłuchowski[1],
and Jara Suárez de Puga García[3]

[1] Systems Research Institute, Polish Academy of Sciences, Warsaw, Poland
{maria.ganzha,marcin.paprzycki,pawel.szmeja,katarzyna.wasielewska,
bartlomiej.solarz-niesluchowski}@ibspan.waw.pl
[2] Faculty of Mathematics, Physics, and Informatics,
University of Gdańsk, Gdańsk, Poland
wieslaw.pawlowski@inf.ug.edu.pl
[3] Departamento de Comunicaciones, Universitat Politècnica de València,
Valencia, Spain
jasuade@dcom.upv.es
[4] Warsaw University of Technology, Warsaw, Poland
[5] Warsaw Management Academy, Warsaw, Poland

Abstract. One of "urban legends" of today's computer science is: *use of semantic technologies can become a serious performance bottleneck*. It is even possible that this, widely spread, belief is one of the reasons of slow progress in adopting semantic technologies in real-world applications. Since, obviously, IoT scenarios involve fast flowing streams of sensor data, will use of semantic technologies be "efficient enough" to not to adversely affect the effectiveness of the whole Internet of Things (IoT) ecosystem. The aim of this contribution is to provide an initial response to this question.

1 Introduction

It is rather rare when semantic technologies materialize in real-world/industrial grade projects/deployments. Instead, they are one of poster children of academic research. It is easy to find publications claiming that, for instance, ontologies will become a silver bullet for problems of e-commerce [3], or that semantics combined with software agents will deliver novel form of intelligent systems [2]. It can be stipulated that one of the reasons of this situation is a, widely held, belief that semantic technologies result in poor performance of applications. However, very few tests of this claim, for specific deployments, have been run.

In this context, in the (EU-funded) INTER-IoT project it was decided that semantic technologies will facilitate high-level interoperability between IoT artifacts (platforms, middlewares, applications, etc.). As reported in [4–6,10] the proposed approach can be summarized as follows. Assume that (1) multiple artifacts have to communicate (exchange/send/receive) messages within an IoT

G. Fortino et al. (Eds.): InterIoT 2017/SaSeIoT 2017, LNICST 242, pp. 67–74, 2018.
https://doi.org/10.1007/978-3-319-93797-7_9

ecosystem; and (2) majority of them use different internal data representation (syntax and semantics). Then, to facilitate interoperability, the following steps need to be undertaken. (1) Semantics of each artifact has to be represented in the form of an OWL-based ontology. This may require "lifting" other data representations to OWL ontologies [4,7]. (2) Uni- or bi-directional syntactic translators have to be implemented, to translate data from the artifact's internal syntax to the RDF representation (and, possibly, back). Note that when an artifact already uses RDF, the process is reduced to wrapping the message into a "proper structure". Need for uni- or bi-directional translation depends on the flow of information to be used. (3) Central modular ontology, covering the "core concepts of the IoT" as well as "domain specific" aspects of the deployment, has to be designed (from modules recommended by INTER-IoT, or other external ontologies). Modularity of the central (OWL-based) ontology assures that individual message flows can be easier managed, if they concern different "aspects" of the ecosystem. (4) Semantic translation mechanism, based on ontology alignments [5,10], has to be facilitated for translations between ontologies representing semantics of individual artifacts and the central ontology (and back). Here, again, need for uni- or bi-directional translation depends on the flow of messages between artifacts. The latter functionality has been conceptualized and implemented in the Inter-Platform Semantic Mediator (IPSM) component. The translation rules are defined in an alignment persisted in the INTER-IoT Alignment Format.

The aim of this contribution is to described preliminary experiments measuring performance of the IPSM. In the next section we introduce the architecture of the IPSM. We follow with results of throughput testing and conclude with proposed future work.

2   Inter-Platform Semantic Mediator

The role of the Inter-Platform Semantic Mediator is to facilitate alignment-based translation between source and target artifacts' semantics. Specifically, for each "communicating artifact" it's ontology is aligned with the central ontology. Note that there is no need to define complete alignments between ontologies. It is enough to capture correspondences between parts (or modules) used in communication. Specifically, while an alignment can represent number of correspondences (for a pair of ontologies), only the actually used ones are included. Alignments are represented in the INTER-IoT Alignment Format (for details see [5,10]). This format is based on the Alignment API[1] and influenced by the EDOAL[2].

The architecture of the IPSM is depicted in Fig. 1, where one can "follow" the translation process. Briefly, IPSM offers *translation channels* and communication infrastructure, based on Apache Kafka[3]. An input RDF message, expressed in the source ontology, is published to a preconfigured *input topic* associated with

---

[1] http://alignapi.gforge.inria.fr/format.html.
[2] http://alignapi.gforge.inria.fr/edoal.html.
[3] https://kafka.apache.org/.

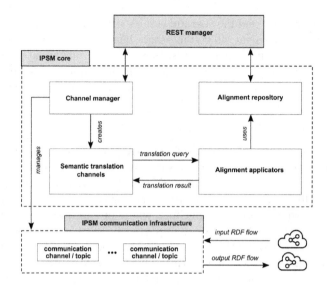

Fig. 1. IPSM architecture

a translation channel. Next, it gets translated to an RDF message, in the target ontology, and published to a preconfigured *output topic* of the channel, from where it can be consumed. Operations, for alignments and channel management, are exposed via a REST API. Each communication channel has a number of configuration parameters, including input and output topic names, alignment from source to central ontology, alignment from central to target ontology, and a "parallelism factor" of the channel. A more detailed description of the IPSM inner structure and the translation process can be found in [6].

3   IPSM Throughput Testing

Let us now discuss results of experimental testing of performance of the IPSM. Since IPSM is used to translate messages, we have decided to focus on throughput of the translation process. In other words, we assess how fast messages are translated. Due to the limited space, we report only a single set of experiments.

3.1   Experimental Setup

Let us introduce the setup used for carrying the experiments. We have used three different "machines". (A) Desktop PC with dual-core AMD Athlon 64 X2 processor and 4 GB of RAM, (B) Desktop PC with a quad-core Intel Core2 processor running at 2.4 GHz, with 4 GB of RAM, and (C) MS Azure VM exposing a "dual-core subset" of the Intel Xeon E5-2673 processor[4], and 8 GB of RAM.

---

[4] 12-core Xeon E5-2673 offers two logical cores for each physical one, resulting in 4 (logical) cores available to the Azure VM.

Translation involved real-life size and complexity messages, including geospatial data. In each experiment, 40,000 messages have been generated (with actual payload, differing by randomly chosen sensor data and numerical values of latitude and longitude). IPSM was set up to log the individual message processing time using Apache Kafka. Monitoring data was analyzed using R[5] framework.

3.2   Results and Analysis

In Fig. 2, a comparative histogram of message processing times for all three testing environments is presented. Specifically, we show how many messages have been processed within 5 ms, 15 ms , 25 ms, etc. As expected, the Azure VM was the most efficient, with a majority of messages processed within 5–15 ms. The next was the quad-core Intel machine, where processing time of majority of messages was between 5–25 ms. More importantly, even in the case of a weak, approximately 8 years old Athlon-based machine, the processing time of a vast majority of messages was less than 35 ms. This seems to contradict that general view that semantic technologies have to introduce bottlenecks to applications running them.

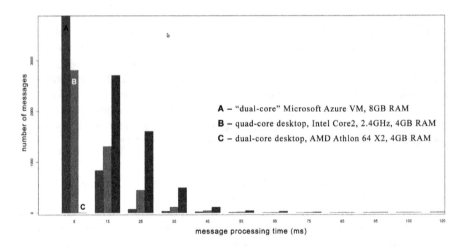

A – "dual-core" Microsoft Azure VM, 8GB RAM
B – quad-core desktop, Intel Core2, 2.4GHz, 4GB RAM
C – dual-core desktop, AMD Athlon 64 X2, 4GB RAM

Fig. 2. IPSM message processing time(s) – comparative histogram

Interestingly, we have observed (but have no space to depict) that performance of the Azure-based infrastructure was somewhat "erratic". Specifically, in each run there was a (small) number of individual messages that took relatively large amount of time to be translated. For instance, 3–5 messages took around 200 ms each, to be processed. We believe that this is an effect of Azure being a virtual machine, running together with other processes/VMs on a shared hardware, and competing for resources. No similar "obvious processing time peaks"

---

[5] https://www.r-project.org/.

were observed for the "physical machines". The figure shows that the IPSM performance "gently degrades" in accordance with the hardware specification of the machines used for testing.

The next series of experiments concerned possibility of further utilizing potential of the underlying hardware. We started by testing the influence of *internal parallelism* of translation channels. This time, we have concentrated solely on the Azure VM, as the most powerful environment in our setup. Results of experiments have been summarized in Fig. 3. Once again, we have streamed 40 thousand randomly generated, parametrized messages through a single translation channel, with a "parallelism factor" ranging from 1, up to 32. Figure 3 shows, for each of the tested factor values, a relationship between the message processing time *median*, and the *total time* needed to translate the whole stream.

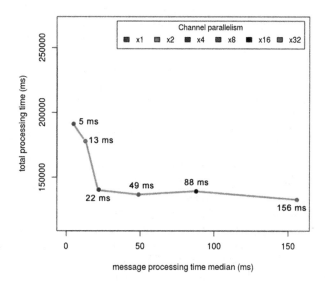

Fig. 3. Processing 40k messages via channel with internal parallelism on Azure VM

As can be seen, "performance gain" (represented as reduction of total processing time for all messages) has a "sweet spot" for the channel parallelism factor equal to 4. Further attempts at increasing the channel internal parallelism either result in substantial increase of the median or do not bring (sufficient) reduction of the total processing time. In other words, in-channel 4x parallelism exhausted resources of hardware used in our experiments. Obviously, for different hardware, it may be possible to further (in-channel) parallelize flow of messages.

Finally, in the last series of experiments, we have used multiple 1–16 (purely sequential) IPSM channels. As before, each run involved 40.000 messages (Fig. 4).

The results show that the sweet spot is, again, reached for four channels, where the underlying hardware became "saturated". Together with the results of the channel internal parallelism tests this shows that the IPSM translation

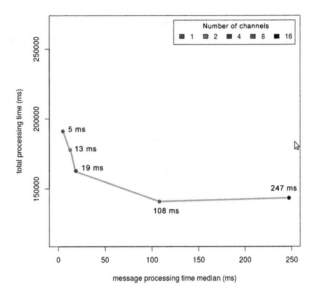

Fig. 4. Processing 40k messages via multiple channels on Azure VM

infrastructure is able to efficiently utilize the "native threads" (logical cores) of the VM's CPU.

All completed, thus far, performance test show that the IPSM architecture is not only efficient, but also scales very well "vertically", i.e., the more powerful the available hardware, the better translation throughput can be observed. Here, let us note that IPSM has been implemented using Scala programming language [9] and the actor-based [1,8] Akka[6] toolkit. Thanks to the well known properties of Akka and Apache Kafka, which was used to organize the IPSM communication infrastructure, and due to the fact that IPSM is component that can be deployed in multiple instances, it should also be highly scalable "horizontally".

4   Conclusions and Future Work

In this contribution we have attempted at experimentally addressing the question: is it really the case that use of semantic technologies results in serious performance bottlenecks? The context for seeking an answer was provided by the semantic translation that is being implemented in the IPSM component, developed within the framework of the INTER-IoT project.

The results are quite promising, since even when running the IPSM on an almost obsolete computer hardware, the processing time is reasonable. Therefore, we believe that semantic technologies can be used for information processing (e.g. semantic translation) even in the case relatively fast data flows.

---

[6] https://akka.io/.

Obviously, it is possible that more complex semantic translation scenarios than the ones used in our tests, will be needed. As a matter of fact, such translations are very likely to materialize within the scope of the INTER-IoT project. Therefore, we will continue our research and study performance of the IPSM in such cases. We will also see, which elements of the IPSM can be optimized to further improve its performance (in case of complex semantic translations). To even further improve the horizontal scalability of our solution we plan to investigate the possibility of forming IPSM clusters, where multiple IPSM instances can be administered and utilized in a uniform way.

Acknowledgment. This research was partially supported by the European Union's "Horizon 2020" research and innovation program as part of the "Interoperability of Heterogeneous IoT Platforms" (INTER-IoT) project under Grant Agreement No. 687283.

References

1. Agha, G.A.: Actors: A Model of Concurrent Computation in Distributed Systems. MIT Press, Cambridge (1986)
2. Allemang, D., Handler, J.: Semantic Web for the Working Ontologist, Second Edition: Effective Modeling in RDFS and OWL. Morgan Kaufmann Publishers Inc., San Francisco (2008)
3. Fensel, D.: Ontologies: Silver Bullet for Knowledge Management and Electronic Commerce. Springer, Heidelberg (2001). https://doi.org/10.1007/978-3-662-04396-7
4. Ganzha, M., Paprzycki, M., Pawłowski, W., Szmeja, P., Wasielewska, K.: Towards semantic interoperability between Internet of Things platforms. In: Gravina, R., Palau, C.E., Manso, M., Liotta, A., Fortino, G. (eds.) Integration, Interconnection, and Interoperability of IoT Systems. IT, pp. 103–127. Springer, Cham (2018). https://doi.org/10.1007/978-3-319-61300-0_6
5. Ganzha, M., Paprzycki, M., Pawłowski, W., Szmeja, P., Wasielewska, K.: Alignment-based semantic translation of geospatial data. In: Proceedings of the 3rd International Conference on Advances in Computing, Communication & Automation (ICACCA) (in press)
6. Ganzha, M., Paprzycki, M., Pawłowski, W., Szmeja, P., Wasielewska, K.: Streaming semantic translations. In: Proceedings of the 21st International Conference on System Theory, Control and Computing, ICSTCC (in press)
7. Ganzha, M., Paprzycki, M., Pawłowski, W., Szmeja, P., Wasielewska, K., Palau, C.E.: From implicit semantics towards ontologies–practical considerations from the INTER-IoT perspective (submitted for publication). In: Proceedings of 1st Edition of Globe-IoT 2017: Towards Global Interoperability Among IoT Systems (2017)
8. Hewitt, C., Bishop, P., Steiger, R.: A universal modular ACTOR formalism for artificial intelligence. In: Proceedings of the 3rd International Joint Conference on Artificial Intelligence, IJCAI 1973, pp. 235–245. Morgan Kaufmann Publishers Inc., San Francisco (1973)

9. Odersky, M., Spoon, L., Venners, B.: Programming in Scala, 3rd edn. Artima Press, USA (2016)
10. Ganzha, M., Paprzycki, M., Pawłowski, W., Szmeja, P., Wasielewska, K.: Declarative ontology alignment format for semantic translation. In: 3rd International Conference on Internet of Things: Smart Innovation and Usages (IoT-SIU 2018) (submitted)

Assessing the Impact of Mobility on LoRa Communications

Óscar Alvear[1,2], Jorge Herrera-Tapia[1,3], Carlos T. Calafate[1],
Enrique Hernández-Orallo[1], Juan-Carlos Cano[1], and Pietro Manzoni[1(✉)]

[1] Department of Computer Engineering,
Universitat Politècnica de València, Valencia, Spain
`jorge.herrera@live.uleam.edu.ec, pmanzoni@disca.upv.es`
[2] Department of Electrical Engineering, Electronics and Telecommunications,
Universidad de Cuenca, Cuenca, Ecuador
`oscar.alvear@alttics.com`
[3] Universidad Laica Eloy Alfaro de Manabí, Manta, Ecuador

Abstract. The use of LPWAN (Low Powered Wide Area Network) technologies in the scope of the Internet of Things have become the best alternative to send data between devices and cloud systems. Among these technologies, LoRa stands out as a novel and promising system that could be used in areas with a high device density, and in locations where other technologies do not provide enough communications range. In the past, most research works have made experiments in static scenarios, without taking the mobility of the things into account.

Our research is focused in analyzing the impact that mobility will have in LoRa communications performance, with the objective to determine the adequacy of this technology for vehicular scenarios oriented to data sensing, or in applications where small pieces of data are transmitted over long distances.

Experimental results show that both the mobility and the message size affect LoRa communications, despite still allowing to reach an acceptable coverage range.

Keywords: LoRa · Long range communications · Internet of Things
Sensors

1 Introduction

The Internet of Things (IoT)[1] is a novel paradigm where massive data collection and analysis has become a hot topic, especially when we are selecting the data transmission system to be adopted. Among the most widely used technologies, a few stand out, including WiFi, Bluetooth, NB-IoT, CAT-M1, and cellular communication. It is hard to choose the best option because one solution can achieve a good performance in a specific case, but perform poorly in other situations.

---

[1] www.internet-of-things-research.eu.

© ICST Institute for Computer Sciences, Social Informatics and Telecommunications Engineering 2018
G. Fortino et al. (Eds.): InterIoT 2017/SaSeIoT 2017, LNICST 242, pp. 75–81, 2018.
https://doi.org/10.1007/978-3-319-93797-7_10

In most of the cases, the short data messages generated by IoT devices derive from sensors mounted on such devices, and must meet different requirements in terms of communications performance, including long range, low power consumption, and low cost. As an example of solutions where sensor data is remotely retrieved, authors in [1] selected vehicles that, combined with fixed nodes located at strategic places, allow the data acquisition range to be extended. More recently, Alvear et al. [2] proposed a more sophisticated implementation where flying drones are used for sensing tasks. The above alternatives aim at addressing the sensor location problem, especially when the distances involved are high. There is a set of implementations and protocols named LPWAN (Low Powered Wide Area Network) [3,4] that accomplish and offer these requirements. In this group of technologies we can find SigFox, Random Phase Multiple Access (RPMA), Weightless, and the new technology LoRa (Long Range). Notice that only some of these are proprietary, while others are open source. LPWAN systems are currently the best alternative for sensing applications in dense locations where long term monitoring is necessary, sending small data packets in a wide area, and preserving battery life for a long period of time; these features are the differentiating factor between LPWAN and any other kind of wireless network.

In this paper we focus on the LoRa technology [5], which has been designed to transmit small data packets at large distances. In fact, according to the authors in [6], the transmission range can reach up until 50 km in rural areas if line of sight conditions are met, and up to 2 km in urban areas. In this work, we analyze the LoRa transmission range in both stationary and mobile environments. The rest of this paper is organized as follows: in Sect. 2 we refer to related works. An overview of LoRa is provided in Sect. 3. The testbed used in this work is presented in Sect. 4, and the obtained results are then discussed in Sect. 5. Finally, Sect. 6 presents the conclusions and refers to future work.

2   Related Work

Since LPWAN solutions emerged as an enabling technology allowing "things" to communicate, several researchers have focused their efforts on studying and improving these technologies. In [7] authors provide a detailed description of LPWAN, highlighting the advantages and disadvantages of this new model for IoT, and characterizing it in terms of efficiency, effectiveness, and architectural design for typical smart city applications.

In [8] the authors refer to it merely as LPWA (avoiding the network concept associated to the "n"). They offer a comparison between this type of protocols from a machine-to-machine (M2M) communications perspective, finding that this type of data transmission solutions is a potential candidate in ubiquitous computing contexts. Furthermore, they provide examples about specific scenarios where LPWA could be applied.

In the scope of LPWAN protocols, LoRa is a novel promising member, and many authors have analyzed this IoT-related solution from different points of view. For instance, in [9], authors evaluate the physical and data link layers of the LoRa technology through both field tests and simulations, proposing some improvements.

In [10], LoRa is adopted for sensing applications where the researchers tested the LoRa and LoRaWAN communications in urban areas with a high building density and irregular topography conditions. Using devices mounted in Raspberry and Arduino boards, the results show that, by using multiples gateways, the signal can span over certain areas that other radio technologies are unable to reach. A similar experiment is made in [11,12], where the authors analyze the LoRa properties in both indoor and outdoor scenarios, exploring how the environment affects its core communication properties. The result obtained is better than other alternatives that offer data transmission for alerts or sensing.

Overall, we find that there are many exciting research studies about LoRa, and in all of them the authors highlight both the benefits and the limitations of this novel technology. It is also worth pointing out that most of these articles have focused on data transmission under stationary conditions. In our research instead we present the results achieved when LoRa transmissions are performed under mobility conditions, and taking into account both the transmitter-receiver distance and the actual speed. Our ultimate goal is to determine the feasibility of adopting LoRa as a vehicular communications technology.

3   LoRa Technology Feature

LoRa is a LPWAN (Low–Power Wide-Area Networks) designed to optimize different aspects such as communication range, battery lifetime, and costs, supporting thousands of devices headed for the Internet of Things in several domains such as sensing, metering, and machine-to-machine (M2M) communications.

Theoretically, LoRa achieves a transmission range of more than 15 km in rural environments, and more than 2 km in dense urban zones. Its bandwidth ranges between 250 bps and 50 Kbps in different frequencies: 169 MHz, 433 MHz, and 868 MHz in Europe, and 915 MHz in North America.

LoRa Technolgy significantly increases the communications range thanks to the chirp spread spectrum modulation technique adopted. This communication system has been used in military activities for several years due to the long transmission distances that can be achieved, and also due to their robustness to interference.

The LoRa Spreading Factor is the "duration of the chirp" operating at various levels, from SF7 to SF12, where each level doubles the "duration" to the previous one, causing the bitrate to vary from 250 bps to 5.47 Kbps for a bandwidth of 125 kHz.

In this work, we are interested in long-range communications in vehicular networks. Low power is a bonus, but it is not a substantial requirement for our target application since in vehicular scenarios energy is not a critical factor.

4   Experimental Setup

In this section we detail the experiments undertaken using a LoRa-based data communications system under diverse mobility conditions. Our purpose is to determine to which degree do speed and distance affect data transmission. To achieve it, we analyze the transmission between a gateway and a mobile node using LoRa.

Fig. 1. Test architecture.

Figure 1 provides an overview of the testbed we have used. As shown, we have acquired Pycom modules[2] for our experiments. Both devices have nearly the same features. As a static gateway we configured a Pysense expansion board including a LoPy module and SD memory. Since we are interested in determining the impact of mobility on communications performance, the second device works as a mobile node that is equipped with a GPS receiver (Pytrack expansion board).

In our tests, we locate a gateway (Pysense equipped with a LoPy module) in a fixed position (39.480590 −0.346855, next to Universitat Politecnica de Valencia). To analyze how the speed affects the packet delivery ratio, we install the mobile node in a vehicle moving along the Tarongers Avenue (Valencia, Spain) under medium-high traffic levels, and at speeds up to 60 km/h, as shown Fig. 2.

In the gateway, we store all the data received from the mobile node, and in the mobile node we send and store two message types: (i) a large message - 30 bytes -, with an identifier and the GPS position, and (ii) a short message - 3 bytes -, carrying the identifier alone.

The LoRa radio configuration depends on the application scenario to be implemented. The most relevant configuration parameters are the Spreading Factor, the power, and the bandwidth. In our experiments, the power was set to the maximum value, the bandwidth to 125 MHz, and the Spreading Factor was changed from the minimum value 7 (recommended for short distance line-of-sight propagation), up to the maximum value 12 (for large distances and non-line-of-sight scenarios). In our experiments, we vary these parameters to determine what is the most optimal setting when operating under mobility. In the next section we describe the experiments made, and discuss the achieved results.

---

[2] www.pycom.io.

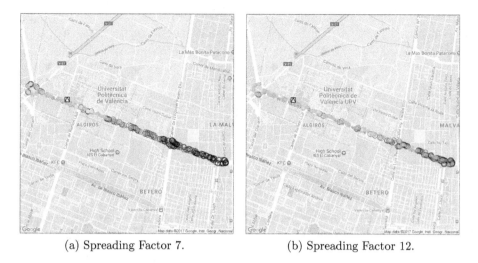

(a) Spreading Factor 7.   (b) Spreading Factor 12.

Fig. 2. Delivered (colored points) and lost (black circles) packets for different values of the Spreading Factor. (Color figur online)

5 Mobility Test and Results

In this section we present the LoRa performance results achieved under different conditions.

Figure 2 shows two maps that illustrate packet loss (black circles) and packet reception (colored points) when using a Spreading Factor of 7 (see Fig. 2a), or when using a Spreading Factor of 12 (see Fig. 2b). It becomes clear that a high Spreading Factor increases robustness when distances are high, as expected according to theory.

Figure 3 presents the analysis of the delivery ratio versus distance between Gateway and Node. Figure 3a shows the delivery ratio behaviour of the node installed in the vehicle (moving up to 60 km/h) when a Spread Factor of 7 is used. To analyze the impact of mobility on the packet delivery ratio, the figure also shows the delivery ratio with a static node at different distances, and for both message sizes (large -30 bytes-, and short -3 bytes-). We can observe that higher degrees of mobility cause the delivery ratio to be degraded. Moreover, the message size affects the maximum coverage area. The maximum range at which the delivery ratio remains higher than 75% is 520 m and 660 m for message sizes of 30 bytes and 3 bytes, respectively.

In Fig. 3b we make a similar results analysis when adopting a Spreading Factor of 12. We find that the results are similar: both message size and mobility have an impact on the LoRa range, achieving up to 860 m and 1250 m for message sizes of 30 bytes and 3 bytes, respectively.

In general we find that, as expected, using a Spreading Factor equal to 12 allows achieving better results than a Spreading Factor of 7, but its bit rate is much smaller: 250 bits/s against 5470 bits/s. Also, when using the Spreading

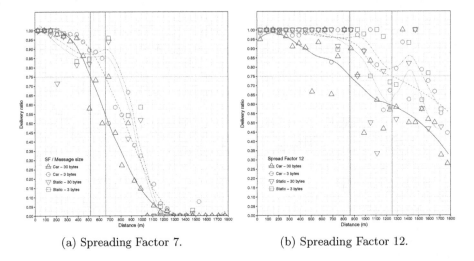

(a) Spreading Factor 7.   (b) Spreading Factor 12.

Fig. 3. Delivery ratio vs. range comparing: (i) Car (60 Km/h) and large messages, (ii) Car (60 Km/h) and short messages, (iii) Static and large messages, and (iv) Static and short messages for different values of the spreading factor.

Factor of 12, the loss variability is much higher than when using a Spreading Factor of 7.

It is worth pointing out that our objective was to analyze the performance of LoRa in a real urban scenario, and so the tests were made in an avenue with medium-high traffic levels, including an abundant number of cars, buses and trains moving along the avenue, which cause the loss rate levels and the variability to increase. Under ideal conditions, without line-of-sight obstructions, much better results are expected.

6   Conclusions and Future Work

In this paper we evaluated the combined use of LoRa communications with mobility to determine its applicability to vehicular networks in urban scenarios. Specifically, we wanted to determine the impact of the data size, the covered distance and the receiver speed on the packet delivery ratio. We found that both mobility and message size deteriorate the Lora performance. In addition, we changed the Spreading Factor in the LoRa devices, and found that the Spreading Factor provides a trade-off between transmission rate and packet loss.

Based on the obtained results, we conclude that the applicability of the LoRa technology in vehicular sensing scenarios is feasible as long as suitable parameters are set in the LoRa radio configuration. Our future work is focused in analyzing the performance of LoRa in different scenarios, and to perform exhaustive vehicular network simulations.

Acknowledgments. This work was supported by the *Ministerio de Economía y Competitividad, Programa Estatal de Investigación, Desarrollo e Innovación Orientada a los Retos de la Sociedad, Proyectos I+D+I 2014*, Spain, under Grant TEC2014-52690-R, the *Generalitat Valenciana*, Spain, the Secretaría Nacional de Educación Superior, Ciencia, Tecnología e Innovación del Ecuador (SENESCYT), the Universidad de Cuenca, and the Universidad Laica Eloy Alfaro de Manabí, Ecuador.

References

1. Herrera-Tapia, J., Förster, A., Hernández-Orallo, E., Udugama, A., Tomas, A., Manzoni, P.: Mobility as the main enabler of opportunistic data dissemination in urban scenarios. In: Puliafito, A., Bruneo, D., Distefano, S., Longo, F. (eds.) ADHOC-NOW 2017. LNCS, vol. 10517, pp. 107–120. Springer, Cham (2017). https://doi.org/10.1007/978-3-319-67910-5_9
2. Alvear, O.A., Zema, N.R., Natalizio, E., Calafate, C.T.: A chemotactic pollution-homing UAV guidance system. In: 2017 13th International Wireless Communications and Mobile Computing Conference (IWCMC), no. i, pp. 2115–2120 (2017)
3. Raza, U., Kulkarni, P., Sooriyabandara, M.: Low Power Wide Area Networks: A Survey, pp. 1–15 (2016). http://arxiv.org/abs/1606.07360/
4. Link-Labs: A Comprehensive look at Low Power, Wide Area Networks For 'Internet of Things' Engineers and Decision Makers (2016)
5. LoRa Alliance: A technical overview of LoRa and LoRaWAN, pp. 1–20, November 2015
6. Adelantado, F., Vilajosana, X., Tuset-peiro, P., Martinez, B., Melià-seguí, J., Watteyne, T.: Understanding the limits of LoRaWAN. IEEE Commun. Mag. (2017)
7. Zanella, A., Zorzi, M.: Long-range communications in unlicensed bands: the rising stars in the IoT and smart city scenarios. IEEE Wirel. Commun. 60–67 (2016)
8. Xiong, X., Zheng, K., Xu, R., Xiang, W., Chatzimisios, P.: Low power wide area machine-to-machine networks: key techniques and prototype. IEEE Commun. Mag. **53**(9), 64–71 (2015)
9. Augustin, A., Yi, J., Clausen, T., Townsley, W.M.: A study of LoRa: long range & low power networks for the Internet of Things. Sensors 1–18 (2016)
10. Wixted, A.J., Kinnaird, P., Larijani, H., Tait, A., Ahmadinia, A., Strachan, N.: Evaluation of LoRa and LoRa WAN for wireless sensor networks. IEEE Sensors 2016, 5–7 (2016)
11. Iova, O., Murphy, A.L., Picco, G.P., Ghiro, L., Molteni, D., Ossi, F., Cagnacci, F.: LoRa from the city to the mountains : exploration of hardware and environmental factors. In: International Conference on Embedded Wireless Systems and Networks (EWSN) 2017, pp. 317–322 (2017)
12. Herrera-Tapia, J., Hernández-Orallo, E., Tomás, A., Calafate, C.T., Cano, J.C., Zennaro, M., Manzoni, P.: Evaluating the use of sub-gigahertz wireless technologies to improve message delivery in opportunistic networks. In: Proceedings of the 2017 IEEE 14th International Conference on Networking, Sensing and Control, ICNSC 2017, pp. 305–310 (2017)

SaSeIoT Track

A Reinforcement Protection Game
in the Internet of Things

Andrey Garnaev[1,2]($\boxtimes$) and Wade Trappe[2]

[1] Saint Petersburg State University, St. Petersburg, Russia
garnaev@yahoo.com
[2] WINLAB, Rutgers University, North Brunswick, USA
trappe@winlab.rutgers.edu

Abstract. The vast scale of the Internet of Things (IoT), combined with its heterogeneous nature involving many different types of devices and machines, could lead the IoT to be vulnerable to a variety of security threats and malicious attacks. Addressing the broad array of threats requires that different security mechanisms are deployed at appropriate locations within the broader IoT communication network. In this paper, we examine this problem by applying a resource allocation approach involving a game-theoretical framework to model: (a) an attack aimed to maximize total damage to the network, and (b) an attack aimed to compromise at least one of the devices. To evaluate the probability of a successful attack we apply a contest success function, and found the associated equilibrium strategies in closed form. Additionally, we note an interesting relationship between equilibrium strategies in security reinforcement games and OFDM transmission games under hostile jamming. A criteria is designed that allows one to determine whether an IoT controller's resources is sufficient to protect all of the IoT devices it manages.

Keywords: IoT · Security · Compromised devices · Nash equilibrium

1 Introduction

The Internet of Things (IoT) is an emerging technology consisting of countless devices that were not traditionally associated with the Internet (such as TVs, thermostats, lighting appliances, coffeemakers, etc.), but are now being attached to the broader Internet. As these devices are deployed alongside next generation network protocols, they will be remotely accessible, allowing them to be monitored, updated, and reprogrammed. Unfortunately, with this increased connectivity comes the increased likelihood that they will be the target of malicious attacks.

Due to the large scale and heterogeneous nature of the devices involved (especially as many will have varying security capabilities), the IoT could end up more vulnerable to variety of security threats (such as cyber attacks or radio interference attacks [24]) than the Internet we have been familiar with. The recent the

© ICST Institute for Computer Sciences, Social Informatics and Telecommunications Engineering 2018
G. Fortino et al. (Eds.): InterIoT 2017/SaSeIoT 2017, LNICST 242, pp. 85–95, 2018.
https://doi.org/10.1007/978-3-319-93797-7_11

WannaCry virus attack [11] and demonstration of a thermostat ransomware hack [22], where the thermostat was set to 99°, and control would only be returned if the target paid Bitcoin to the cyber attackers, illustrated that such cyber attack will have unprecedented speed and scale, and might be especially dangerous as they can influence the physical world around us.

The large scale and heterogeneity of security capabilities makes developing and deploying anti-adversary strategies more challenging than in traditional networks [3]. One of the tools that has been used extensively in the literature to model different adversarial attacks on the IoT, as well as in the other networks, is game theory [13]. This is motivated by the fact that in such a security problem, there are at least two agents (e.g., the IoT controller and the adversary) that are present, and each of them has its own objective. For such a multi-agent problem, game theory supplies the foundations for developing and understanding the form that solutions should take [13]. As examples, we refer the readers to [17] for a Colonel Blotto game formalism, that arrives at a lower bound on SINR as a criteria for successful communication, and an evolutionary algorithm is devised that involves a centralized anti-jamming approach for an OFDM-based IoT system, where the IoT controller faces an adversarial attack aimed at maximizing the number of devices that cannot communicate with each other. In [15], signaling games were used to model honeypot-based deception mechanism to ensure security. In [16], a model motivated by low throughput networks was presented that models an attack where the adversary wants to maximize the number of compromised nodes while avoiding detection. In [18], a bi-matrix game was employed to model a choice of the subset of prosumers to share data if one of the prosumers can be compromised. In [19], an anomaly detection technique for low-resource IoT devices based on Nash equilibrium was suggested.

In this paper, motivated by the recent (and extremely rapid world-wide spread) WannaCry virus attack, in which many IoT devices were compromised throughout the world, we look at IoT security from a different angle. Namely: *how should the IoT controller allocate its protection reinforcement efforts in a heterogeneous network to minimize possible damage?* Here we quantify the damage involved by either the total number of compromised devices or the possibility that just one device will be compromised. The last scenario is important since, if a device inside of a corporate network is compromised, it makes it much easier for thieves to gain access to workstations and servers, and thus it is desirable to minimize the likelihood of a single device being compromised. To model the problem, we apply a resource allocation approach, which has been used extensively to model different network/communication security problems. As examples, we refer the readers to [21] for design multiband transmission protocol under jamming, to [6] for modeling one-time spectrum coexistence in dynamic spectrum access, to [23] for fair and efficient resource allocation in cloud computing, to [5,7–9] for bandwidth scanning strategy and to [2] for network protection.

The organization of this paper is as follows: in Sect. 2, two game-theoretical models for security reinforcement are formulated. In Sect. 3, for the first model dealing with minimizing the total damage (number of devices) to the network, equilibrium strategies are found. In Sect. 4, for the second model dealing with maximizing probability for the network not to be compromised, equilibrium strategies are designed. Finally, in Sect. 5, discussion of the obtained results is offered, and, in Appendix, the proofs of the obtained results are given.

2   Model

In the paper, we consider an IoT system consisting of a set of IoT devices located in a (protected) zone, connected to each other for the purpose of communicating and sharing data. We will abstract the notion of the network and not specify any particular topology, but instead consider just a subset D of the protected zone. This set consists of a finite number (say, n) of devices, i.e., $D = \{1, \ldots, n\}$. The devices are under attack by an adversary attempting to intrude on the protected zone in order to perform a damaging action (e.g. to steal data). To perform intrusion, the adversary also has some resources, for example this might be a number of compromised devices attacking the network. The total adversary's resources are X. To reinforce the network's protection, the IoT controller also has some resources (e.g., it can be related to the amount of time devoted to remote scanning and attestation of a device). The total IoT controller's resources is Y. Let y_t be the reinforcement effort the IoT controller applies to protect device t, and x_t be the resource applied by the adversary to infect/intrude into the device t. Thus, the set of feasible strategies to the adversary is $\Pi_A = \{x = (x_1, \ldots, x_n) \in \mathbb{R}_+^n : \sum_{t \in D} x_t = X\}$. Similarly, the set of feasible strategies for the IoT controller is $\Pi_C = \{y = (y_1, \ldots, y_n) \in \mathbb{R}_+^n : \sum_{t \in D} y_t = Y\}$. Let $P_t(x, y)$ be the probability of a successful intrusion into a device t of the network, when the protection effort x_t and intrusion effort y_t are employed. In this paper, we assume that this probability is proportional to the fraction of effort put into the attack, that is

$$P_t(\boldsymbol{x}, \boldsymbol{y}) = \alpha_t x_t / (d_t + \alpha_t x_t + \beta_t y_t), \tag{1}$$

where d_t is an initial level of the device's security, α_t and β_t are coefficients associated with the protection sensitivity to attack and protection efforts. The provability (1) is given by the ratio form contest success function commonly used in the attack-defense literature [4,12,14,20].

To avoid bulkiness in formulas we introduce the notation: $\alpha_t := \alpha_t / d_t$ and $\beta_t := \beta_t / d_t$. In the new notation, (1), reflects the probability of a successful attack on the device t, and becomes

$$P_t(\boldsymbol{x}, \boldsymbol{y}) = \alpha_t x_t / (1 + \alpha_t x_t + \beta_t y_t). \tag{2}$$

Then, the probability that no device has been compromised, is

$$Q(\boldsymbol{x}, \boldsymbol{y}) = \prod_{t \in D} (1 - P_t(\boldsymbol{x}, \boldsymbol{y})). \tag{3}$$

We now consider the two different goals for the IoT controller.

The goal of the IoT controller is to minimize total damage to the network. Let R_t be the value of device t, which reflects the reward to the adversary for successful intrusion of the network at node t. Then, the expected total damage is given as follows:

$$v_A(\boldsymbol{x}, \boldsymbol{y}) = \sum_{t \in D} R_t P_t(\boldsymbol{x}, \boldsymbol{y}). \tag{4}$$

In particular, for $R \equiv 1$, v_A is the expected number of devices that might be compromised by the adversary's attack. The v_A can be considered as a payoff to the adversary, which he aims to maximize. For the IoT controller, on the other hand, it is a cost function to be minimized. We assume that the agents have complete information about the parameters of the networks, i.e., α, β and R as well as on the total resources X and Y they have in their disposition. This scenario is described by a zero-sum game, and we look for an equilibrium [13]. Recall that, for a pair of strategies $(\boldsymbol{x}_*, \boldsymbol{y}_*)$ is an equilibrium in a zero-sum game if and only if the following inequalities hold for each $(\boldsymbol{x}, \boldsymbol{y})$:

$$v_A(\boldsymbol{x}, \boldsymbol{y}_*) \leq v_A(\boldsymbol{x}_*, \boldsymbol{y}_*) \leq v_A(\boldsymbol{x}_*, \boldsymbol{y}), \tag{5}$$

where $v_A(\boldsymbol{x}_*, \boldsymbol{y}_*)$ is called the value of the game. Even if there are several equilibria, each of them returns the same value of the game, i.e., the value of the game uniquely defined by (5).

The goal of the IoT controller is to maximize the probability that no device will be compromised. In this case, the payoff to the IoT controller is $Q(\boldsymbol{x}, \boldsymbol{y})$, while for the adversary this is its cost function. Again, this is a zero sum game and we look for the equilibrium strategies.

3   The Minimizing Total Damage Game

In this section, we find the equilibrium strategies for the game involving minimizing the total damage.

Theorem 1. *(a) In the minimizing total damage game, each equilibria has to have the form $(\boldsymbol{x}, \boldsymbol{y}) = (\boldsymbol{x}_{\omega,\nu}, \boldsymbol{y}_{\omega,\nu})$ where ω and ν are positive parameters and*

$$x_{\omega,\tau,t} = \begin{cases} R_t \alpha_t \beta_t \tau / (\omega (\tau \alpha_t + \beta_t)^2), & t \in I^{11}_{\omega,\tau}, \\ \left(\sqrt{R_t \alpha_t / \omega} - 1 \right) / \alpha_t, & t \in I^{10}_{\omega,\tau}, \\ 0, & t \in I^{00}_{\omega,\tau}, \end{cases} \tag{6}$$

$$y_{\omega,\tau,t} = \begin{cases} R_t \alpha_t \beta_t / (\omega (\alpha_t \tau + \beta_t)^2) - 1/\beta_t, & t \in I^{11}_{\omega,\tau}, \\ 0, & t \notin I^{11}_{\omega,\tau}, \end{cases} \tag{7}$$

where

$$I^{00}_{\omega,\tau} := \{t : R_t \alpha_t / \omega \leq 1\}, \quad I^{10}_{\omega,\tau} := \left\{ t : 1 < \sqrt{R_t \alpha_t / \omega} \leq 1 + (\alpha_t / \beta_t) \tau \right\},$$

$$I^{11}_{\omega,\tau} := \left\{ t : 1 + (\alpha_t \beta_t) \tau < \sqrt{R_t \alpha_t / \omega} \right\}. \tag{8}$$

*(b) Functions $S_x(\omega, \tau) := \sum_{t \in D} x_{\omega, \tau, t}$ and $S_y(\omega, \tau) := \sum_{t \in D} y_{\omega, \tau, t}$ have the
following properties:*

*(b-a) For a fixed $\tau > 0$, $S_y(\omega, \tau)$ is continuous on ω and decreasing from infinity
    for $\omega \downarrow 0$ to zero for $\omega \geq \max_t \alpha_t / (1 + \alpha_t \tau / \beta_t)^2$.*
*(b-b) For a fixed $\omega > 0$, $S_y(\omega, \tau)$ is continuous on τ and decreasing from
    $S_y(\omega, 0) = \sum_{t \in D} (1/\beta_t) \lfloor R_t \alpha_t / \omega - 1 \rfloor_+$ for $\tau = 0$ to zero for large τ.*
(b-c) For a fixed τ there is a unique $\Omega(\tau)$ such that

$$S_y(\Omega(\tau), \tau) = Y. \tag{9}$$

*Moreover, due to the monotonicity properties given in (a), the $\Omega(\tau)$ can be
found by bisection method.*
*(b-d) $\Omega(\tau)$ is a continuous and decreasing function from Ω_0 for $\tau = 0$ to zero,
    while τ tends to infinity, where Ω_0 is the unique positive root of the equation:
    $\sum_{t} {}_D (1/\beta_t) \lfloor R_t \alpha_t / \Omega_0 - 1 \rfloor_+ = Y$.*
*(b-e) $\Omega(\tau) \sim \Omega_\infty / \tau^2$ for τ tending to infinity, where Ω_∞ is the unique positive
    root of the equation: $\sum_{t \in D} \lfloor R_t \beta_t / (\alpha_t \Omega_\infty) - 1/\beta_t \rfloor_+ = Y$.*

*(c) The value of the parameters, ω and τ, can be found based on the condition
    that the resource budgets have to be fully utilized by both agents, i.e., as a
    solution of equations $S_x(\omega, \tau) = X$ and $S_y(\omega, \tau) = Y$ in two steps:*
(c-a) For each τ, find $\omega = \Omega(\tau)$ as the unique root of (9) by bisection method.
*(c-b) Since $S_x(\Omega(0), 0) = 0$ and $S_x(\Omega(\tau), \tau)$ tends to infinity for τ tending to
    infinity, τ can be found as the root of the equation $S_x(\Omega(\tau), \tau) = X$ by bisection method.*

Here, we can observe that the IoT controller, due to the restricted resources,
generally applies reinforcement partly, namely to a subset of devices I^{11} which
were not originally protected in a reliable manner, relying on initial level of
security for the others devices. While the adversary, besides attacking initially
less protected devices will, if he has enough resources, also exhibit a tendency
to take a chance among a subset I^{10} of the originally reliable protected devices.
A similar phenomena was also observed in the OFDM jamming problem, where
in general SNR regime the jammer can generally jam fewer subcarriers than the
user employs for transmission [1,10].

The theorem, beyond giving an algorithm to design equilibrium strategies,
also implies a criteria needed to establish whether the IoT controller's resources
are sufficient to reinforce all the devices.

Theorem 2. *In the game to minimize damage, the IoT controller can reinforce
all of the devices if the following condition holds:*

$$\tau < X \min_{t \in D} \frac{R_t \alpha_t}{(\tau \alpha_t / \beta_t + 1)^2} \Big/ \sum_{t \in D} \frac{R_s \alpha(s) / \beta_s}{(\tau \alpha_s / \beta_s + 1)^2}, \tag{10}$$

where

$$\tau = X / (Y + \sum_{t \in D} 1/\beta_t). \tag{11}$$

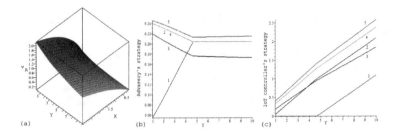

(a)   (b)   (c)

Fig. 1. (a) The payoff to an adversary aimed at maximizing the total damage, as functions of X and Y; (b) the strategy of the adversary and (c) the strategy of the IoT controller as functions of Y for $X = 1$.

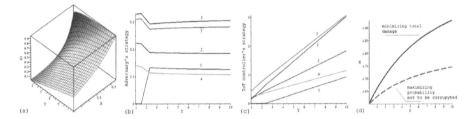

(a)   (b)   (c)   (d)

Fig. 2. (a) The payoff for the IoT controller that is aimed at maximizing the probability that the network is not compromised, as a function of X and Y; (b) the strategy of the adversary and (c) the strategy of the IoT controller as functions of Y for $X = 1$; and (d) the switching lines in the plane (X, Y) for the zones where the IoT controller's resources are enough to reinforce all of the devices.

Then, the equilibrium strategies are given by the first lines (6) and (7) with

$$\omega = \frac{\tau}{X} \sum_{t \in D} \frac{R_s \alpha_s / \beta_s}{(\tau \alpha_s / \beta_s + 1)^2}. \tag{12}$$

4   Maximizing Probability Not to Be Compromised

In this Section, we consider the game where the IoT controller wants to maximize the probability that none of the devices are compromised.

Theorem 3. *In the maximizing probability not to be compromised game, there is a unique equilibrium given by $(\boldsymbol{x}_{\omega,\tau,t}, \boldsymbol{y}_{\omega,\tau,t})$ where*

$$x_{\omega,\tau,t} = \begin{cases} \dfrac{\alpha_i \tau}{(\alpha_t \tau + \beta_t)\omega}, & t \in I^{11}_{\omega,\tau}, \\ \dfrac{1}{\omega} - \dfrac{1}{\alpha_t}, & t \in I^{10}_{\omega,\tau}, \\ 0, & t \in I^{00}_{\omega,\tau} \end{cases} \qquad y_{\omega,\tau,t} = \begin{cases} \dfrac{\alpha_t}{(\alpha_t \tau + \beta_t)\omega} - \dfrac{1}{\beta_t}, & t \in I^{11}_{\omega,\tau}, \\ 0, & t \notin I^{11}_{\omega,\tau} \end{cases}$$

$$\tag{13}$$

with $I_{\omega,\tau}^{00} := \{t : \alpha_t \leq \omega\}$, $I_{\omega,\tau}^{10} := \{t : \alpha_t \beta_t/(\alpha_t \tau + \beta_t) \leq \omega < \alpha_t\}$ and
$I_{\omega,\nu}^{11} := \{t : \omega < \alpha_t \beta_t/(\alpha_t \tau + \beta_t)\}$.

Astonishingly, these strategies coincide with OFDM transmission strategies when facing jamming [10]. This coincidence with OFDM transmission strategies implies that the value of parameters can be uniquely defined by superposition of bisection methods from the condition that the strategy must employ all of the resources, as was done in Theorem 1. Here, as in Theorem 1, as parameters we use the Lagrange multiplier ω, while as the other parameter τ we use ratio of Lagrange multipliers that arise to solve the corresponding best response equations. This allows, similar to Theorem 2, to show that if the following condition holds then the IoT controller's resources are enough to reinforce all of the devices:

$$\tau < X \min_{t \in D}(\alpha_t \beta_t)/(\tau \alpha_t + \beta_t)/\sum_{t \in D} \alpha(s)/(\tau \alpha_s + \beta_s) \text{ where } \tau \text{ is given by (11).}$$

(14)

5   Discussions

As an example, let us consider a network consisting of $n = 5$ devices and $\alpha = (1, 2, 2.1, 2.8, 3.2)$, $\beta = (1.5, 2, 1.2, 5, 2)$, and $R = (1, 1, 1, 1, 1)$. Since $R \equiv 1$, the payoff v_A, i.e., the expected total damage, reflects the expected number of compromised devices. Figure 1(a) illustrates that the total damage is decreasing with respect to an increase in Y, and it is increasing with respect to an increase on X. Figure 2(a) illustrates that the probability for the network to not be compromised is increasing with an increase in Y and it is decreasing with an increase in X. Figures 1 and 2 illustrate that the adversary's strategy for compromising at least one device is more distributed among the devices than for the case where the objective is to maximize the total damage.

Note that, by (11), the left-side of condition (10) tends to zero for Y tending to infinity, while its right-side tends to $\min_{t \in D} R_t \alpha_t / \sum_{s \in D} R_s \alpha_s / \beta_s > 0$. Thus, for each fixed X there is a Y such that the resource is enough to reinforce all of the devices. By (14), a similar conclusion holds for maximizing the probability that the network is not compromised. Figure 2(d) illustrates, in the plane (X, Y), the switching line between the zone where the IoT controller has enough resources to reinforce all of the devices and the zone where the resources only allows one to maintain partial reinforcement. In particular, this confirms that, in the game to maximize the probability for the network to not be compromised, the IoT controller must employ a strategy to reinforce all of the devices under a smaller resource budget than in the game to minimize total damage.

Appendix

Proof of Theorem 1. (a) By (5), (x, y) is an equilibrium if and only if x and y are the best response strategies to each other, i.e., they are the solution of the best response equations: $x = \mathrm{BR}_A(y) = \arg\max_{x \in \Pi_A} v_A(x, y)$ and $y =$

$BR_C(x) = \arg\min_{y \in \Pi_C} v_A(x, y)$. Since $v_A(\boldsymbol{x}, \boldsymbol{y})$ is concave on $\boldsymbol{x}$ and convex on $\boldsymbol{y}$, a pair of strategies $(\boldsymbol{x}, \boldsymbol{y})$ is the solution of the best response equations if and only if there are ω and ν (Lagrange multipliers) such that the following conditions hold:

$$\frac{R_t \alpha_t (1 + \beta_t y_t)}{(1 + \alpha_t x_t + \beta_t y_t)^2} \begin{cases} = \omega, & x_t > 0, \\ \leq \omega, & x_t = 0, \end{cases} \quad \frac{R_t \alpha_t \beta_t x_t}{(1 + \alpha_t x_t + \beta_t y_t)^2} \begin{cases} = \nu, & y_t > 0, \\ \leq \nu, & y_t = 0. \end{cases} \tag{15}$$

By (15), $\nu > 0$ and $\omega > 0$. Also, by the second relation of (15), if $x_t = 0$ then $y_t = 0$, since otherwise $\nu = 0$. Thus, we have to consider separately only three cases: (a-i) $x_t = 0$, $y_t = 0$, (a-ii) $x_t > 0$, $y_t = 0$ and (a-iii) $x_t > 0$, $y_t > 0$.

(a-i) Let $x_t = 0$, $y_t = 0$. Then, (15) is equivalent to $t \in I_{\omega,\nu}^{00} := \{t : R_t \alpha_t / \omega \leq 1\}$.

(a-ii) Let $x_t > 0$, $y_t = 0$. Then, (15) is equivalent to

$$R_t \alpha_t / ((1 + \alpha_t x_t)^2) = \omega, \tag{16}$$

$$R_t \alpha_t \beta_t x_t / (1 + \alpha_t x_t)^2 \leq \nu. \tag{17}$$

Solving (16) implies that

$$x_t = \left(\sqrt{R_t \alpha_t / \omega} - 1 \right) / \alpha_t. \tag{18}$$

Then, since $x_t > 0$, (18) implies that

$$\omega < R_t \alpha_t. \tag{19}$$

By (16), (17) is equivalent to

$$\beta_t x_t \leq \nu / \omega. \tag{20}$$

Substituting x_t given by (18) into (20) implies $\sqrt{R_t \alpha_t / \omega} \leq 1 + (\alpha_t / \beta_t)(\nu / \omega)$. This, jointly with (19), gives that $t \in I_{\omega,\nu}^{10} := \{t : 1 < \sqrt{R_t \alpha_t / \omega} \leq 1 + (\alpha_t / \beta_t)(\nu / \omega)\}$.

(a-iii) Let $x_t > 0$, $y_t > 0$. Then, (15) is equivalent to

$$R_t \alpha_t (1 + \beta_t y_t) / ((1 + \alpha_t x_t + \beta_t y_t)^2) = \omega, \tag{21}$$

$$R_t \alpha_t \beta_t x_t / ((1 + \alpha_t x_t + \beta_t y_t)^2) = \nu. \tag{22}$$

Dividing (21) by (22) implies

$$1 + \beta_t y_t = (\omega / \nu) \beta_t x_t. \tag{23}$$

Substituting (23) into (22) yields $x_t = R_t \alpha_t \beta_t / \left(\nu (\alpha_t + \beta_t \omega / \nu)^2 \right)$. Clearly, such x_t is positive. Substituting this x_t into (23) implies that $y_t = R_t \alpha_t \beta_t / (\omega (\alpha_t \nu / \omega + \beta_t)^2) - 1/\beta_t$. Then, the condition that such y_t is positive is equivalent that $t \in I_{\omega,\nu}^{11} := \left\{ t : 1 + (\alpha_t / \beta_t)(\nu / \omega) < \sqrt{R_t \alpha_t / \omega} \right\}$.

Finally, let us introduce an auxiliary notation $\tau := \nu/\omega$. In this notation x, y, I^{00}, I^{10} and I^{11} have the form given by (6), (7) and (8), and (a) follows.

(b-a) and b-(b) follow in a straightforward manner from (7) and (8) and the fact that $S_y(\omega, \tau) = 0$ if and only if the set $I^{11}_{\omega,\tau}$ is empty. (b-c) and (b-d) follow from (b-a) and (b-b).

(b-e) By (7) and (8), $S_y(\omega, \tau) = Y$ is equivalent to

$$\sum_{t \in D} \left\lfloor R_t \alpha_t \beta_t / ((\omega/\tau^2)(\alpha_t + \beta_t/\tau)^2) - 1/\beta_t \right\rfloor_+ = Y. \tag{24}$$

Then, substituting $\omega = \Omega(\tau)$ into (24) and taking τ to infinity we obtain that (24) is asymptotically equivalent to $\sum_{t \in D} \lfloor \beta_t / ((\Omega(\tau)/\tau^2)\alpha_t) - 1/\beta_t \rfloor_+ = Y$. This implies (b-e), and (b) follows.

(c) By (8), $I^{10}_{\omega,0}$ is empty. Thus, by (6) and (b-d), $S_x(\Omega(0),0) = S_x(\Omega_0, 0) = 0$. By (7) and (6), $I^{11}_{\Omega(\tau),\tau}$ is not empty for any τ. By (6) and (b-e), for large τ

$$x_{\Omega(\tau),\tau,t} \sim R_t \alpha_t \beta_t \tau^3 / (\Omega_\infty(\alpha_t \tau + \beta_t)^2) \sim R_t \beta_t \tau / (\alpha_t \Omega_\infty) \text{ with } t \in I^{11}_{\Omega(\tau),\tau}.$$

Thus, $\lim_{\tau \uparrow \infty} S_x(\Omega(\tau), \tau) = \infty$, and the result follows. ∎

Proof of Theorem 2. Since $I^{11}_{\omega,\tau} = \{1, \ldots, n\}$, x and y are given by the first lines in (6) and (7). Summing up these $x_{\omega,\tau,t}$ divided by τ on t, summing up these $y_{\omega,\tau,t}$ on t, and taking into account that $\boldsymbol{x}_{\omega,\tau} \in \Pi_A$ and $\boldsymbol{y}_{\omega,\tau} \in \Pi_C$ imply (11). Then, by (11), summing up these $x_{\omega,\tau,t}$ implies (12). Finally, (12) and the fact that $I^{11}_{\omega,\tau} = \{1, \ldots, n\}$ yields (10). ∎

Proof of Theorem 3. It is clear that the problem of maximizing (minimizing) $Q(\boldsymbol{x}, \boldsymbol{y})$ is equivalent to the problem of maximizing (minimizing) $\ln(Q(\boldsymbol{x}, \boldsymbol{y}))$. Using this simple observation implies that a pair of strategies $(\boldsymbol{x}, \boldsymbol{y})$ is the solution of the best response equations if and only if there are ω and ν (Lagrange multipliers) such that the following conditions hold:

$$\frac{\alpha_t}{1 + \alpha_t x_t + \beta_t y_t} \begin{cases} = \omega, & x_t > 0, \\ \leq \omega, & x_t = 0, \end{cases} \quad \frac{\alpha_t \beta_t x_t}{(1 + \beta_t y_t)(1 + \alpha_t x_t + \beta_t y_t)} \begin{cases} = \nu, & y_t > 0, \\ \leq \nu, & y_t = 0. \end{cases}$$

Astonishingly, these conditions coincide with the conditions for designing a transmission strategy under hostile jamming in OFDM communication [10]. Then, introducing a new variable $\tau = \nu/\omega$, in variables τ and ω the result follows. ∎

References

1. Ara, M., Reboredo, H., Ghanem, S.A.M., Rodrigues, M.R.D.: A zero-sum power allocation game in the parallel Gaussian wiretap channel with an unfriendly jammer. In: IEEE International Conference on Communication Systems (ICCS) (2012)
2. Baston, V.J., Garnaev, A.Y.: A search game with a protector. Naval Res. Logistics **47**, 85–96 (2000)

3. Fragkiadakis, A.G., Tragos, E.Z., Askoxylakis, I.G.: Survey on security threats and detection techniques in cognitive radio networks. IEEE Commun. Surv. Tutorials **15**, 428–445 (2013)
4. Garnaev, A., Baykal-Gursoy, M., Poor, H.V.: Security games with unknown adversarial strategies. IEEE Trans. Cybern. **46**, 2291–2299 (2016)
5. Garnaev, A., Trappe, W.: Stationary equilibrium strategies for bandwidth scanning. In: Jonsson, M., Vinel, A., Bellalta, B., Marina, N., Dimitrova, D., Fiems, D. (eds.) MACOM 2013. LNCS, vol. 8310, pp. 168–183. Springer, Cham (2013). https://doi.org/10.1007/978-3-319-03871-1_15
6. Garnaev, A., Trappe, W.: One-time spectrum coexistence in dynamic spectrum access when the secondary user may be malicious. IEEE Trans. Inf. Forensics Secur. **10**, 1064–1075 (2015)
7. Garnaev, A., Trappe, W.: A bandwidth monitoring strategy under uncertainty of the adversary's activity. IEEE Trans. Inf. Forensics Secur. **11**, 837–849 (2016)
8. Garnaev, A., Trappe, W.: Bandwidth scanning when facing interference attacks aimed at reducing spectrum opportunities. IEEE Trans. Inf. Forensics Secur. **12**, 1916–1930 (2017)
9. Garnaev, A., Trappe, W., Kung, C.-T.: Optimizing scanning strategies: selecting scanning bandwidth in adversarial RF environments. In: 8th International Conference on Cognitive Radio Oriented Wireless Networks (CROWNCOM), pp. 148–153 (2013)
10. Garnaev, A., Trappe, W., Petropulu, A.: Equilibrium strategies for an OFDM network that might be under a jamming attack. In: 51st Annual Conference on Information Systems and Sciences (CISS), pp. 1–6 (2017)
11. Gerstein, D.M.: The WannaCry virus, a lesson in global unpreparedness. The National Interest, 17 May 2017. http://nationalinterest.org/feature/the-wannacry-virus-lesson-global-unpreparedness-20719
12. Guan, P., Zhuang, J.: Modeling resources allocation in attacker-defender games with "warm up" CSF. Risk Anal. **36**, 776–791 (2016)
13. Han, Z., Niyato, D., Saad, W., Basar, T., Hjrungnes, A.: Game Theory in Wireless and Communication Networks: Theory, Models, and Applications. Cambridge University Press, New York (2012)
14. Hausken, K., Levitin, G.: Review of systems defense and attack models. Int. J. Performability Eng. **8**, 355–366 (2012)
15. La, Q.D., Quek, T.Q.S., Lee, J., Jin, S., Zhu, H.: Deceptive attack and defense game in honeypot-enabled networks for the Internet of Things. IEEE Internet Things J. **3**, 1025–1035 (2016)
16. Margelis, G., Piechocki, R., Tryfonas, T., Thomas, P.: Smart attacks on the integrity of the Internet of Things: avoiding detection by employing game theory. In: IEEE Global Communications Conference (GLOBECOM) (2016)
17. Namvar, N., Saad, W., Bahadori, N., Kelleys, B.: Jamming in the Internet of Things: a game-theoretic perspective. In: IEEE Global Communications Conference (GLOBECOM) (2016)
18. Rontidis, G., Panaousis, E., Laszka, A., Dagiuklas, T., Malacaria, P., Alpcan, T.: A game-theoretic approach for minimizing security risks in the Internet-of-Things. In: IEEE International Conference on Communication Workshop (ICCW), pp. 2639–2644 (2015)
19. Sedjelmaci, H., Senouci, S.-M., Bahri, M.A.: A lightweight anomaly detection technique for low-resource IOT devices: a game-theoretic methodology. In: IEEE International Conference on Communication (ICC), pp. 1–6 (2016)

20. Skaperdas, S.: Contest success functions. Econ. Theory **7**, 283–290 (1996)
21. Song, T., Stark, W.E., Li, T., Tugnait, J.K.: Optimal multiband transmission under hostile jamming. IEEE Trans. Commun. **64**, 4013–4027 (2016)
22. Storm, D.: Hackers demonstrated first ransomware for IoT thermostats at DEF CON. ComputerWorld, 8 August 2016. http://www.computerworld.com/article/3105001/security/hackers-demonstrated-first-ransomware-for-iot-thermostats-at-def-con.html
23. Xu, X., Yu, H.: A game theory approach to fair and efficient resource allocation in cloud computing. Math. Prob. Eng. **2014**, 1–14 (2014)
24. Zhou, L., Chao, H.-C.: Multimedia traffic security architecture for the Internet of Things. IEEE Netw. **25**, 35–40 (2011)

Safety-Related Wireless Communication via RF Modules for Industrial IoT Applications

Samer Telawi$^{(\boxtimes)}$, Ali Hayek, and Josef Börcsök

Department of Computer Architecture and System Programming,
University of Kassel, Wilhelmshöher Allee 71-73, 34121 Kassel, Germany
{samer.telawi,ali.hayek,j.boercsoek}@uni-kassel.de

Abstract. The major trend of *IoT* concept in the recent years is this technology being widely engaged into the industrial applications where the principles of critical safety are the essential concerns. Moreover, the great advantages and the rapid development of wireless communication technologies have driven them to form the backbone of *IoT* applications. Therefore, these wireless technologies must comply additional safety-related requirements in order to make their great features available for industrial applications. This research work is a complement work to the research introduced by Hayek et al. [1] and it describes a conceptual design of a safety-related wireless communication protocol based on *RF* technology, that fulfills the needed requirements as well as implements the safety approaches defined in the related safety standards to achieve all enhancements that make this technology suitable to be used in industrial internet of things applications.

Keywords: Frequency band · Frequency Hopping Spread Spectrum
Gateway · Industrial Internet of Things · Jamming
Safe communication · Safety integrity level · Safety-related
Sensor node · Threats · Wireless sensor networks

1 Introduction

The terminologies of smart and intelligent devices or systems that are being expanded and integrated in our daily life's details, such as smart homes, intelligent monitoring and transportation, represent systems that connect our physical world more than we ever imagined possible. These systems are commonly associated with the concept Internet of Things *(IoT)*, where through the utilization of different sensors types, the entire physical environments are coupled and connected closely in order to transmit a massive amount of sensory data via communication technologies. In such sophisticated systems used to provide intelligent monitoring, management and control, many embedded devices are interconnected to transmit the required information and instructions via distributed sensor networks. Consequently, a Wireless Sensor Network *(WSN)* defines the

© ICST Institute for Computer Sciences, Social Informatics and Telecommunications Engineering 2018
G. Fortino et al. (Eds.): InterIoT 2017/SaSeIoT 2017, LNICST 242, pp. 96–112, 2018.
https://doi.org/10.1007/978-3-319-93797-7_12

large number of interconnected sensor nodes that are equipped with a big range of sensors to detect and capture different factors as well as physical conditions and phenomena such as temperature, pressure, humidity, gas, human body pointers, motion, vibration, etc.

However, the term Internet of Things was introduced by Kevin Ashton in 1999 [2] which recognizes all the objects that are uniquely identified and have their own virtual existence in an "internet-like" structure. There are tremendous possibilities for these objects, so they can be anything starting from large buildings, vehicles, planes, machines, any type of products, to humans and animals or even a specific part of their bodies.

As a matter of fact, both *IoT* and *WSNs* were developed in parallel, and while *IoT* does not require or assume any specific kind of the available communication technologies, the wireless technology have the capabilities to play the major and most important role in *IoT* applications. Furthermore, the *WSNs* are recognized as a revolutionary approach for capturing and gathering environmental data that is used to structure efficient and reliable systems. Moreover, their features such as flexibility, fast deployment of devices comparing with wired networks, rapid development, and availability of the inexpensive miniaturized low power consumption components like microprocessors, radios and sensors that are integrated together to form System on Chip *(SoC)*, lead to involve and integrate *IoT* in the smallest objects installed in any kind of environments and applications. This integration is the major evolution which drives *WSNs* to become the backbone and the key technology for *IoT*.

However, the wide utilization of industrial internet of things *(IIoT)* in different fields, where the safety of human is a critical issue, requires safety-related communication. Nowadays, variety of efforts focus on this promising field to have the advantages of wireless communication in the industrial applications and provide more sophisticated, reliable, and safe approaches that meet the safety requirements of different relevant international standards. This research work introduces a new approach to achieve the safe wireless communication based on providing hardware redundancy which requires redundant communication channels, in addition to the conceptual protocol that meets the standardized safety requirements and manages the redundant channels. This proposed approach targets the safety-related *IIoT* applications.

The next two subsections of this paper provide an overview about the key concept of *IoT* which is the wireless communication networks, also a review of the related research works is introduced. Section 2 of this paper roughly reviews the standardized requirements of safety related communications and how to integrate them in wireless communications. Section 3 explains how to overcome different challenges of the wireless sensor networks. Section 3.2 introduces the conceptual safety-related wireless protocol and Sect. 4 includes a summary of experiments and tests in addition to the conclusion of this research work.

1.1 Wireless Sensor Networks

Commonly, *WSNs* identify the type of sensor networks that utilize the wireless communication, and consist of a base station (gateway) and sensor nodes that capture the physical parameters or events and convert them into a digital representation giving us the ability to monitor the physical environment around us. A sensor network can be composed of one or a large number of sensor nodes partially distributed and deployed closely to the phenomenon or the event to be monitored. Consequently, the purpose of these nodes is to collect the relevant sensory data and route them back to the sink which will utilize this data.

Wireless sensor node integrates many capabilities such as sensing, on-board processing, communications, and storage together on a very small miniaturized board [3]. With these enhancements, a wireless sensor node can often play different roles in addition to the main role of capturing sensory data, such as in-network analysis which requires collaborating with other nodes in order to propagate the sensory data toward the base station, and fusion of its own sensory data with the data of other nodes. Sensor node in *WSNs* can have different variations, in that, it can be a simple sensor node to monitor a single physical factor or a complex device that combines many sensing techniques e.g., acoustic, optical, magnetic. Moreover, they can utilize different communication capabilities and technologies like ultrasound, infrared, or radio frequency.

WSNs have two different types according to their routing structure which is affected by the geographical distribution [3]:

(i) Single hop (Star Topology)
(ii) Multi hop (Mesh Topology)

Accordingly, *WSNs* offer many great advantages, such as reducing the mass and volume by eliminating cables, the wireless components can be embedded in different materials, the cost effective and rapid deployment of sensor nodes, the ability to penetrate many materials without the need of actual physical penetration, and in some applications the wireless might provide a redundant layer for functions that is insensitive to failures in the system structure. Hence, providing developers and designers with more flexibilities and abilities that might be very important in some industries like avionics systems, vehicles, and energy.

1.2 Related Work

WSNs have inspired the system designers to introduce a tremendous applications. Some of them are futuristic like the research work introduced by Alena et al. [4] which investigates and evaluates the *ZigBee* technology and its capabilities to be used in avionics and aerospace industry, while a large number of them are in use and practically useful. The applications in the latter category show a remarkable diversity according to the ability of *WSNs* in providing a continuous real-time autonomous data acquisition, a combined data from a wide variety of sensors, an improved data accessibility, a better data management, and the analysis of data to predict and prevent unlikely events. Such applications are noticeable in different fields of industries as the following:

(i) Home automation or smart home.
(ii) Emerging smart energy markets: like the smart network project to monitor the electricity usage of homes, which is carried out by *WEL Networks* the electricity distribution company in *New Zealand* [5].
(iii) Monitoring of underground working Environment: to detect and capture the environmental factors of the coal mines introduced by Tejashri et al. [6], and Raghram et al. [7].
(iv) Transportation: to monitor the physical environment of the railways introduced by Victoria et al. [8].
(v) Monitoring of human activities and health as in the work provided by Lu et al. [9].
(vi) Monitoring of nature such as active volcanoes, forests in order to protect them from fire as introduced by Jadhav et al. [10], weather, etc.
(vii) Monitoring of pipelines (water, oil, gas), structural health, supply chain management, etc.

Nonetheless, the mentioned research works introduce systems involved with the safety of human life; which is the most important concern; they only focus on showing the efficiency of using *WSNs* in such applications and they evaluate different factors and parameters of the systems, such as network topologies, communication quality, power management, and routing algorithms. Besides, these systems are not safety-related even those that are proposed to be used in hazardous working environments, conversely, the systems that are engaged in a critical environments and whose failure might endanger the human safety or the environment itself must be safety-critical systems, thus the systems must fulfill the safety requirements that consist of functional part and safety-integrity level *(SIL)* part which determines the required level of risk reduction [11–13], likewise, achieving a safe communication.

Meanwhile, many noticeable efforts are involved in introducing different approaches to provide safe wireless communication for industrial or human safety relevant applications, such as the *SafeCOP ECSEL* project that provides an approach to the safety assurance by use of safe wireless communication. This project implements the defined requirements in the well known standards e.g. *IEC 61508* [11], and *ISO 26262* [14] to achieve the safe communication. Furthermore, a remarkable effort is introduced by Pendli et al. in which the researchers provided a complete approach with all mathematical models and analysis for utilizing the *Bluetooth* technology and implementing the defined requirements in the mentioned standards to achieve the safe communication that can be used in safety-related systems [15, 16].

However, the efforts that aim to achieve a safe wireless communication comply the safety requirements defined in different standards by adding a new safety-layer to the stack of the involved communication protocol, in that they mainly focus on implementing those requirements at the software layer. This research work introduces an approach to fulfill the safe communication by providing a hardware redundancy as well as the required improvements to the protocol to manage the safety communications and the redundant channels.

The next section provides an overview about the safety standards and fundamental requirements that are needed to be considered and integrated to achieve the safe wireless communications. These standards identify the challenges that form the sources of failures and errors in wireless communications, in addition to the proposed procedures and policies to overcome and manage these sources of errors.

2   Safety-Related Wireless Communications

Regarding the increased demand on safe communication for safety-related systems in industrial applications, the necessity to develop the available industrial network technologies that do not provide safe communication such as *Profinet, Interbus, Profibus, Ethernt* and *CAN-Open* comes into a considered meaning. Consequently, to achieve a safe communication these technologies have been developed and new versions have been issued accordingly as *Profinet-Safety, Interbus-Safety, Profibus-Safety, Safe-Ethernet* and *CANOpen-Safety*. These safety protocol fulfill the special requirements for safety-related industrial applications such as high reliability, high safety integrity level up to *SIL 3*. Nevertheless, the great advantages of the wireless communication it cannot totally replace the previous industrial wired technologies. But when the wireless communication become a mandatory requirement for some applications that need mobility or special physical structures in which the physical penetration for the cables is not likely, this technology must be analyzed to implement the safety methods according to the European standard *EN 50159-2* [17]. In that, two major issues must be taken into account in order to adopt the wireless communication in industrial safety-related applications, that are security and safety.

Although the safety standards and analysis frameworks of data communication were originally intended for wired network, they can also be implemented and applied to the wireless communications referring that the wireless communications do not produce any new types of errors, but the only differentiation is in the probabilities of errors [18]. The next subsection provides a rough summary about the required safety issues and standards to overcome the failures and errors produced by the wireless communications in order to achieve the safe communication.

2.1   Fundamental Requirements for Safety-Related Communications

The distributed nature of industrial Internet of things applications requires more effective and uninterrupted communication methodologies between all sensor nodes. Therefore, additional safety layers are added to fulfill the necessary special requirements that are fault tolerant and safety. When implementing safety-related applications, it is important to utilize two safe hardware ends that are the source and destination nodes in addition to the safe protocol. Moreover, all standards for functional safety demonstrate that the reliability of such systems is achieved by adopting redundancy in addition to the technical and non-technical measurements for fault detection of the safety system, but redundancy is not sufficient to achieve faults free systems while this can be impaired by the random failures of single components, in that the best approach is to control these unavoidable failures based on a redundancy that does not lead to the failure or it can diagnose the failures so early [19,20].

The main challenges of a safe communication can be categorized according to their type into two categories [19,20]:

(i) Functional requirements of the process: this category concerns many factors such as the response time of the safety-related system controller, the amount of data that are needed to be processed and the operation mode of the application whether it should operate in a high or low demand mode.
(ii) Qualitative measures against failures: the most important issues in safety-related systems are the transmission errors, such as repetition of a message, loss of a complete message, insertion of an unwanted message due to an error, wrong sequence of messages, data corruption and delay.

Similarly, the standards of safe communications such as *EN 50159-1* and *EN 50159-2* describe the suitable defense methods to control and overcome the previews challenges. Table 1 shows descriptions of the threats and corresponding defense methods.

Furthermore, the concept of data integrity is considered as the most important challenge in the safety-related systems, thus this integrity can be assured using the redundancy method which assumes that both sender and receiver have two communication channels, and the received messages are compared to check the correctness of transmission. Hence, detecting any difference between the two copies of the same message represents an error. Adopting this hardware redundancy method eliminates and detects many threats such as retransmission, packet loss, malicious insertion and wrong sequence. Consequently, this hardware redundancy must implement one of the four defined architectural models [19–21], and these models that are presented in Fig. 1 describes how the channels are connected and the communication is managed over the adopted redundancy model through across different layers of the communication stack.

(i) Model *A* represents a single channel of controller for both safety-related end nodes.
(ii) A complete redundant system is described in model *B*, in which the safeguard and the transmission layers are designed dual. This model is adopted for this research work.
(iii) Model *C* corresponds to Model B with a single-channel transmission medium. The transmission layers and the safeguards are existed in both safety channels of the safety-related end node.
(iv) Model *D* presents two-canal link layers via a single-channel of transmission layer, and both link layers have the ability to access the transmission layer independently.

So far, the presented methods were introduced to provide safety for wired communication, but while the wireless communication does not produce any new

Table 1. Description of the defense methods against threats [22]

Defense method	Description	Threat
Sequence number	Each message is identified by a consecutive number	Repetition, deletion, insertion, incorrect sequence
Time stamp	Each message has the sending time	Repetition, incorrect sequence, delay
Source and destination identifier	Source and destination addresses are included in the message	Insertion
Acknowledgments	Receiver send sends a positive or negative acknowledgment	Insertion
Identification	Identity check must be done for all network members before the system starts up	Insertion
CRC cyclic redundancy check	CRC is calculated for the message bits and included with it	Corruption
Encryption	Apply authentication and add the cryptographic code into the message	Corruption, malicious attacks
Membership control	The network members monitor each other	Inconsistency
Atomic broadcast	To ensure that all sent messages are delivered in the same order to all receivers	Inconsistency
Hamming distance to addresses and message identifiers	To detect the case of single bit failure in the address or in the message identifier	Insertion

type of errors, these methods are capable to be adopted in the wireless communication technologies. Regarding the different physical transmission medium used in wireless communications more threats need to be considered, and the next subsection overviews these threats with the correspondence defense methods.

2.2   Safe Requirements for WSNs

Due to the broadcasting nature and the deployment of wireless sensor nodes, they are exposed to different types of threats that might affect the confidentiality, integrity and availability of sensory data. These threats are categorized based on the affected layer of the wireless communication protocol stack and the objectives into the following:

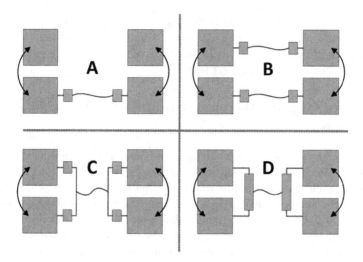

Fig. 1. Communication models

(i) Sabotage attack: *WSNs* are widely distributed making them an easy targets for different types of attacks. The first type called passive attack in which the attacker listens to the channel and steals the packets that may include important information, thus they only seek information without disturbing the communication or damaging the network, and this attack targets the higher layers of the protocol stack. The defense methods against this type of threat are encryption and keys management algorithms [3,23].

(ii) Denial of service attack: usually this type targets the physical layer which contains the operating frequencies, the capability to turn ON/OFF the transceiver and channel selection. However, the most spread type of such attack is jamming that disturbs the transmission communication by inserting a severe intervention to occupy the channels and block the receivers. Jamming attack either continuously emits a high energy signal on the channel in that always found busy by the sender, or transmits regular packets to force the receiver to receive junk packets all the time [24]. Hence protection against jamming attack requires an efficient prevention mechanism like Frequency Hopping Spread Spectrum *(FHSS)* where the data packets are transmitted with different carrier frequencies bands at different intervals of time. Therefore, the two parties have to go through a negotiation phase in order to agree on the switching sequence before the real data transmission starts [25].

(iii) Interference and multi-path: *RF* interference is the main reason for packet errors while it disrupts the ability to interpret received packets, also the existing of reflecting metals in the environment at which the wireless nodes are deployed is the main reason for duplicating the messages. It is possible to overcome these threats by using addressing and sequence number in addition to select the right carrier frequency band that has no interference.

The mentioned methods have to be implemented according to the required *SIL* applying the approaches defined in the standard *IEC 61508* that regards the probability of failure of the whole hardware of the system. These approaches will be defined in more details next section.

3   Concept of Safe Wireless Communication Using RF Modules

This section introduces in more details the proposed design of the safety-related wireless communication system for *IIoT* applications. The first subsection includes a short review about some required basic concepts, characteristics and approaches that are involved in achieving the target system according to the standard *IEC 61508-2*. The second subsection introduces the hardware components as well as the software design and how the safety requirements for safe communication are managed in both software and hardware. Finally, the last section summarizes some experiments conducted by the researchers to test the conceptual system.

3.1   Safety-Related Concepts and Approaches

The digital systems designed to operate in safety-critical environments must comply some functional, nonfunctional, and technical conditions; in particular fail-safe architecture, reliability and fault-tolerance. The reliable system requires to implement hardware redundancy which integrates more components than required to perform the same function. In case of failure in one component the system will switch into a defined safe-mode after activating the correspondence replacement of the failed component. The fail-safe architecture is the frame which holds the previous concepts, and the safety structure X *out of* Y in which Y stands for the existed number of independent paths; the path is a group of hardware components responsible to perform specific function; while X is the minimum necessary number of paths for the system to operate correctly. Consequently, the adopted structure of the investigated system in this research work is *1oo2* where one of the two channels is sufficient for the safety function to fulfill its task [12, 13].

Designing of the communication system is a combination of hardware and software. Therefore, the methods of *IEC 61508-2 (hardware)* and *IEC 61508-3 (software)* should be satisfied to achieve a safe communication. The standard *IEC 61508-2* addresses that when implementing a safety function that requires any form of data communication the probability of undetected failure of the communication process must be calculated considering the previously mentioned threats. This probability is taken into account when estimating the probability of dangerous failure of the safety function. Moreover, two approaches were defined in this standard:

(i) *White channel:* all the subsystems hardware as well as software used in safe communication should meet the relevant requirements of *IEC 61508*.

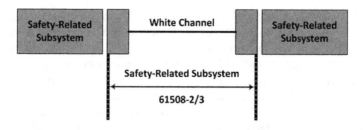

Fig. 2. White channel approach [22]

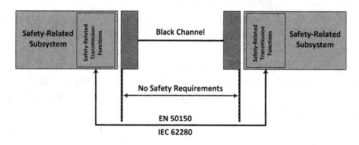

Fig. 3. Black channel approach [22]

Figure 2 shows a block diagram for the concept of a white channel that is adopted in this research work.

(ii) *Black channel:* the required measures to provide a safe data communication are implemented in the subsystems that represent the sender and the receiver. Thus, there are no safety requirements on other part of the safety-related communication systems. The concept of black channel approach is shown in the term of block diagram in Fig. 3. This is the approach of standards *EN 50159-1,-2, IEC 62280* and it was extended in *IEC 61508* to include the calculations of probability of dangerous failures.

The next subsection provides a detailed overview about the target safe communication system, in that the utilized hardware components are introduced and how they are integrated together in order to fulfill the safety requirements and implement the adopted standardized approach in order to achieve the safe communication functionality.

3.2   Conceptual Safe Wireless Communication System

This research work utilizes a *SIL 3* safety-related chip which integrates two subsystems together, the first subsystem is the safety system and it includes two processors in order to achieve the *1oo2* safe-architecture as well as a hardware comparator between these two processors that is responsible to provide diagnosis functionality, in that achieving an enhanced safe-architecture which is *1oo2D*. Furthermore, the second subsystem in this chip is the com system that includes only one processor and it is responsible to provide the safe part of this chip with the required communication interfaces with the external environment implementing the approach introduced in Fig. 3. All of these components are integrated together on a single chip to form a System on Chip.

Accordingly, in order to provide the physical wireless transmission medium for the safety-related chip, the *RFM69* modules are used where they provide many features drive them to be suitable solution for high performance sensor networks, such as the extremely low-cost solutions, very small size, low mass, narrow-band and wide-band communication modes, the major parameters of *RF* communication are programmable, lower power consumption, two transmission modes (continuous and packet), *SPI* communication interface, and the most important that is the module provides some built in functions that fulfill the safe requirements [26].

Furthermore, in order to complete the structure of the wireless sensor node an acceleration sensor is used and combined with the safety-related chip. Thus, any type of sensors can be used even the node can combine more than one type of sensors to be able to detect more than one factor of the monitored environment. However, regardless what sensor type is used to build up this node, these sensors must be structured according to *1oo2* safe-architecture.

This research work starts with the simplest structure of the wireless sensor network that consists of only two ends, the gateway and the sensor node. As mentioned previously in order to achieve a safe communication both ends must be safety-related designed, in that the hardware redundancy is achieved by implementing the *1oo2* safe-structure along the path from the source to the sink according to the white channel approach shown in Fig. 2. The detailed design of this conceptual system is presented in Fig. 4 that shows the safety architecture of both safety-gateway and safety-node in addition to the safe wireless communication. According to the white channel approach this whole system consists of three safety-related subsystems:

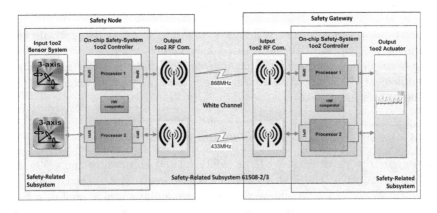

Fig. 4. Structure of the safe wireless communication system

(i) The first subsystem exists in the safety node and it includes the safety-related sensor system and the safety-related controller which is implemented in the utilized safety-chip. Each sensor is interfaced with a specific processor in the controller via an independent *SPI* interface fulfilling the *1oo2* architecture to obtain a safe sensory data.

(ii) The second subsystem exists in the safety gateway and similarly it includes the safety-related controller that is connected to some safety-related actuator via some interface.

(iii) The third subsystem exists in both safety ends and it includes the communication parts of both sides. This communication part consists of two *RFM69* modules connected via *SPI* interfaces independently to each processor in the controller according to safe-architecture *1oo2*. Besides, one *RF* module operates at frequency band of 868 MHz and the second one operates at 433 MHz to implement; with cooperation of the *RF* modules on the other end; a redundant communication channel. These two communication parts on both ends represent the white channel approach.

However, each end in the presented design can be viewed as a sequence of input-controller-output. Thus, for safety node the *1oo2* sensor system represents the input, the safe part of the safety-related chip represents the *1oo2* controller, the *RF* communication represents the *1oo2* output. Likewise, for safety gateway the *RF* communication represents the *1oo2* input, the safe part of the safety-related chip represents the *1oo2* controller, and the safe actuators represent the *1oo2* output.

Figure 5 presents a prototype of the introduced system where all involved hardware components are integrated together and the *RFM69* modules are

Fig. 5. Prototype of safe wireless communication system

mounted to a board with correspondent antennas, in addition the second board includes the safety-related chip and the acceleration sensors. Besides, the two boards are interfaced together via *SPI* using wires.

Table 2. Frequency bands ranges [26]

Frequency band	Min	Max
433 MHz	424	510
868 MHz	862	890

However, the denial of service attack based on jamming is one of the most important challenges that this system must overcome using one of the proposed defense method such as frequency hopping in which the underlying basics are to change the carrier frequency to assure that the data is transmitted over one frequency band for a short time. Therefore, the frequency band of the transceiver should be divided into channels and the communication protocol will hop between these different channels with respect to the hopping period and the sequence pattern of the channels. However, this research work utilizes two *RF* modules operate at two different frequency bands 433 MHz and 868 MHz where their possible frequencies are shown in Table 2, so these two bands can be divided into different number of frequency channels based on the utilized step which can be one of the next values 200 kHz, 1 MHz, 5 MHz, 7 MHz, 12 MHz, 20 MHz, 25 MHz [26]. Thus the suitable number of channels and the hopping period will be determined based on experiments while many issues should be considered such as response time, processing load, and complexity.

Regarding, the previous issues and the great built-in functionalities of *RFM69* modules, the challenges and the requirements that this system must overcome and comply accordingly are managed and distributed between hardware and software as presented in Table 3.

Furthermore, the wireless communication protocol for this simple network structure where only two ends are involved, should follow different phases before the transmission of safe sensory data starts. However, at the beginning when the wireless sensor node is powered up it is considered as an orphan and autonomous node while it is not a member yet of any network, then this node should broadcast a join request packet with a predefined identification code to enable the wireless gateway to recognize this node and answer back with an acceptance and a specific *ID* of this node. Next the node accepts the *ID* and acknowledges the operation to move into the next phase that is negotiation about the parameters of this communication channels and so on. Regarding the existence of two frequency bands, the protocol can follow different scenarios to structure the network like broadcasting on one channel or two channels at a specific frequency.

While the *RFM69* is designed to build the data packet automatically after the processor writes payload data into the *RF* module buffer and triggers the transmit mode, in that any other functionality like sequence number or message

Table 3. Implementation of defense methods against threats

Defense method	Implementation	Description
Sequence number	Software	Monitor the messages received on both channels
Time stamp	Software	Should be synchronized between both ends at startup
Source and destination identifier	Hardware/Software	RFM69 provides 8-bytes for network ID and 1-byte for node ID, more Flags can be added in software
Acknowledgments	Software	Each packet type should have a special Acknowledgment
Identification	Software	Not needed with the simple structure of networks
CRC cyclic redundancy check	Hardware	RFM69 provides 2-bytes for CRC
Encryption	Hardware/Software	Hardware: a symmetric-key block cipher to provide cryptographic, 128-bit long fixed key. Software: encryption models and schemes [23]
Membership control	Software	When there is no available data to transmit
Atomic broadcast	Software	Not needed with simple network structure
Hamming distance	Software	Monitor bit failure in addresses
Keys management	Software	At startup key should be negotiated
Denial of service (Jamming)	Software	Frequency Hopping Spread Spectrum: hopping pattern is negotiated at startup

type should be added into the payload before writing them into the *RF* buffer. Consequently, different types of messages can be defined and recognized based on their unique code, such as joint request, acknowledgment, battery level, sensor message, etc. Moreover, on the receiving side also many scenarios can be followed based on the application requirements, for example the basic scenario is the node should receive the same correct message on both channels otherwise the system must trigger the safe mode. But it might be accepted in case of losing one communication channel for some reason to inform the other end by using the second available channel to recover the lost one by following some procedure like changing the frequency. Furthermore, an important factor need to be considered which is the synchronization among both communication channels, in that many experiments are needed with respect to response time.

3.3   Experiments and Tests

The software part of this prototype for a safe wireless communication system is still under development. Moreover, the utilized safety chip provides a certified *SIL3* software package that includes an operating system and a middle ware to enable the developer to use all the safety functions provided by the chip, in that the application of this protocol is written using this software package. Consequently, some basic experiments were performed to check the capability of this prototype to function correctly, in that the researchers tested each channel independently and the transmission is successfully fulfilled, in addition, the redundant communication is also tested successfully. However, some packet errors were detected, but changing the cycle time of each transmission and improving the code reduced this error rate. Besides, the frequency bands of the redundant channel are detected by utilizing *RTL SDR* radio receiver which captures and converts the analog signal into digital data to be visualized with a supportive software called *SDRsharp* as illustrated in Fig. 6. The left part shows the captured signal for 868 MHz band and the right part shows the captured signal for 434 MHz band. The continuous development process of the software requires more experiments such as permanent monitoring of packet errors, investigating the values of Received Signal Strength Inductor of the receiver *(RSSI)*, testing the frequency hopping functionality, monitoring the behavior and response time in case of errors, and investigating the influence of metal parts on the transmission procedure such as positioning the node inside a metal box.

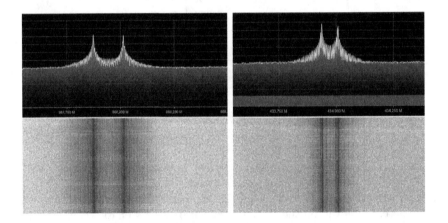

Fig. 6. Frequency bands of redundant communication

4   Results and Conclusion

The introduced prototype has revealed a potential capability to provide a robust safe wireless communication utilizing the *RF* technology which opens a wide range of opportunities for *IoT* to be used in industrial applications especially with those that are criticized as safety-related applications and where the safety of human life is the major concern, in addition to the efficiency in providing an effective cost system with safe functionality.

Moreover, there are many challenges that can be outlined as a future work for this research such as enhancing the communication protocol to manage the other topologies of the networks such as star and mesh with concerning the ability to handle the mobile sensor nodes that are mounted on some moving objects like robots or vehicles. Furthermore, this prototype introduces the main frame for designing another prototype for a new wireless safety-chip that includes all the components in one miniaturized single chip to form a system on chip, hence making this system a great option for applications such as safe monitoring of human motion.

The unique design of the utilized safety chip that includes three processors; two of them represent the *1oo2* safety-system and the third one represents the com system; opens a new potential opportunity to introduce another design involving the com processor, in that the safe part of this chip will be responsible only for obtaining the safe sensory data while the safe communication functionality will be moved into the com processor that will transmit the same message via the redundant channel, but this approach requires the com processor to perform some other functions like comparing to assure the data integrity. Figure 7 shows a rough design of this new approach.

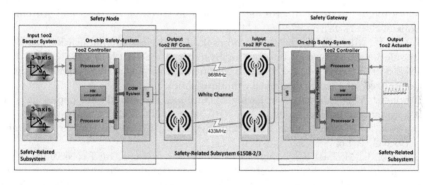

Fig. 7. Safe wireless communication with both parts of the safety chip

References

1. Hayek, A., Telawi, S., Bieler, C., Börcsök, J.: Adoption of miniaturized safety-related systems for industrial internet-of-things applications. In: 3rd EAI International Conference on Safety and Security in Internet of Things, Paris (2016)
2. Shu, Y., et al.: Internet of Things: Wireless Sensor Networks. IEC Market Strategy Board, Beijing (2014)
3. Waltenegus, D., Christian, P.: Fundamentals of Wireless Sensor Networks Theory and Practice. Wiley, Chichester (2010)

4. Richard, A., Ray, G., Jarren, B., Thom, S., Pete, W.: Fault tolerance in ZigBee wireless sensor networks. In: IEEEAC Paper #1480 (2010)
5. Samrtbox project. https://www.wel.co.nz
6. Tejashri, D.D.: Application of the wireless sensor network based on ZigBee technology in monitoring system for coal mine safety. Int. J. Eng. Res. Manag. (IJERM) (2015). ISSN: 2349–2058
7. Raghram, P., Veeramuthu, V.: Enhancing mine safety with wireless sensor networks using ZigBee technology. J. Theor. Appl. Inf. Technol. **37**(2), 261–267 (2012)
8. Victoria, J.H., Simon, O., Michael, W., Anthony, M.: Wireless sensor networks for condition monitoring in the railway industry: a survey. IEEE Trans. Intell. Transp. Syst. **16**(3), 1088–1106 (2015)
9. Lu, J., Van Den Bossche, A., Campo, E.: An IEEE 802.15.4 based adaptive communication protocol in wireless sensor network: application to monitoring the elderly at home. Wirel. Sens. Netw. **6**, 192–204 (2014)
10. Jadhav, P.S., Deshmukh, V.U.: Forest fire monitoring system based on ZIG-BEE wireless sensor network. Int. J. Emerg. Technol. Adv. Eng. **2**, 187–192 (2012). ISSN: 2250-2459
11. IEC 61508: Functional safety of electrical/electronic/programmable electronic safety-related systems. International Electrotechnical Commission (2010)
12. Josef, B.: Electronic Safety Systems Hardware Concepts, Models, and Calculations. Hüthig GmbH and Co. KG, Heidelberg (2004)
13. Josef, B.: Functional Safety. Hüthig GmbH and Co. KG, Heidelberg (2004)
14. ISO 26262 - Road vehicles-functional safety. International Organization for Standardization/Technical Committee 22 (ISO/TC 22) (2009)
15. Pavan, P., Michael, S., Hans, W., Börcsök, J.: Safe wireless communication for safety related systems. In: Recent Advances in Circuits, Systems and Automatic Control (2013). ISBN: 978-960-474-349-0
16. Pavan, P., Michael, S., Hans, W., Börcsök, J.: Wireless communication modeling for safety related system. Int. J. Circ. Syst. Sig. Process. (2014). ISSN: 1998-4464
17. EN 50159–2: Safety-related communication in open transmission system. European Committee for Electro Technical Standardization
18. Howlader, M.K., Dionand, J., Ewing, P.D.: Issues associated with deploying wireless systems in nuclear facilities. In: NPIC and HMIT, Las Vegas, Nevada (2010)
19. Börcsök, J.: Introduction in Safety Bus Systems. HIMA Paul Hildebrandt GmbH + Co KG, Brühl
20. Börcsök, J., Michael S.: Principles of safety bus systems. In: Proceedings of the International Conference on Networking, International Conference on Systems and International Conference on Mobile Communications and Learning Technologies (ICNICONSMCL 2006) (2006)
21. FAET; FAEM III, BIA, Proposal of a Guideline for the Test and Certification of "Bus Systems for the Transmission of Safety Relevant Messages" Stand, 28 May 2000
22. Jarmo, A., Marita, H., Timo M.: Safety of digital communications in machines. In: VTT Industrial Systems (2004)
23. Sklavos, N., Zaharakis, I. D.: Cryptography and security in Internet of Things (IoTs): models, schemes, and implementations. In: 8th IFIP International Conference on New Technologies, Mobility and Security (NTMS), pp. 1–2 (2016)
24. Avionics Department: Electronic Warfare and Radar Systems Engineering Handbook, 4th edn. Wiley, Chichester (2013)
25. Andreas, F.M.: Wireless Communications, 2nd edn. Wiley, Chichester (2011)
26. HOPERF ELECTRONIC: RFM69 ISM Transceiver Module Datasheet V1.1

Blockchain and IoT: Mind the Gap

Anass Sedrati[1,2], Mohamed Ahmed Abdelraheem[2], and Shahid Raza[2(✉)]

[1] INPT, Rabat, Morocco
sedrati@inpt.ac.ma
[2] RISE SICS, Stockholm, Sweden
{mohamed.abdelraheem,shahid.raza}@ri.se

Abstract. Blockchain, the core technology behind the first decentralized cryptocurrency, Bitcoin, has been recently proposed as a promising solution to create a viable decentralized network of Internet of Things (IoT) with good security and privacy properties. This survey investigates the currently proposed Blockchain-IoT solutions and examines their suitability for IoT devices.

1 Introduction

Blockchain is the core technology behind the decentralized Bitcoin cryptocurrency which operates in a trustless peertopeer network without the need to a centralized trusted party dictating the operations executed in the network. However, as indicated in many reports such as the UK government [1], Blockchain applications go far beyond Bitcoin as it can be used to turn a centralized application running by a trusted party to a decentralized application where the trust is distributed across the entire peer-to-peer network. The security behind the bitcoin blockchain relies on incentivising the participants in its peer-to-peer network who successfully accomplish specific assigned tasks by performing a certain amount of work.

Based on the Bitcoin blockchain concept, many alternative cryptocurrencies have been proposed by tweaking some parameters and/or adding new functionalities such as programs that execute autonomously on blockchains which are called smart contracts. An important new cryptocurrency that added new functionality represented in executing smart contracts is the Ethereum cryptocurrency. Anyone can participate in the trading of these alternative cryptocurrencies without any prior registration or permission and therefore are called public blockchains. When the participants of a blockchain are known, a so-called private or permissioned blockchain are more suitable and efficient choice. A private blockchain inherits the public blockchain features such as consensus-based transactions and creation of smart contract. However, private blockchains lose the true notion of distributed trust as it requires a single or group of entities to grant permissions to participate in the blockchain operations.

Internet of Things (IoT), a network of globally identifiable heterogeneous physical objects or things, are by nature a distributed network with very loose

© ICST Institute for Computer Sciences, Social Informatics and Telecommunications Engineering 2018
G. Fortino et al. (Eds.): InterIoT 2017/SaSeIoT 2017, LNICST 242, pp. 113–122, 2018.
https://doi.org/10.1007/978-3-319-93797-7_13

or no centralized control. Therefore, blockchain could be a most suitable choice to perform secure and privacy-preserved device-to-device or device to back-end (cloud) transactions. In general, blockchain technology can be used to create decentralized applications where the trust is distributed across a peer-to-peer networks. However, this capability comes with increased and redundant use of resources. Most IoT devices, on the other hand, have limited processing, storage and communication capabilities. Also, most IoT deployments are within or close to human surroundings and sense physical environments; therefore, IoT have more stringent privacy requirements. Furthermore, compared with traditional Internet hosts, IoT devices are more vulnerable to unforeseen attacks. In this paper, we review different blockchain-based solutions proposed or claimed for IoT and investigate their suitability for different classes of IoT devices. We also discuss different blockchain technologies and IoT use cases where these technologies could be used.

The paper is organized as follows. In Sect. 2, we discuss IoT networks and their security challenges. In Sect. 3, we review blockchain technologies. In Sect. 4, we survey current blockchain technologies proposed or claimed for IoT. Section 5 concludes the paper.

2   IoT Devices and Networks

IoT Security: Providing security is challenging in the Internet, but even more challenging in the IoT as the devices are expected to have IPv6 and web support, globally accessible, heterogeneous (consisting of things, smartphones, standard computers, clouds), often deployed in unguarded environments, and most of them lack conventional user interface (keyboard, display, etc.). In addition, constrained environments in the IoT inherit the constraints of conventional Wireless Sensor Networks (WSNs) such as limited energy and processing resources, lossy wireless links, and multi-hop communication. A number of security solutions are proposed for these low-power and lossy IoT networks [2,3]. IoT deployments that deal with personal or sensitive data have the following security challenges.

- *Confidentiality and Integrity*: End-to-End encryption and unnoticed modification protection, while IoT data is in transit through a wireless multi-hop networks and at rest (stored in an IoT), is hard but necessary.
- *Availability*: Compared with traditional Internet hosts, due to unattended IoT deployments it is easier to compromised IoT devices, and due to low-power wireless connectivity it easier to interfere with or jam IoT networks.
- *Authenticity*: Source authentication is important but challenging because the limited IoT resources may not always permit digital signatures.
- *Compliance*: It is very challenging to ensure new EU GDPR compliance when ubiquitous environment-sensing IoT devices sense personal data.
- *Freshness*: Often connection-less data transfer protocols are used in IoT; it is therefore necessary that old packets are not replayed.

IoT Devices: IoT devices have heterogeneous capabilities in terms of processing power, storage, and energy; therefore, the definition of an IoT device varies across different sectors and use cases. However, there are two general categories of IoT devices: (i) long-lasting battery-powered and (ii) continuously powered or frequently chargeable. IETF, the organization who standardizes the base Internet protocols (IP, TCP, UDP, TLS/SSL, etc.), has also classified different IoT devices [4] and has standardized different novel protocols for these devices namely 6LoWPAN, CoAP, and RPL. In the current classification, IETF only considers battery-powered IoT devices and divides them into three classes. *Class 0* includes highly constrained devices with RAM size *less* than 10 KiB and ROM size *less* than 100 KiB. These devices will probably not be able to establish a secure global communication channel using sophisticated security protocols such as Datagram TLS (DTLS) [5]. They typically join the Internet through a more powerful device (e.g., a gateway). *Class 1* includes devices with RAM size close to 10 KiB and ROM size close to 100 KiB. These devices can use strong Internet security protocols such as DTLS but only with pre-shared keys and cannot have digital signature processing capabilities. *Class 3* includes devices with RAM close to 50 KiB and ROM close to 250 KiB. These devices can use fully-fledged DTLS with digital signature. We have recently shown the feasibility of DTLS in battery-powered IoT devices with digital signatures [6].

It is evident that the IETF classified IoT device categories cannot themselves run blockchain mining or even digital signatures for each transaction. On the other hand, these devices may rely on a third party for blockchain operations; however, this is against the philosophy of distributed blockchain where no trusted third party exists. Even when IoT devices are continuously powered and have more resources (such as a TV, refrigerator, and an ECU in a vehicle) they are not general-purpose computers and it will be insane to use them as blockchain minors. They can however create a blockchain transaction and can themselves perform digital signatures, ensuring end-to-end security.

Centralized vs Decentralized IoT: IoT architectures can be classified into two categories: centralized and decentralized. In most centralized architectures, IoT devices are passive and sense and send raw data to trusted cloud backends. Such an architecture requires a protected communication channel between an IoT device and cloud where the actual processing (or integration with for example blockchain) happens in a powerful machine. On the other hand, fully distributed IoT devices retrieve, process, combine and provide data and services to other entities, enabling direct device-to-device communication. When device resources permit, blockchain would be suitable choose to establish trust in distributed IoT.

3   Blockchain Technologies

Blockchain is a distributed authenticated data structure in a peer-to-peer network where blocks of data are added according to a consensus protocol. The blocks of data are interlinked with each other through the use of cryptographic hash functions in way that creates a hash chain in order to make it difficult to modify by adversaries. Two main blockchain-based distributed ledgers are Bitcoin and Ethereum.

Bitcoin. Blockchain is the core technology behind the Bitcoin cryptocurrency and it was introduced in 2008 [7]. Bitcoin runs a consensus a protocol where any participant node that is able to solve a proof-of-work (POW) hash puzzle is allowed to add new blocks containing new transactions to the blockchain. A distributed consensus protocol must satisfy: *Agreement* all honest nodes decide for the same value; *Termination* all honest nodes must terminate in finite time; and *Validity* a decision value must be the input value of an honest node.

Bitcoin's consensus protocol is secure under the assumption that 51% of the participants are honest. While being secured and decentralized via a proof-of-work hash puzzle, Bitcoin's proof-of-work system has led it to become a centralized system as currently few miners have the privilege to add more blocks thanks to their huge investment in sophisticated and powerful hardware equipments to "mine" new bitcoins. Moreover, the proof-of-work system is estimated to require as much electricity as all of Denmark by 2020 [8]. This has led to many proposals other than the proof-of-work system such as proof-of-stake where a user's mining power depends on the amount of Bitcoin owned by the user. Also many alternative coins have been created by forking Bitcoin's source code and changing the cryptographic hash function under use (i.e. SHA256) to another hash function that is difficult to optimize in hardware such as scrypt. For example, Zerocash [9], a new promising cryptocurrency with strong privacy guarantees uses Equihash [10] proof-of-work algorithm to prevent any possible centralization of the mining process. Another concern regarding Bitcoin's scalability is the growing size of its blockchain and the few number of transactions (maximum 7 transactions/sec [11]) being processed in one second compared to standard credit card payment through the internet.

Ethereum. Besides the financial sector, blockchain can have different applications. One attempt to generalize the use of blockchains into different domains is Ethereum. It is a blockchain technology proposed by Vitalik Buterin where a transaction-based state machine is built [12]. Ethereum views smart contract as their first-class element. A smart contract is the transaction-based state machine generalization of the blockchain. Each node in the network is considered to be a singleton state machine that can switch between different states. Each state transition can be seen as a transaction and is added to a block that will be in the blockchain. In a smart contract context The machine updates then the states in the network depending on the current information in the blocks. Ethereum builds into the blockchain a Turing-complete instruction set to allow smart-contract programming and a storage capability to accommodate on-chain state [13].

Blockchain's Privacy. In Bitcoin's paper, it is mentioned that privacy can be maintained by keeping the public key (Bitcoin addresses) anonymous which would not enable linking a transaction to anyone. However, several papers [14–16] have investigated the anonymity of Bitcoin and the conclusion is that

Bitcoin is only pseudonymous. Obviously if anyone can link the different public key addresses to the real world identity of their owner, then all your transaction history is linked to your identity. In fact, many companies are offering de-anonymization services to financial and law enforcement agencies. Two main directions to achieve anonymity in cryptocurrencies. The first direction is using mixing/tumbler services which is specific for anonymizing Bitcoin. Many solutions exist such Coinshuffle [17], Mixcoin [18] and Blindcoin [19], to name a few. The second direction is to build "Anonymous Decentralized Cryptocurrencies". Recently two such cryptocurrencies have been proposed Zerocoin [20] and Zerocash [9]. Zerocoin [20] was originally proposed for providing anonymity in Bitcoin but it can be used in any cryptocurrency. However, it does not hide the meta data about the transactions. It uses cryptographic accumulators, commitment schemes and zero knowledge proofs to achieve anonymity. It is a semidecentralized cryptocurrency as it requires a trusted setup to generate large prime numbers used in its scheme. Zerocash [9] is an independent cryptocurrency with strong privacy properties. It can also be integrated with Bitcoin or any other altcoins. It uses zk-SNARKS (Zero Knowledge Succinct Non Interactive Arguments of Knowledge) [21] a special kind of zero knowledge proof. It can also be considered as a semi-decentralized cryptocurrency as it also needs a trusted setup to generate its public parameters which was done recently in a ceremony where the random numbers involved in the setup procedure had been destroyed in order to prevent counterfeiting of Zerocash.

Private Blockchains. Bitcoin and Ethereum's blockchains are decentralized and permission-less public systems. This publicity comes at the cost confidentiality by revealing all the transactions history for everyone. It also leads to the privacy issues pointed above. Thus another solution that might be suitable for enterprises and financial institutions is to have a private blockchain. Such blockchain will operate in a closed network where a participant needs a permission to join the network. A private blockchains is a kind of shared database where all the interesting functions of public blockchains (i.e. consensus protocol, authenticated distributed data structure, smart contracts) are applied. However, they operate in a closed centralized network where the blockchain is accessible only by permissioned nodes.

4 Blockchains for IoT

Blockchain technology can provide a reasonable solution to some of the previously mentioned security and privacy problems existing in decentralized IoT networks [22]. In addition to security, blockchain offers the following to the IoT: data management and support for micro-transactions between IoT devices based on the exchange of data and services [22]. Next, we list possible use cases where blockchain-IoT combination can be useful.

4.1   Blockchain Use Cases in IoT

IoT was originally defined as a network of globally identifiable physical objects. Currently, IoT has become a generic term for any distributed connected devices/services. However, broadly speaking, IoT devices can be categorized as *devices having continuous power source* and *battery-powered or energy harvesting devices*. IoT in an enabling technology behind smart cities, smart homes, industry 4.0, etc. IoT and blockchain can go hand-in-hand in all those cases where the availability or use of a central entity is cumbersome or practically not possible, and most importantly the entity is not trustworthy. For completeness, we present some use cases where IoT can benefit from blockchain.

Supply Chain is one of the most hyped blockchain use case. Distributed IoT sensors (e.g. in smart containers) will be a major part of future supply chain management system.

Device-to-Device Communication in connected vehicles, future 5G-enabled devices, and wearable devices in another use case where blockchain can solve the painful cybersecurity authentication problem.

Software updates in billions of distributed IoT devices can be achieved using blockchain, where community built open source software for IoT can be distributed to devices without trusting or relying on a single software distribution entity.

4.2   Blockchain-IoT Solutions

In the following, we give a brief description about the currently proposed blockchain-IoT solutions.

IOTA. It is a public (or permission-less) cryptocurrency that does autonomous machine-2-machine transactions to enable technological resource trade which includes computational power, storage, data, bandwidth, electricity. Its core invention is a Directed Acyclic Graph (DAG) called the tangle [23] where all the transactions are stored. To issue a transaction, a user needs to verify and approve another two issued transactions chosen randomly beside solving a cryptographic hash puzzle [24] to stop spam and sybil attacks. IOTA was using a hash function called Curl [25] which has been recently replaced by the well-known SHA-3 hash function (Keccak) due to the recent practical collision attacks [26] on the Curl hash function. IOTA uses Winternitz hash-based signatures [27] in order to make it possible for IoT devices to sign transactions since IoT devices do not have the computational power to process the heavy mathematical operations existing in the standard digital signatures based on public key cryptography such as RSA, DSA and ECDSA. Moreover, hash-based signature also makes IOTA quantum-resistant which could be a major advantage in the future over standardized digital signatures.

KSI Guardtime. Key less Signature Infrastructure (KSI) [28] provides data integrity through the use of hash-based digital signatures [29] similar to IOTA.

Its blockchain is private (or permissioned) and thus it uses a scalable distributed consensus protocol to add new issued transactions.

IBM Private Blockchain. Enables IoT devices to send its data or transactions to a private blockchain network (e.g. hyperledger fabric [30]). Using a consensus protocol such as Practical Byzantine Fault Tolerance (PBFT) where an n nodes network can withstand $(n-1)/3$ non-honest nodes, IBM's private blockchain enables business partners involved to reach an agreement about any transaction executed in the network without the need for third-party authentication and validation. According to IBM, this allows the creation of more efficient and profitable business networks. However, IBM's private blockchain uses digital signatures based on public key cryptography which might not be suitable for constrained IoT devices.

ENIGMA. Storing, managing and using sensitive data collected by IoT devices in a decentralized fashion is one of Enigma's many applications suggested in [31]. It is a decentralized platform enabling private computations of data by employing secure multi-party computations (MPC). Private data is divided between different nodes which securely compute functions without leaking information to other nodes. It is not a cryptocurrency but a personal data management platform supporting privacy. Its incentive is not based on mining rewards as done in public blockchains but on fees where nodes are paid for computational resources. It uses a distributed hash table (DTH) accessible from the blockchain to store references of the location of data. Sensitive data are encrypted at the client side before being stored and its corresponding access policy are encoded in the blockchain. Encrypted data are stored in an off-chain distributed database shared by a number of nodes where each node has a distinct view of shares. Off-chain nodes perform secure multiparty computations to process the encrypted data. Security deposits are paid by nodes in order to join a multiparty computation in order to punish malicious nodes.

Discussion. *Data integrity* in IOTA's public network and Guardtime's private network is provided via the use of Hash-based signatures, which enable lightweight IoT devices to sign their issued transactions. However, IOTA's public network employs a hash puzzle proof-of-work mechanism to prevent sybil attacks. While a lightweight IoT device can sign transactions using a hash-based signature scheme such as Winternitz's one-time signature [27], solving a hash puzzle consumes a lot of energy and thus will not be possible using energy-limited IoT devices.

Confidentiality of IoT's data can be provided using ENIGMA, but one problem here is that secure MPC are not scalable even for standard computing devices let alone IoT devices in terms of computation time and communication size. Thus, the IoT use case in ENIGMA provides integrity to public non-sensitive data on its blockchain can only be suitable for *Class 2* IoT devices. However, *confidentiality* can be supported, in *Class 1* IoT devices where *only* symmetric cryptographic operations can be performed (e.g. subclass of *Class 1*), through the use of pre-shared symmetric keys in case of small scale IoT network with limited number of users. Table 1 shows how current blockchain-IoT solutions are different from each other.

Though there are few blockchain solutions targeting IoT devices, blockchain for IoT is still in inception stage and there is lot to do before we can take full advantages of blockchain in resource-constrained IoT. On top the to-do list are lightweight privacy-enabled consensus protocols and permission management for private blockchain without a central permission granting entity.

Table 1. The table shows the difference between some Blockchain-IoT solutions. Proof-of-work is a requirement for public networks. Guardtime's KSI private blockchain uses an unspecified distributed consensus protocol without employing proof-of-work.

Solution	Network	Signature scheme	Security features	Consensus
IOTA	Public	hash-based (Winternitz [27])	Data integrity only	Proof-of-work
KSI	Private	hash-based (KSI [29])	Data integrity only	Not specified
IBM	Private	standard	Data integrity only	PBFT
ENIGMA	Public	standard	Confidentiality/integrity	Proof-of-work

5   Conclusion

Public blockchains use a proof-of-work consensus and thus they have a number of efficiency limitations represented in (a) the waste of energy done by the proof-of-work consensus mechanism, (b) limited number of transactions processed per second. Another concern in public blockchains is the growing size of the blockchain which makes auditing difficult for new nodes. However, a public blockchain with a secure proof-of-stake consensus algorithm might enable light clients such as IoT devices to join the network and add new blocks [32]. Moreover, confidentiality of transactions and privacy of users are major issues that halt the adoption of public blockchains in business enterprises. But even with a pro-privacy cryptocurrency such as Zerocash, the limited number of processed transactions per second will remain to be an issue that needs to be addressed in public blockchains.

Blockchain-IoT solutions can be useful in IoT applications where data integrity is needed but confidentiality and privacy are not needed for the users involved in the network. Due to employing a proof-of-work mechanism, public Blockchain-IoT solutions such as IOTA suffer from high energy consumption as well as a fewer number of transactions processed per second compared to standard payment systems such as VISA. Therefore, private blockchains using hash-based signatures (e.g. Guardtime's KSI) instead of standard digital signatures to provide data integrity are the most appropriate choice for IoT applications since they do not need to employ a proof-of-work mechanism and thus could enable energy-limited IoT devices where symmetric cryptographic operations can be performed to join the network.

Acknowledgments. This work is funded by the VR Strategic Research Area (SRA) Information and Communication Technology - The Next Generation (ICT TNG) program.

References

1. Office of Science UK Government Chief Scientific Advisor. Distributed ledger technology: beyond block chain (2016)
2. Bagci, I.E., Raza, S., Roedig, U., Voigt, T.: Fusion: coalesced confidential storage and communication framework for the iot. Secur. Commun. Netw. **9**(15), 2656–2673 (2016). sec.1260
3. Raza, S., Wallgren, L., Voigt, T.: SVELTE: real-time intrusion detection in the Internet of Things. Ad Hoc Netw. **11**(8), 2661–2674 (2013)
4. Bormann, C., Ersue, M., Keranen, A: Terminology for constrained-node networks. Technical report (2014)
5. Rescorla, E., Modadugu, N.: Datagram transport layer security version 1.2 (2012)
6. Raza, S., Helgason, T., Papadimitratos, P., Voigt, T.: Securesense: end-to-end secure communication architecture for the cloud-connected Internet of Things. Future Gener. Comput. Syst. **77**, pp. 40–51. Elsevier (2017)
7. Nakamoto, S.: Bitcoin: A peer-to-peer electronic cash system (2008)
8. Deetman, S.: Bitcoin could consume as much electricity. https://web.archive.org/web/20160828092858/http://motherboard.vice.com/read/bitcoin-could-consume-as-much-electricity-as-denmark-by-2020
9. Sasson, E.B., Chiesa, A., Garman, C., Green, M., Miers, I., Tromer, E., Virza, M.: Zerocash: Decentralized anonymous payments from bitcoin. In: 2014 IEEE Symposium on Security and Privacy, pp. 459–474. IEEE (2014)
10. Biryukov, A., Khovratovich, D.: Equihash: Asymmetric proof-of-work based on the generalized birthday problem (2017)
11. Croman, K., Decker, C., Eyal, I., Gencer, A.E., Juels, A., Kosba, A., Miller, A., Saxena, P., Shi, E., Gün Sirer, E., Song, D., Wattenhofer, R.: On scaling decentralized blockchains. In: Clark, J., Meiklejohn, S., Ryan, P.Y.A., Wallach, D., Brenner, M., Rohloff, K. (eds.) FC 2016. LNCS, vol. 9604, pp. 106–125. Springer, Heidelberg (2016). https://doi.org/10.1007/978-3-662-53357-4_8
12. Wood, G.: Ethereum: A secure decentralised generalised transaction ledger. Ethereum Project Yellow Paper, 151 (2014)
13. Azaria, A., Ekblaw, A., Vieira, T., Lippman, A.: MedRec: Using blockchain for medical data access and permission management. In: International Conference on Open and Big Data (OBD), pp. 25–30. IEEE (2016)
14. Ron, D., Shamir, A.: Quantitative analysis of the full bitcoin transaction graph. In: Sadeghi, A.-R. (ed.) FC 2013. LNCS, vol. 7859, pp. 6–24. Springer, Heidelberg (2013). https://doi.org/10.1007/978-3-642-39884-1_2
15. Meiklejohn, S., Pomarole, M., Jordan, G., Levchenko, K., McCoy, D., Voelker, G.M., Savage, S.: A fistful of bitcoins: characterizing payments among men with no names. In: Proceedings of the 2013 Conference on Internet measurement Conference, pp. 127–140. ACM (2013)
16. Androulaki, E., Karame, G.O., Roeschlin, M., Scherer, T., Capkun, S.: Evaluating user privacy in bitcoin. In: Sadeghi, A.-R. (ed.) FC 2013. LNCS, vol. 7859, pp. 34–51. Springer, Heidelberg (2013). https://doi.org/10.1007/978-3-642-39884-1_4

17. Ruffing, T., Moreno-Sanchez, P., Kate, A.: CoinShuffle: practical decentralized coin mixing for bitcoin. In: Kutyłowski, M., Vaidya, J. (eds.) ESORICS 2014. LNCS, vol. 8713, pp. 345–364. Springer, Cham (2014). https://doi.org/10.1007/978-3-319-11212-1_20

18. Bonneau, J., Narayanan, A., Miller, A., Clark, J., Kroll, J.A., Felten, E.W.: Mixcoin: anonymity for bitcoin with accountable mixes. In: Christin, N., Safavi-Naini, R. (eds.) FC 2014. LNCS, vol. 8437, pp. 486–504. Springer, Heidelberg (2014). https://doi.org/10.1007/978-3-662-45472-5_31

19. Valenta, L., Rowan, B.: Blindcoin: blinded, accountable mixes for bitcoin. In: Brenner, M., Christin, N., Johnson, B., Rohloff, K. (eds.) FC 2015. LNCS, vol. 8976, pp. 112–126. Springer, Heidelberg (2015). https://doi.org/10.1007/978-3-662-48051-9_9

20. Miers, I., Garman, C., Green, M., Rubin, A.D.: Zerocoin: Anonymous distributed e-cash from bitcoin. In: 2013 IEEE Symposium on Security and Privacy (SP), pp. 397–411. IEEE (2013)

21. Ben-Sasson, E., Chiesa, A., Tromer, E., Virza, M.: Succinct non-interactive zero knowledge for a von neumann architecture. Cryptology ePrint Archive, Report 2013/879 (2013). http://eprint.iacr.org/2013/879

22. Brody, P., Pureswaran, V.: Device democracy: Saving the future of the Internet of Things. IBM, September 2014

23. Popov, S.: The tangle (2016). https://iota.org/IOTA_Whitepaper.pdf

24. IOTA infosheet // blockchain 3.0. http://iotanodes.org/IOTA_Infosheet_dec_2016_revised.pdf

25. Sønstebø, D.: The transparency compendium. https://blog.iota.org/the-transparency-compendium-26aa5bb8e260

26. Heilman, T.D.E., Narula, N., Virza, M.: IOTA vulnerability report: Cryptanalysis of the curl hash function enabling practical signature forgery attacks on the IOTA cryptocurrency (2017). https://github.com/mit-dci/tangled-curl

27. Buchmann, J., Dahmen, E., Ereth, S., Hülsing, A., Rückert, M.: On the security of the winternitz one-time signature scheme. In: Nitaj, A., Pointcheval, D. (eds.) AFRICACRYPT 2011. LNCS, vol. 6737, pp. 363–378. Springer, Heidelberg (2011). https://doi.org/10.1007/978-3-642-21969-6_23

28. Guardtime. KSI blockchain technology. https://guardtime.com/technology/ksi-technology

29. Buldas, A., Kroonmaa, A., Laanoja, R.: Keyless signatures' infrastructure: how to build global distributed hash-trees. In: Riis Nielson, H., Gollmann, D. (eds.) NordSec 2013. LNCS, vol. 8208, pp. 313–320. Springer, Heidelberg (2013). https://doi.org/10.1007/978-3-642-41488-6_21

30. Cachin, C.: Architecture of the hyperledger blockchain fabric. In: Workshop on Distributed Cryptocurrencies and Consensus Ledgers (2016)

31. Zyskind, G., Nathan, O., Pentland, A.: Enigma: Decentralized computation platform with guaranteed privacy (2015). arXiv preprint arXiv:1506.03471

32. Buterin, V.: Light clients and proof of stake (2015). https://blog.ethereum.org/2015/01/10/light-clients-proof-stake/

Lightweight X.509 Digital Certificates for the Internet of Things

Filip Forsby[1,3], Martin Furuhed[2], Panos Papadimitratos[3], and Shahid Raza[1(✉)]

[1] Security Lab, RISE SICS, Stockholm, Sweden
shahid.raza@ri.se
[2] Technology Nexus Secured Business Solutions, Stockholm, Sweden
martin.furuhed@nexusgroup.com
[3] Networked Systems Security Group, KTH, Stockholm, Sweden
{forsby,papadim}@kth.se

Abstract. X.509 is the de facto digital certificate standard used in building the Public Key Infrastructure (PKI) on the Internet. However, traditional X.509 certificates are too heavy for battery powered or energy harvesting Internet of Things (IoT) devices where it is crucial that energy consumption and memory footprints are as minimal as possible.

In this paper we propose, implement, and evaluate a lightweight digital certificate for resource-constrained IoT devices. We develop an X.509 profile for IoT including only the fields necessary for IoT devices, without compromising the certificate security. Furthermore, we also propose compression of the X.509 profiled fields using the contemporary CBOR encoding scheme. Most importantly, our solutions are compatible with the existing X.509 standard, meaning that our profiled and compressed X.509 certificates for IoT can be enrolled, verified and revoked without requiring modification in the existing X.509 standard and PKI implementations. We implement our solution in the Contiki OS and perform evaluation of our profiled and compressed certificates on a state-of-the-art IoT hardware.

Keywords: X.509 certificate · IoT · CBOR · 6LoWPAN · Contiki

1 Introduction

Most IoT standards [1,2] specify the use of digital certificates. We have recently shown that even though conventional X.509 certificates fit into state-of-the-art IoT hardware [3], they have significant overhead in terms of energy consumption on battery-powered IoT devices. Conventional certificate standards are developed for workstations and servers in mind, where factors like computational power, memory footprint and energy consumption are not main concerns. However, in battery powered and energy harvesting IoT devices, these factors are crucial and it is therefore important to adapt these standards to be more suitable for IoT. We have already adapted the Internet communication security standards

© ICST Institute for Computer Sciences, Social Informatics and Telecommunications Engineering 2018
G. Fortino et al. (Eds.): InterIoT 2017/SaSeIoT 2017, LNICST 242, pp. 123–133, 2018.
https://doi.org/10.1007/978-3-319-93797-7_14

to IoT by providing the 6LoWPAN header compression mechanisms for these standards, namely IPsec [4] and DTLS [5]. In the previous work, we have either used pre-shared keys or standard X.509 certificates. There are already efforts to compress digital certificates [6] without breaking the compatibility, which uses conventional compressing methods and dictionaries with reoccurring and frequently used text strings to compress X.509 certificates. A modified version of *gzip* uses the DEFLATE [7] compression algorithm with a dictionary consisting of a typical certificate with unpopulated cryptographic fields. These solutions are designed for conventional Internet hosts; however, they can be complementarily employed along with the solutions proposed in this paper.

This paper investigates and proposes a lightweight implementation of a digital certificate with properties such as low memory footprint, low computational complexity and minimised data transfer as the main concerns. The solution proposed in this paper consists of two parts. The first part is an X.509 Profile for IoT which specify the necessary field that must be included when communicating with IoT devices, without compromising the security and standard compliance. To further reduce the size, the second part specifies compression mechanisms for the profiled X.509 certificate fields, which are applied when a certificate travels within 6LoWPAN networks. Certificates conforming to this profile will be fully valid X.509 certificates and can be processed by any entity that can process regular X.509 certificates. However, new IoT devices cannot process the legacy X.509 certificates that are generated without using the guidelines detailed in this paper. Certificates for IoT devices have to be explicitly issued using the specification of this profile. Legacy devices can get new lightweight X509 certificates that conforms to this profile.

We implement our IoT X.509 profile in Contiki, a state-of-the-art operating system for IoT. Our implementation consists of (i) traditional, (ii) profiled, and (iii) compressed X.509 certificates and their processing. We also perform empirical evaluation of our solution using a state-of-the-art IoT hardware, the ARM's Cortex M3 MCU packaged in the TI's CC2538 system on chip. Our evaluation consists of energy, memory and packet overhead, and shows significant improvements over the traditional X.509 certificates.

2   Background Technologies

2.1   X.509 Certificates

The X.509 [8] certificates has been around for a long time and are a part of many standards such as Datagram TLS [9] and IKEv2 [10]. An X.509 certificate essentially consists of three parts: *(i)* information about the subject, issuer and details about the certificate such as serial number and validity dates; *(ii)* the public key of the subject and its cryptographic algorithm; and *(iii)* a signature from the issuing Certificate Authority (CA). The latest version (X.509 version 3) has opened up for optional extensions, which can be marked as critical and thus has to be processed by the receiver. An X.509 certificate is specified and encoded using the Abstract Syntax Notation One (ASN.1) [11] Distinguished Encoding Rules (DER), and then converted to Base64 before it is stored or transmitted.

2.2 CBOR and CDDL

Concise Binary Object Representation (CBOR) [12] is a lightweight encoding scheme with support for binary data. CBOR is designed to be extremely lightweight in terms of code and message sizes. CBOR is based on JSON [13] and fully supports the JSON syntax and data types. Even though CBOR does not rely on a specific schema in order to encode and decode messages, the CBOR Data Definition Language (CDDL) [14] was specified in order to describe and constrain CBOR structures. We use CBOR to encode and ultimately compress our profiled X.509 certificate.

2.3 IoT Protocols: 6LoWPAN, CoAP, DTLS

IPv6 over Low power Wireless Personal Area Networks (6LoWPAN) [15] is a transmission protocol that enables IPv6 communication over low-powered and lossy networks, such as the IEEE 802.15.4 protocol. The Constrained Application Protocol (CoAP) [16] is a web protocol (similar to HTTP) standardised for IoT. Secure CoAP (CoAPs) mandates Datagram TLS (DTLS) [17]. CoAP has some restrictions on how the certificates must be constructed. Section 9.1.3.3 of the CoAP standard specifies the cipher suits and subject names to be used, which we take into consideration when designing a certificate for IoT. The DTLS Profile for IoT [9] specifies the use of DTLS protocol in constrained environments. This profile also specifies the use of certificates and their contents, where restrictions have been made to keep the certificates smaller. Our work is in line with these guidelines.

3 X.509 Profile for IoT

In this section, we propose the X.509 certificate profile for IoT and discuss individual fields and their compression mechanisms. In our design, we also use the guidelines from the DTLS profile for IoT [9] standard.

Version. The current (since 2008) version is 3, which introduces optional extensions. Version 3 is also the only valid version used in the DTLS Profile for IoT. In our profiled certificate too we fixed the version value to 3. Restricting the version number allows us omitting this field while a certificate travels within 6LoWPAN networks. When a certificate leaves a 6LoWPAN network, the version field is set to 3.

Serial Number. A CA chooses the serial number during the certificate enrollment process. We do not make any restriction on the serial number value; however, we suggest low numbers and the size is reduced by encoding it in the CBOR format. Relying on the DTLS IoT profile guidelines we also use only unsigned values.

Signature and signatureAlgorithm. These fields specify the signature algorithm that a CA uses to sign a certificate. Both the signature and signatureAlgorithm fields contain the same value. We omit both the signature and the signatureAlgorithm fields, and fix the signature algorithm to ecdsaWithSHA256, which is also used in the DTLS IoT profile. The field is populated back to ecdsaWithSHA256 by the 6LoWPAN border router when the certificate leaves 6LoWPAN networks.

Issuer. It is a non-empty sequence of name-value pairs that is used to identify the issuing CA. Though the issuer is a key field to map a given certificate to a certain CA, the range of possibilities to identify an issuer is extensive and using full range is not suitable for IoT devices. We therefore restrict this field to common name (CN) of the UTF8String type. However, the name must not be the same as for any other known CA. Our CBOR coding of this field reduces the example "Root CA" to 8 bytes from 20 bytes.

```
-- Compressed CBOR -- (8 bytes)
0x67    // Text string of size 7
0x52 0x6F 0x6F 0x74 0x20 0x43 0x41 // Value "Root CA"
```

Validity. It is a sequence of two dates: the start date and the end date, which can be represented in multiple formats. The ASN.1 representations used in conventional X.509 certificates are the longest of them all, with up to almost six times more bytes needed than UnixTime. We compress the textual format to UnixTime that requires the least amount of bytes to represent a date: four bytes before January 2038 and 5 bytes after that. Since UTCTime is implied, the structural specifiers are omitted.

Subject. Similar to the Issuer field, the subject field represents the entity with the given public key. A subject can be another CA or an end-user. In both cases it must be a non-empty Distinguished Name (DN). Relying on the DTLS IoT profile guidelines, the subject field in our profile contains the CN represented in the EUI-64 format when the certificate is issued to an IoT device. We represent the CN in the UTF8String format that is used in the IEEE Guidelines for EUI-64 [18]. Within 6LoWPAN networks, we compress the CN to the binary representation and CBOR format, which brings the size down to 9 bytes from 36 bytes. The CBOR format is represented below.

```
-- Compressed CBOR -- (9 bytes)
0x48    // Byte array of size 8
0x01 0x23 0x45 0x67 0x89 0xAB 0xCD 0xEF  // Value 0x0123456789ABCDEF
```

Subject Public Key Info. It contains the public key in a bit string and the algorithm the key is used with. For our profiled certificate we fix the algorithm to the 256-bits ECC keys from the curve prime256v1; we therefore omit the algorithm information when a certificate travels within 6LoWPAN networks. We compress the ECC public keys using the Miller's approach [19]. Compression is done by omitting the y-value and providing an information byte, depending on the characteristics of y. The information byte will either be 0x02 or 0x03 when the key is compressed. Since the equation of the given curve is known $(y^2 = x^3 + ax + b)$, y be calculated from x as the square root of $x^3 + ax + b$. The details of compression and decompression of ECC public keys can be found in [20] Sects. 2.3.3 and 2.3.4, respectively. To further reduce the key size within 6LoWPAN networks we encode the compressed key into the CBOR format, which in total reduces its size from 91 to 35 bytes.

```
-- Compressed CBOR --   (35 bytes)
0x58 0x21    // Byte string of size 33
0x0* [ECC value X] // Where * is 2 or 3, depending on y value)
```

Issuer Unique ID and Subject Unique ID. These fields are only valid for version 2 or 3, and are only necessary if the issuer or subject are duplicated. In our solution, subjects are inherently unique, and issuers must use unique names, which makes these fields unnecessary. We therefor omit these fields in the profiled certificate.

Extensions. Extensions consist of three parts; an OID, a boolean telling if it is critical or not, and a ASN.1 DER encoded bit string as the value. We compress the OIDs by omitting the first two bytes that will always be 0x551D. The rest of the OID bytes are used as a tag for the CBOR structure which has the format: [tag, critical*, value], where `critical` is a true or false value and is the same as in ASN.1. The value will contain the DER encoded bit string, as a compression mechanism for all possible extensions and their variants will be too complex to fit in this simple protocol. Any extension is allowed in this profile. Here is an example of the compressed extension field [[1, true, 0x3000], [15, 0x03020284]].

```
-- Compressed CBOR --     (14 bytes)
0x82  /* Array of size 2 */       0x83  // Array of size 3
0x13  /* Value 1 */               0xF5  // Value true
0x42  /* Byte sting of size 2 */  0x30 0x00  // Value
0x82  /* Array of size 2 */       0x0F  // Value 15
0x44  /* Byte string of size 4 */ 0x03 0x02 0x02 0x84  // Value
```

Signature. This is an encoded bit string that represents the actual digital signature of a CA. We use the ECDSA-Sig-Value format described in RFC5480 [21]. The r and s values in an ECDSA signature are both 256 bits (32 bytes) unsigned integers, when using the *prime256v1* curve. Unlike the x and y values of an ECC public key, r and s are not points on the curve and therefore cannot be compressed in the same way. There are however patented solutions for compressing ECDSA signatures, for example *Compressed ECDSA signatures* (patent number US 8631240 B2) [22], where the s value is replaced by a smaller value c. Within 6LoWPAN networks, we omit the signatureAlgorithm value (as it is fixed) and compress the signature by encoding it to the CBOR format, which reduces the size from 75 to 66 bytes.

```
-- Compressed CBOR --    (66 bytes)
0x58    /*Byte array*/ 0x40    // Size 64
[32 bytes r value] [32 bytes s value]
```

Table 1 shows the summary of all the X.509 certificate fields and their values in our profile.

Table 1. Summary of certificate field contents in the X.509 Profile for IoT.

Field	Value
Version	3
Serial number	Unsigned integer
Signature	ecdsaWithSHA256
Issuer	CommonName containing CA name as UTF8String
Validity	UTCTime in format YYMMDDhhmmssZ
Subject	CommonName containing CA name or EUI-64 as UTF8String
Subject public key info	ecPublicKey followed by prime256v1 and 64 byte uncompressed ECC public key
Issuer and subject unique ID	Not present
Extensions	Any extension
Signature algorithm	ecdsaWithSHA256
Signature	ECDSA-Sig-Value ::= SEQUENCE {r INTEGER, s INTEGER}

4   Implementation and Evaluation

We implement our proposed IoT X.509 profile in Contiki, an operating system for IoT. Our implementation supports our proposed compression, decompression, verification of compressed certificates and creation of new certificates. In our implementation, a certificate can be in three different states: Uncompressed, Compressed, and Decoded. An *uncompressed* certificate is our profiled X.509 certificate, which is used outside 6LoWPAN networks. It is represented as a byte array containing the ASN.1 DER encoded structure. A *compressed* version of a certificate is our profiled certificate compressed and encoded with the techniques specified in Sect. 3. It is used when a certificate travels within 6LoWPAN networks. It is represented as byte array containing the CBOR encoded structure. A *decoded* certificate is a C struct with all the fields from the compressed certificate. This struct is used when the certificate is verified and certain fields need to be accessed. The transitions between these stages are performed using a number of functions. We implement the X.509 parser for encoding, decoding and working with X.509 certificates. We use two external libraries: *cn-cbor*[1] for encoding/decoding a certificate, and *micro-ecc*[2] for ECC public key creation and compression. Our Contiki app is called *xiot* (X.509 for IoT) and is placed in the Contiki/apps/xiot directory. All functions and types have the *xiot_* prefix. Figure 1 highlights the Contiki app.

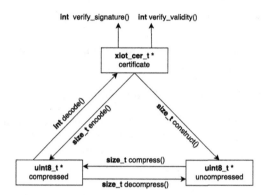

Fig. 1. Structure of our Contiki app, with functions and their interactions.

We also perform the evaluation of our profiled and compressed certificates in order to determine the overheads and gains of our solution. We measure the certificate size, per field gain, and energy consumption of our solution and compare it with the standard X.509 certificate. We perform the evaluation on the Zolertia Firefly[3] motes that uses ARM® Cortex®-M3 TI CC2538 MCU, up to 32 MHz core clock, 32 KB RAM memory, 512 KB flash memory, and power consumption from 7 mA at 16 MHz clock speed without peripherals and 20 mA or 24 mA with active radio in receive or transmit mode, respectively. It also provides hardware support for AES and ECC crypto. The full specifications can be found in the CC2538 datasheet [23] and on the Zolertia Firefly GitHub page [24].

4.1   Memory Usage

Memory overhead is evaluated in two ways: the actual size of a certificate, and the size of the compiled code. For certificate size comparison we use three different certificates: a regular X.509 certificate, a certificate conforming to the X.509 Profile for IoT, and a compressed version of the same profiled certificate. The sizes of these three certificates are shown in Fig. 2. In this case,

---

[1] https://github.com/cabo/cn-cbor.
[2] https://github.com/kmackay/micro-ecc.
[3] http://zolertia.io/product/hardware/firefly.

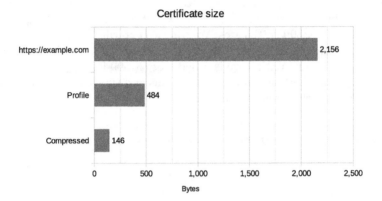

Fig. 2. The size in bytes for different example certificates.

Table 2. Size of individual fields for different certificates.

Field	Field size (Bytes)		
	No profile	Uncompressed	Compressed
Overhead	8	7	1
Version	5	5	0
Serial number	18	3	2
Signature	15	12	0
Issuer	114	20	8
Validity	32	32	11
Subject	168	36	9
Subject public key info	294	91	35
Issuer and subject unique ID	0	0	0
Extensions	596	31	14
Signature algorithm	15	12	0
Signature	261	75	66
Total	**1526**	**324**	**146**

the regular X.509 certificate is a generic example taken from the Internet web page https://www.example.com. The profiled certificate is self generated with an EUI-64 as subject and with 2 extensions. Both the profiled certificate and the example.com certificate are base64 encoded surrounded with the strings -----*BEGIN CERTIFICATE*----- and -----*END CERTIFICATE*-----, while the compressed certificate is pure binary. Base64 encoding increases the size by one third, or by ~33%, since it takes 3 bytes and converts them to four printable characters, where each character is 1 byte. The size of a certificate can be broken down into sizes of individual fields. Table 2 shows the field sizes for the different types of certificates. These are the binary sizes without base64 encoding, and the total sizes are therefore less than what is shown in Fig. 2. The table shows where the most bytes are used and where compression does not do much difference. It also shows for example the *subject* and *issuer* fields are greatly reduced with the profile, and so are the cryptographic parts and the extensions. The fields *version, serial number, signature, validity* and *signature algorithm* are very little affected by our profile, if any at all.

We measure the code size using the *arm-none-eabi-size* program provided for the ARM Cortex M3 platform. For the compiled code size, adding compression mechanisms on top of the regular library adds about 1.3 kB on the text area, 0.8 kB on the data area and 2 kB on the bss area.

4.2   Energy Comsumption

To measure energy, we use the Energest tool, available in the Contiki OS. Energest measures the time individual peripherals are active, and calculates power consumption using the current and voltage levels provided in the CC2538 datasheet [23]. Energest returns the time in *ticks* that must be divided by the number of ticks per second to retrieve the time in seconds. The formula for calculating energy usage is therefore: *Energy = ticks/(ticks/second) * Voltage * Current.*

Figure 3 (left) shows the energy consumption for different operations with uncompressed and compressed certificates. When no hardware support for ECC operations is used, the verification step is by far the most dominant consumer. In this case, the gain from smaller size is not as evident as when hardware crypto is used. Without hardware crypto, the uncompressed certificate consumes ∼2.2% more energy than the compressed, whereas with hardware support the uncompressed certificate consumes ∼23.4% more energy. In multi-hop 6LoWPAN networks, a digital certificate travels through multiple nodes. Figure 3 (right) shows the total energy consumption for intermediate nodes plus the end node for multiple hops. This includes decoding and verification by the end node.

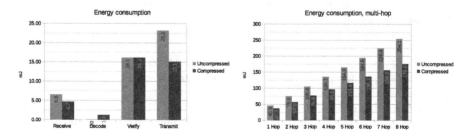

Fig. 3. *Left:* Energy consumption for different certificate handling steps, with hardware crypto. *Right:* Combined energy consumption with multiple hops.

4.3   Compatibility with the X.509 Standard

In order to prove that our profiled certificates are valid X.509 certificates, we parsed them with the well-known OpenSSL library. Our certificates pass the parsing without any errors and are X.509 compatible. For parsing an X.509 certificate with the name `certificate.crt`, the OpenSSL command we used is *openssl x509 -in certificate.crt -text -noout*.

5   Conclusion

We have specified a lightweight version of the X.509 certificate for IoT and provided compression and encoding schemes for our profiled certificate. An important feature is the compatibility with the X.509 standard, meaning that our lightweight certificate can be used in any existing PKI solutions. Our implementation for constrained environments and evaluation using a real IoT hardware show significant gains in terms of size and energy consumption.

Acknowledgement. This research is funded by VINNOVA under the Eurostars SecureIoT project.

References

1. Shelby, Z., Hartke, K., Bormann, C.: The Constrained Application Protocol (CoAP). RFC 7252, June 2014. http://www.ietf.org/rfc/rfc7252.txt
2. Schaad, J.: CBOR Object Signing and Encryption (COSE). RFC 8152, July 2017
3. Raza, S., Helgason, T., Papadimitratos, P., Voigt, T.: SecureSense: end-to-end secure communication architecture for the cloud-connected internet of things. Elsevier, June 2017. https://doi.org/10.1016/j.future.2017.06.008
4. Raza, S., Duquennoy, S., Höglund, J., Roedig, U., Voigt, T.: Secure communication for the Internet of Things - a comparison of link-layer security and IPsec for 6LoWPAN. Secur. Commun. Netw. **7**(12), 2654–2668 (2014)
5. Raza, S., Shafagh, H., Hewage, K., Hummen, R., Voigt, T.: Lithe: lightweight secure CoAP for the Internet of Things. IEEE Sens. J. **13**(10), 3711–3720 (2013)
6. Pritikin, M., McGrew, D.: The Compressed X.509 Certificate Format, May 2010
7. Deutsch, P.: RFC 1951 - DEFLATE Compressed Data Format Specification version 1.3, May 1996
8. Housley, P., Ford, W., Polk, T., Solo, D.: Internet X.509 public key infrastructure certificate and CRL profile. RFC 2459, RFC Editor, January 1999. http://www.rfc-editor.org/rfc/rfc2459.txt
9. Tschofenig, H., Fossati, T.: Transport layer security (TLS)/datagram transport layer security (DTLS) profiles for the Internet of Things. RFC 7925, RFC Editor, July 2016
10. Kaufman, C., Hoffman, P., Nir, Y., Eronen, P., Kivinen, T.: Internet Key Exchange Protocol Version 2 (IKEv2). STD 79, RFC Editor, October 2014. http://www.rfc-editor.org/rfc/rfc7296.txt
11. International Telecommunication Union ITU. Introduction to ASN.1
12. Bormann, C., Hoffman, P.: RFC 7049 - concise Binary Object Representation (CBOR), October 2013

13. W3Schools. JSON Introduction
14. Vigano, C., Birkholz, H.: CBOR data definition language (CDDL): a notational convention to express CBOR data structures, September 2016
15. Kushalnagar, N., et al.: RFC 4944 - transmission of IPv6 Packets over IEEE 802.15.4 Networks, September 2007
16. Shelby, Z., Hartke, K., Bormann, C.: The Constrained Application Protocol (CoAP), March 2013
17. Rescorla, E., Modadugu, N.: RFC 6347 - Datagram Transport Layer Security Version 1.2, January 2012
18. Lambert, K.A.: Guidelines for 64-bit Global Identifier (EUI-64), January 2015
19. Miller, V.S.: Use of elliptic curves in cryptography. In: Williams, H.C. (ed.) CRYPTO 1985. LNCS, vol. 218, pp. 417–426. Springer, Heidelberg (1986). https://doi.org/10.1007/3-540-39799-X_31
20. Brown, D.R.L.: Standards for Efficient Cryptography 1 (SEC 1), May 2009
21. Turner, S., Yiu, K., Brown, D.R.L., Housley, R., Polk, T.: RFC 5480 - Elliptic Curve Cryptography Subject Public Key Information, March 2009
22. Vanstone, S.A.: Compressed ECDSA signatures, November 2007
23. Texas Instruments. CC2538 Powerful Wireless Microcontroller System-On-Chip for 2.4-GHz IEEE 802.15.4, 6lowpan, and ZigBee© Applications, December 2012
24. Zolertia, S.L.: Firefly - Zolertia/Resources Wiki, January 2017. https://github.com/Zolertia/Resources/wiki/Firefly

Privacy Preserving and Resilient Cloudified IoT Architecture to Support eHealth Systems

Jarkko Paavola[(✉)] and Jani Ekqvist

Turku University of Applied Sciences, Joukhaisenkatu 3, Turku, Finland
{jarkko.paavola, jani.ekqvist}@turkuamk.fi

Abstract. Significant improvement in eHealth services in both quality and financial points of view are possible if public cloud infrastructures could be utilized in storing and processing personal health information (PHI) from IoT devices monitoring and collecting data from persons. The challenge is that personal health records are highly sensitive and health related organization are not willing to trust the cybersecurity of public clouds. Another challenge is that strict regulation is in place regarding the physical location of PHI. This paper addresses these issues by proposing tokenization architecture and crypto-implementation for personal identity number (PIN). This will allow the storage and processing of the personal health information (PII) in the public cloud as the data cannot be identified to a specific person. The proposal follows the general data protection regulation (GDPR) by offering secure and highly resilient architecture for the separation of health data and person identity.

Keywords: IoT · Cloud · eHealth · Information security · Resiliency
Privacy · Tokenization

1 Introduction

Industrial Internet consortium (IIC) envisions the emergence on industrial internet in five different sectors: energy & utilities, manufacturing, transportation, public sector, and *health care*. IIC estimates that the Industrial Internet can help globally drive down annual healthcare costs by roughly 25%, or about $100 billion a year [1].

There are several visions what industrial Internet, or Internet-of-Things (IoT), could offer for health care. For example, Microsoft envisions transforming patient care with IoT [2], which could provide health organizations with the ability to leverage the cloud in new ways to transform their operations for reducing operational costs through predictive maintenance, real-time asset monitoring, or utilizing data across the entire continuum of care with analytics.

Cost-efficient global business operations require sophisticated utilization of cloud-based information system tools. Cloud computing is an approach to control the consumption of computing resources. It involves groups of remote servers and networks that allow centralized data storage and online access to computer services or resources. Clouds can be classified as public, private or hybrid. Another classification is whether the cloud is utilized as infrastructure, platform, or application. The integration of cloud computing and industrial Internet is an open research question [3].

© ICST Institute for Computer Sciences, Social Informatics and Telecommunications Engineering 2018
G. Fortino et al. (Eds.): InterIoT 2017/SaSeIoT 2017, LNICST 242, pp. 134–143, 2018.
https://doi.org/10.1007/978-3-319-93797-7_15

The source of wide interest on cloud platforms for companies is to expand their businesses geographically around the globe and reduce the operational costs. In the long term, the approach will offer possibilities to utilize e.g. big data to offer novel services. Strategic intent for companies is to offer health care/medical software, products and platforms as a cloud service globally to different countries. Benefit is clear - the return of investment, using the envisioned approach when compared to the traditional approach, is much bigger.

Regulation sets strict demands for information systems processing health related data. The goal is to protect the rights of patients regarding information processing and archiving. Regulatory rules vary from country to country making exporting medical information systems complicated, since they must be tailored to each market and compatibility to regulatory demands must be proven with audit process. These different regulatory demands must be taken into account in very early stage of the development process to ensure that the adaptation to different regulatory demands does not require complex technical changes. This is especially true for new technologies, where legislation may be delayed.

Further, the General Data Protection Regulation GDPR [4] requires "appropriate technical and organisational measures to ensure the level of security appropriate to the risk" from all data processing related to Personally Identifiable Information (PII), and especially sensitive data as Personal Health Information (PHI).

Cloudified IoT and related security challenges has been investigated recently for eHealth applications e.g. in [5–7]. The current literature on the focuses mainly on security protocols for the communications. This paper has a different approach as the privacy will be provided by separating PII from PHI. The information security is protected by extremely resilient architecture, which is designed to minimize the attack surface and to fulfill GDRP requirements.

The work for this paper has been implemented in RAMP (Industrial Internet Reference Architecture for Medical Platform) project, where the approach has been to design open reference architecture, which allows to analyze all required components and services, and to create strategic roadmap for technology and IoT platform selections. A special case considered in the project is that the IoT medical device is located inside hospital. The data to be transferred out from the hospital may be categorized as follows:

- Data related to the conditions of equipment
- Sample data from the patient without identifying information e.g. cell sample for research purposes
- Patient data accompanied with identifying information

Here, we consider the latter case, which is by far the most problematic from the privacy point-of-view as PII and PHI must be separated. When public cloud is utilized, the physical location of the data, in principle, is not anymore under the control of the hospital that has produced the data. To minimize the risk of compromising personal health records in the case data breach within cloud provider this paper proposes

- Architecture for tokenization of personal ID
- Method of cryptographical operations to provide adequate level of security

The proposal has been verified in the real hospital environment pilot as described in Sect. 4.

As an example, this paper presents tokenization architecture and its crypto-implementation for Finnish personal identity number (PIN). This allows the separation of PHI from the PII in the cloud, thus enabling the utilization of public clouds for storing and analyzing patient data even from the hospital environment. The proposed solution is piloted with the hospital in southwest Finland.

The paper is organized as follows: the next Sect. 2 describes the proposed tokenization architecture and cryptographic implementation. Then, in Sect. 3, security analysis for the proposed architecture is presented. Section 4 describes the pilot implementation, and finally, conclusions are drawn in Sect. 5.

2   Tokenization and the Proposed System

Tokenization replaces sensitive information with a surrogate token that does not have any intrinsic value. The purpose of tokenization is to remove sensitive information from the data processing systems and store it in a single protected container.

Here we consider the case of protecting Finnish Personal Identity Number. The PIN is considered sensitive information according to the Finnish Personal Data Act [8] (available only in Finnish and Swedish), and by the General Data Protection Regulation [4]. In our case, it identifies the person whose Personal Health Information is being processed. The PIN is constructed from person's date of birth, a gender identifier, a random number selected from a space of 500, and a checksum character [9] (available only in Finnish and Swedish). A valid example of a PIN is 120188-479P, where '120188' is the date of birth, '-' is the century of birth, '479' is the random identifier (it being an odd number means a male), and 'P' is the checksum calculated over the preceding numbers. It is relatively trivial to find out date of birth and gender, which leaves us with a pool of entropy of only 500 numbers, or about 9 bits. Additionally, numbers 0, 1 and 900–999 are reserved. Therefore, there is a high risk of an attacker being able to reverse the tokenization process if keying is not considered carefully.

Tokenization is widely used in credit card industry for protecting credit card numbers. The proposed architecture follows the approach in PCI DSS standard [10]. However, methods commonly used for credit card number tokenization are not sufficient for storing PIN in the case of PHI. There are less than 10 million PINs currently in use and the whole valid value space from 1900 to 2017 is less than 43 million (the oldest person alive in Finland is 108 years old). If attacker gains access to the token database, he/she will be able to generate a rainbow table of possible PII values and reverse the encryption.

Therefore, we propose an architecture where encryption keys for each PII value are stored in separate server. This provides an added layer of protection without incurring the cost of provisioning a High Security Module (HSM). In addition to improved security, the system is also more resilient than the one in [10].

2.1   Tokenization Architecture

The proposed architecture follows strict separation of duties where a security breach of a single component does not compromise the overall integrity of the system. The architecture is illustrated in Fig. 1, where Processing Cloud denotes any public could used to process PHI.

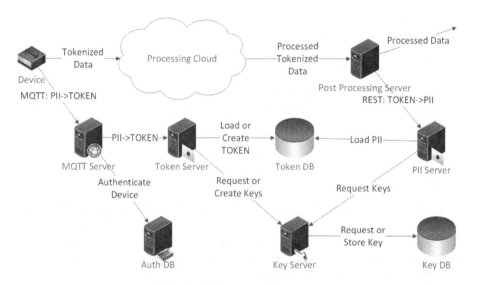

Fig. 1. The system architecture

Message Queue Telemetry Transport (MQTT) [11] was selected as the token query protocol, as it is a lightweight protocol widely used in IoT devices. It provides adequate security for data in transit as it can utilize TLS as transport protection. The architecture requires device authentication so that only trusted devices are able to communicate with a *MQTT server*. A device *Authentication database* is denoted with Auth DB in Fig. 1

The PII is stored encrypted in a *Token Database* (Token DB). Encryption keys for the PII data are stored in a *Key Database* (Key DB). When tokenization is requested from a *Token Server*, it queries encryption keys from a *Key Server*. The Key Server will return a key in constant time for any request to protect the server against timing based side channel attacks. If the key does not exist in the Key DB it will be created. Key mappings in the Key DB are protected using keyed HMAC, which derives the key index from partial PII and authorization keys stored at the Token Server and a *PII Server*. The PII server acts as de-tokenization server.

2.2   Cryptographic Procedure

In our implementation SHA-256 algorithm is used as the hash function for the HMAC construct and AES-256 is utilized in CBC (Cipher Block Chaining) mode of operation for the PII data encryption. Keying is done in four steps as illustrated in Fig. 2, where Requester is the IoT device:

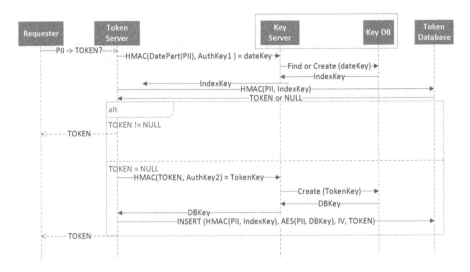

Fig. 2. The keying process

1. Token Server creates Authorization Key 1 (`AuthKey1`) to generate a HMAC construct from the date part of PII data: `HMAC(DATEPART(PII), AuthKey1)`. The authorization key is stored to the Token server and to the PII server.

2. This construct is used to query the Key Server, which will return an existing key (denoted as `IndexKey`) or generates a new one if this was the first request for the given HMAC. In this way, there will be 36525 valid keys in the key database, and thus the Token Database is divided into 36525 separately encrypted partitions. The `IndexKey` is then used to create an index query to the Token DB by utilizing the HMAC construct again, this time with the whole PII data: `HMAC(PII, IndexKey)`.

3. In the third step, assuming the PII data does not exist in the database yet, the Token Server will use a separate Authorization Key 2 (`AuthKey2`) to generate another key request to the Key Server. This HMAC construct hashes the newly generated token into a key identifier: `HMAC(Token, AuthKey2)`. The Key Server will return another key that we denote a `DBKey`. These keys are stored alongside the `IndexKeys` in the Key DB and are indistinguishable from each other.

4. The `DBKey` is finally used to encrypt the PII data in the Token Database. This allows the detokenization server (PII Server) to acquire decryption keys for the PII data utilizing only the `Token` value and `AuthKey2`. The tuple in the Token DB is thus (`HMAC(PII, IndexKey)`, $ENC_{AES}($`PII, DBKey, IV`$)$, `IV`, `Token`). Here, the `HMAC(PII, IndexKey)` is used as an index to allow retrieval of the Token as described previously, `Token` is the generated Token in plain text to allow the PII Server to index the database, $ENC_{AES}($`PII, DBKey, IV`$)$ is the AES encrypted PII data, and the initialization vector `IV` is used to allow tokenization of data exceeding the cipher block size.

The system can be modified to provide additional transport security in case the transport from device to the Token Server cannot be completely trusted. Then, AuthKey1 is distributed to devices, and they calculate the HMAC to access IndexKey. Now, the Token Server can use this HMAC construct to directly query for the IndexKey, and return the Token to the device if it is found. Only if the Token does not exist in the system yet, is the PII data requested from the device. This reduces the window of sensitive data exposure considerably. In the case of small dataset like the Finnish Personal Identity Number, all the Token and Key data can be pre-generated in to the databases. This mode of operation is however susceptible to AuthKey1 leak.

3 Security Analysis of the Proposed System

The General Data Protection Regulation requires "appropriate technical and organisational measures to ensure the level of security appropriate to the risk". The regulation explicitly mentions pseudonymization and encryption of personal data as an advisable technical measure [4]. Our system provides technical measures that fulfils and exceed the requirements for ensuring the security of the PII data during the processing. The security of the system is built on several layers. The requirements of the server architecture follow industry standard best practices such as the PCI DSS Tokenization Guidelines [10] and Cloud Security Alliance Security Guidance [12]. Cryptographic algorithms are selected based on ENISA [13] and NIST [14] guidance. The security of the system requires that the servers and network are configured to allow only authorized access.

3.1 Attack Surface

The tokenization system provides high resilience against intrusions. High emphasis is given on attack surface reduction. The system only has three points of entry for legitimate and illegitimate access: the IoT device, the MQTT Message Server and the Cloud Control Interface. The Cloud platform and control interface are assumed to be protected by industry standard measures, which are outside the scope of this document. The IoT device is the hardest component to protect as it resides outside our control in the customer network. Therefore, material sensitive to the security cannot be stored in the device, and the device must not provide any open services. If attacker has access to the device, he/she will be able collect the PII data at the device input, and thus we cannot protect against it. The protection of the device is manufacturer's and device operator's responsibility. The MQTT Server is the only component that is reachable through Internet. It exposes only the secure-mqtt (TCP 8883) port and service.

3.2 Access Security

Connections to the MQTT Server must be authenticated and verified to be from devices authorized to access the Token Server. All other components of the service must allow connections only from authenticated and authorized components of the system as shown in Fig. 1. The connections between components of the service must be secured using TLS. The network of the Token Service must be separate from other networks, e.g. a separate virtual private cloud in cloud service, and it must only contain servers described in the architecture.

MQTT standard provides only plain username and password based authentication, although the connection is secured using TLS. Device authenticity is enhanced by utilizing an external authentication provider. This allows the system to provision per device credentials automatically instead of using shared key. Passwords are replaced with a key stored using key derivation function. Here, PBKDF2 (Password-Based Key Derivation Function 2) method is selected and parametrized following [12–14].

3.3   Architecture and Cryptographic Resiliency

The security of the PII data in the system is based on standard cryptographic constructs and the strict separation of keys from the protected data. The protected data is stored only in the Token Database and the keys necessary to decrypt it are in the separate Key DB. The authorization keys necessary to access the correct keys in the Key DB are stored in the Token Server and the PII Server, so when data is at rest, unencrypted access to it requires access to three separate servers. When data is in use, it is accessible in the memory of the using server. Thus, the memory must be overwritten as soon as processing ends. It should be noted that as we form the first key indexing value based on the date of birth, attacker is also able to construct this value for retrieving they key if he has access to AuthKey1 and is targeting a known person. The Key Server will return keys only in constant time for any request to protect the server against side channel attacks.

The cryptographic resilience of the system is also based on layered approach. The tokens are generated using secure random number generator, which does not take the PII data as an input and can thus be considered completely separate. The attacker cannot gain any insight into the PII data from the token itself. If attacker has access to the Token Database and can extract the data, he/she has to consider the values of a tuple individually and as a combination. The PII data itself is encrypted using AES-256 in CBC mode using a random initialization vector. The best known attack against the AES-256 can currently recover the key with time complexity of $2^{254.27}$ and data complexity 2^{40} [15], so the algorithm can be considered secure. The Token Database index is created from the PII data using HMAC construct with SHA-256. HMAC security is based on the hash algorithm's resistance against preimage attack and the length of the key used, up to the length of the hash algorithm output. Best known preimage attacks against SHA-256 can discover the input data only on 45 reduced round variant with time complexity of 2^{255} [16]. As long as authentication keys contain at least 256 bits of entropy the algorithm can be considered secure.

Final issue is that the tuple contains the PII data in two forms, encrypted and hashed. There are no known attacks that could utilize a hashed value as a known value to break a symmetric encryption. In our system, the value is further obstructed by the HMAC construct.

4 Architecture and Crypto-System Verification in the Real Hospital Environment Pilot

For the pilot, a device simulating the operation of PerkinElmer GSP product was installed in the medical network of hospital in southwest Finland. The medical network is operated by company providing IT services for the hospital. The pilot implementation was approved in the information security process of the hospital.

The implementation architecture is presented in Fig. 3, which follows the architecture shown in Fig. 1. Device producing the data is located in the hospital network. The outer firewall of the hospital networks has ports open required to access Microsoft Azure and Amazon Web Services (AWS) public clouds. Tokenization operations according the Sect. 3 are implemented in the AWS. However, these operations could be performed in any network e.g. company private network. The main issue is that tokenization operations and data processing are separated to different networks. For data processing Azure cloud is used. IoT Hub is the component responsible for communication with the device in JSON format, and is receiving the data. The data samples are processed with Stream Analytics, stored to Document DB, and visualized with Power BI.

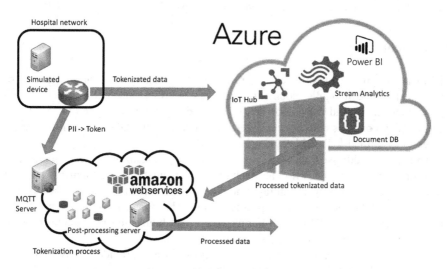

Fig. 3. Pilot implementation structure

A sample of the simulated data in JSON format generated by the device compared to the tokenized data ready for processing in the public cloud is shown in Fig. 4. The figure shows that the PIN value has been changed to the token value.

As the token is static, in addition to comparing single measurements against preset limits, the processing can perform a time-series analysis based on historical data of the same patient. The processing methodology and results are outside the scope of this document. When processing is finished, the data is passed to post-processing server.

This server will query the PII Server of our tokenization system with the token, and replace the token with actual PII data to allow the identification of the patient. The processed data is then forwarded into clinical database for diagnosis.

```
"SpecimenID": "BC123456",             "SpecimenID": "BC123456",
  "Info": {                             "Info": {
    "PIN": "120188-479P",                 "PIN": "oxUKFYC36RdssRE",
    "Tests": [{                           "Tests": [{
      "Test": "hCGb",                       "Test": "hCGb",

      "Concentration": "78.56",             "Concentration": "78.56",
      "Unit": "ng/ml"                       "Unit": "ng/ml"
    },                                    },
    {                                     {
      "Test": "PAPP-A",                     "Test": "PAPP-A",
      "Concentration": "784.3",             "Concentration": "784.3",
      "Unit": "U/ml"                        "Unit": "U/ml"
    }]                                    }]
  }                                     }
}                                     }
```

Fig. 4. Simulated device analysis data and tokenized analysis data compared in JSON format

5   Conclusions

Significant improvement in eHealth services in both quality and financial points of view are possible if public cloud infrastructures and their inherent advantages with global data centers and calculation power in big data analytics can be utilized. However, privacy concerns and especially requirements from the GDPR set difficult challenges to cloudified IoT architectures for eHealth.

This paper addressed these issues by proposing tokenization architecture and crypto-implementation for PII. The example implementation was Finnish PIN. The proposed system will allow the storage and processing of the PHI in the public cloud as the data cannot be identified to a specific person. The proposal follows general data protection regulation (GDPR) by offering secure and highly resilient architecture for the separation of health data and person identity.

The proposal was shown to minimize the attack surface, provide access security as suggested in [12–14], and to provide resilient architecture and cryptographic implementation with layered approach. The system has strict separation of duties where a security breach of a single component does not compromise the overall integrity of the system.

Acknowledgement. This work was supported in part by the Finnish Funding Agency for Innovation (TEKES) under the project "Industrial Internet Reference Architecture for Medical Platforms" (RAMP). The project is partly funded by industry partners Wallac Ltd/PerkinElmer Inc, Etteplan Oyj, Atostek Ltd, and Nextfour Group Ltd.

References

1. Industrial Internet Consortium. http://www.iiconsortium.org/
2. Microsoft. https://www.microsoft.com/en-us/internet-of-things/healthcare
3. Botta, A., de Donato, W., Persico, V., Pescapé, A.: On the integration of cloud computing and Internet of Things. In: 2014 International Conference on Future Internet of Things and Cloud (FiCloud), pp. 23–30. IEEE Press, New York (2014)
4. General Data Protection Regulation (EU) 2016/679. http://eur-lex.europa.eu/legal-content/en/TXT/?uri=CELEX%3A32016R0679
5. Ida, I.B., Jemai, A., Loukil, A.: A survey on security of IoT in the context of eHealth and clouds. In: 11th International Design & Test Symposium (IDT), pp. 25–30. IEEE Press, New York (2016)
6. Supriya, S., Padaki, S.: Data security and privacy challenges in adopting solutions for IOT. In: 2016 IEEE International Conference on Internet of Things (iThings), pp. 410–415. IEEE Press, New York (2016)
7. Sawand, A., Djahel, S., Zhang, Z., Naït-Abdesselam, F.: Multidisciplinary approaches to achieving efficient and trustworthy eHealth monitoring systems. In: IEEE/CIC ICCC 2014 Symposium on Privacy and Security in Communications, pp. 187–192. IEEE Press, New York (2014)
8. Henkilötietolaki 523/1999. http://www.finlex.fi/fi/laki/ajantasa/1999/19990523
9. Valtioneuvoston asetus väestötietojärjestelmästä 25.2.2010/128. http://www.finlex.fi/fi/laki/ajantasa/2010/20100128
10. PCI Data Security Standard Information Supplement: PCI DSS Tokenization Guidelines. https://www.pcisecuritystandards.org/documents/Tokenization_Guidelines_Info_Supplement.pdf
11. ISO/IEC PRF 20922. https://www.iso.org/standard/69466.html
12. Cloud Security Alliance, Security Guidance for Critical Areas of Focus in Cloud Computing. https://downloads.cloudsecurityalliance.org/assets/research/security-guidance/csaguide.v3.0.pdf
13. ENISA: Recommended cryptographic measures – securing personal data. https://www.enisa.europa.eu/publications/recommended-cryptographic-measures-securing-personal-data
14. NIST: Special Publication 800-175B: Guideline for Using Cryptographic Standards in Federal Government: Cryptographic Mechanisms. https://www.nist.gov/publications/guideline-using-cryptographic-standards-federal-government-cryptographic-mechanisms
15. Tao, B., Wu, H.: Improving the biclique cryptanalysis of AES. In: Foo, E., Stebila, D. (eds.) ACISP 2015. LNCS, vol. 9144, pp. 39–56. Springer, Cham (2015). https://doi.org/10.1007/978-3-319-19962-7_3
16. Khovratovich, D., Rechberger, C., Savelieva, A.: Bicliques for preimages: attacks on Skein-512 and the SHA-2 family. In: Canteaut, A. (ed.) FSE 2012. LNCS, vol. 7549, pp. 244–263. Springer, Heidelberg (2012). https://doi.org/10.1007/978-3-642-34047-5_15

Using Physical Unclonable Functions for Internet-of-Thing Security Cameras

Rosario Arjona[✉], Miguel A. Prada-Delgado, Javier Arcenegui,
and Iluminada Baturone

Instituto de Microelectrónica de Sevilla (IMSE-CNM), Universidad de Sevilla,
Consejo Superior de Investigaciones Científicas (CSIC), Seville, Spain
{arjona,prada,arcenegui,lumi}@imse-cnm.csic.es

Abstract. This paper proposes a low-cost solution to develop IoT security cameras. Integrity and confidentiality of the image data are achieved by cryptographic modules that implement symmetric key-based techniques which are usually available in the hardware of the IoT cameras. The novelty of this proposal is that the secret key required is not stored but reconstructed from the start-up values of a SRAM in the camera hardware acting as a PUF (Physical Unclonable Function), so that the physical authenticity of the camera is also ensured. The start-up values of the SRAM are also exploited to change the IV (Initialization Vector) in the encryption algorithm. All the steps for enrollment and normal operation can be included in a simple firmware to be executed by the camera. There is no need to include specific hardware but only a SRAM is needed which could be powered down and up by firmware.

Keywords: Internet of Things (IoT) · Security cameras
Physical Unclonable Functions (PUFs) · Trust and privacy in IoT

1 Introduction

Many IoT (Internet-of-Thing) security cameras employed nowadays are relatively easy to compromise. Some of them communicate without authentication tokens in plain text (even user credentials, including passwords, are transmitted in plain text). Besides, they accept firmware that is not digitally signed. Hence, they can be exploited for malicious purposes, such as spying or acting as remotely controlled bots to spread malware, for example Mirai, which produced a large disruptive DDoS (Distributed Denial-of-Service) attack at the end of 2016 [1]. In addition, they can suffer man-in-the-middle attacks known as virtual camera attacks, through software tools such as Virtual Webcam, ManyCam or Magic Camera, which are able to modify the image captured by the camera and to simulate captures at real time. This kind of attacks is especially problematic in surveillance or access control applications [2].

Thus, it is becoming increasingly important to include security functionalities into networked cameras: (a) authentication to ensure that the images do not come from a counterfeit camera; (b) integrity of the images to ensure that images have not been altered during communication and they are fresh; and (c) confidentiality to safeguard the privacy of sensitive data, which are subject to legal regulations [3–5].

G. Fortino et al. (Eds.): InterIoT 2017/SaSeIoT 2017, LNICST 242, pp. 144–153, 2018.
https://doi.org/10.1007/978-3-319-93797-7_16

Among the forensic techniques used to authenticate a camera, the simplest one is to evaluate the metadata based on the standard Exif (Exchangeable image file format) [3]. However, the Exif information is stored without protection so that it can be modified or removed. A networked camera can be also identified by its MAC (Media Access Control) address. However, MAC address can be also faked. Other more complicated techniques analyze the peculiarities that each particular image sensor could introduce in its images [6].

Cryptographic techniques are the standard techniques to provide security. There are two types of cryptography: symmetric and asymmetric. The symmetric cryptography techniques employ the same key to cipher and decipher, which should be secret for the sender and the receiver. The problem is the communication of secret keys. The asymmetric techniques employ two types of keys: public and private keys. One public key is associated to one private key and it is very difficult to obtain the private key from the public key. As an advantage, nonrepudiation is achieved and the communication of the private keys is not required. As a disadvantage, asymmetric techniques are computationally more complex, particularly for multimedia data. Hence, asymmetric techniques are used to interchange keys and to create digital signatures, and symmetric techniques are used to cipher the data [3–5]. Digital Rights Management (DRM) schemes are widely used to protect video streams on Internet but they employ cryptographic techniques that are computationally intensive for low cost IoT cameras. Hence, new solutions are being provided to integrate security into embedded cameras [5].

In any case, since security lies in the secrecy of the keys, TPMs (Trusted Platform Modules) have been developed which store and process sensitive data in a software protected domain (ARM Trustzone, Texas Instruments M-Shield, etc.) [5]. However, many cameras are deployed in unattended and human-accessible areas and therefore they are vulnerable to physical attacks that are able to read sensitive information from the memories of those modules [7, 8]. In addition to this, TPMs are specific modules that can be costly for many IoT cameras.

In the latest years, there is a new research line oriented to obfuscate secret keys with the aid of PUFs (Physical Unclonable Functions) [9]. PUFs allow reconstructing secret keys whenever required so that there is no need to store them in non-volatile memories. PUFs exploit variability in the manufacturing process of electronic circuits such as SRAMs, latches, D Flip-Flops, arbiters, ring oscillators, etc. Since the manufacturing process variability is random and particular of each device, PUF responses cannot be predicted and generate unique identifiers for each device. Hence, physical attacks as well as introducing fake cameras in the network are much more difficult because the secret keys are not stored but they are generated by PUFs.

In the literature, there are proposals for the application of PUFs to multimedia security which are based on the responses of image sensors. In [10], the PUF is a measured response of pixels to a defined incident light illuminating the charge-coupled device in a CCD sensor. In [11] PUFs are created by the dark signal non-uniformity of fixed pattern noise in a CMOS image sensor. Recently, PUFs extracted from electronic circuits have been applied to multimedia security. In [12] PUFs are based on the comparison of frequency counters of ring oscillators specifically implemented in the FPGA of a trusted visual sensor node. The solution provided in this paper is more general because it exploits PUFs based on an external SRAM, which is a typical component of any camera, so that no specific circuitry has to be included in the camera. The start-up values from the memory cells of the SRAM are employed as PUF. These values are lost when the memory is powered down and generated on the fly whenever required, without any need of storage of sensitive data. Besides, a trustworthy registration and firmware update can be employed with the proposed approach to make IoT cameras highly secure [13].

The paper is structured as follows. Section 2 shows how to use the PUFs in low-cost IoT cameras to cipher and authenticate the images captured. Section 3 summarizes how to obfuscate secret keys with SRAM-based PUFs as well as to generate nonces. Experimental results of a low-cost IoT camera based on a Raspberry Pi 2 model B provided with CMOS SRAM are shown in Sect. 4. Finally, conclusions are given in Sect. 5.

2   Image Integrity and Confidentiality

Data confidentiality is usually addressed by symmetric-key encryption. Since the amount of data is high in the case of images and image sequences, some approaches resort to encrypting compressed data or to the use of partial or selective encryption of specific regions or objects of interest [4, 14, 15]. In any case, encryption algorithms should be selected carefully to provide real-time performance with low-cost IoT cameras, which have constrained computing and memory resources. According to how the data are ciphered, ciphers can be classified into block and stream ciphers. Block ciphers process blocks of bits while stream ciphers encrypt bits individually. Among block ciphers, AES (Advanced Encryption Standard) was approved in 2001 as a US federal standard (FIPS PUB 197) and then, it was included in the ISO/IEC 18033-3 standard. Hence, AES is the dominant symmetric-key algorithm in many commercial applications. Particularly, the hardware of many IoT cameras contains an AES encryption module to off-load the CPU from encryption/decryption tasks.

Concerning integrity, Message Authentication Codes (MACs) are usually employed to obtain authentication tags (or cryptographic checksums). MACs can be obtained from block ciphers or from hash functions. The most popular approach in practice is to use a block cipher such as AES in Cipher Block Chaining (CBC) mode [16]. In this mode, the first iteration of the MAC algorithm is computed with the secret key, an Initialization Vector (IV) and the first block of the data to encrypt. The subsequent plaintext data blocks are xor-ed with the previous ciphertext block before they are encrypted. The MAC of the message is the output of the last round. Chaining mode is preferred to encrypt long messages such as images because each ciphertext block produced not only depends on the plaintext block (and the secret key) but also on the preceding blocks. Encrypting the same plain text using the same key produces the same cipher text if each block is encrypted independently. Chaining mode such as CBC is not usually implemented in hardware. In general, a firmware implementation of the block chaining mode uses the AES hardware accelerator.

CBC mode requires a 128-bit IV and the default key size is 128 bits. The IV should never be reused under the same key because it leaks some information about the first block of the plain text. The IV must also be unpredictable at encryption time. If an attacker knows the IV (or the previous block of the cipher text) before the next plain text is specified, the attacker can try to obtain the plain text of some block that was encrypted with the same key before, which is known as the TLS (Transport Layer Security) CBC IV attack.

Several solutions based on chaos theory, cellular automata and DNA computing have also been reported to authenticate encrypted images [17]. However, they do not follow cryptographic standards, so their security can be compromised [18].

We focus on employing standard authenticated encryption algorithms (such as AES-CBC) in IoT cameras, as illustrated in Fig. 1. The novelty is that the start-up values of the SRAM included in the IoT camera are employed to obfuscate the secret key of 128 bits and to generate the 128 bits for the IV, as will be explained in the following sections. Whenever the user (or a central server) requests image data from the camera, it power-ups the SRAM PUF and uses non-sensitive data to reconstruct the symmetric secret and to generate a nonce for the IV of the authenticated encryption block. Image and authentication and encryption data are obtained when they are requested and, in this way, the freshness of the image is ensured. The camera communicates the authenticated encrypted image data together with the nonce, so that a genuine receiver is able to decipher the information and verify its integrity with the same authenticated encryption algorithm, using the previously shared secret key and the nonce received. Nonces are used because variable IVs are preferred to increase security.

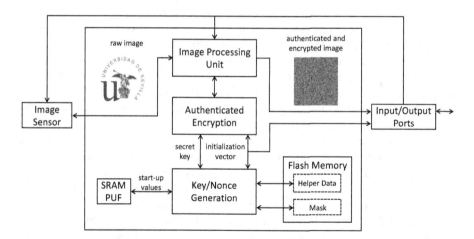

Fig. 1. Authenticated encryption of image data in IoT security cameras.

3 Using PUFs to Reconstruct Pre-shared Secret Keys and to Generate Nonces

Since the SRAM cells are composed of two cross-coupled inverters, their start-up values are imposed by the inverter which begins to conduct. The variations of the physical parameters of the transistors make each memory cell have a particular behavior. Such behavior is difficult to predict, to model mathematically, and to clone physically. When the SRAM is powered up, there are memory cells which tend to take the same value '0' or '1' (referred to as stable or 'A' cells) and other memory cells which do not take always the same value (referred to as unstable or 'B' cells). The start-up values of stable cells are suitable to obfuscate secrets while the start-up values of unstable cells are suitable to generate nonces [19].

The first step to make the secure IoT camera is to register the camera in a controlled environment. The start-up values of the SRAM cells are read several times and the position of 'A' and 'B' cells, $MASK_{AB}$, which is non-sensitive information, is saved in the device or in the central server. Details about the classification procedure can be seen in [19]. The helper data HD_K, also non-sensitive information, associated to a secret key K, are generated and also saved in the device or the central server. The procedure to generate helper data using code-offset techniques is described in [20]. A pre-shared secret key K is encoded using a linear Error Correction Code (ECC), such as a bit repetition code. The result is $K_{coded} = ECC(K)$. The XOR operation is used to obtain $HD_K = XOR[PUF_O, K_{coded}]$, where PUF_O are the start-up values of a set of stable cells. The ECC is needed because stable cells can show bit flipping, although with low probability. The helper data do not reveal information about the secret key if the bit string PUF_O is random. A required condition for randomness is that the number of 1's and 0's in the start-up values should be balanced. Otherwise, a debiasing algorithm should be applied (for instance, von Neumann algorithm) [21].

Once registered, the IoT camera can operate securely in a normal mode. The public data $MASK_{AB}$ and HD_K associated to the camera are employed to reconstruct the shared key K. The camera powers-up the SRAM, selects the same 'A' cells used in the registration phase with the $MASK_{AB}$ and obtains a bit string PUF'_O, which will be very similar to PUF_O. It carries out XOR $[PUF'_O, HD_K] = K'_{coded}$, where K'_{coded} is very similar to K_{coded} so that the last one is recovered (and, hence, the shared secret key) after applying the decoder of the ECC to K'_{coded}. The camera also selects the B cells with the $MASK_{AB}$ and obtains the nonce IV of the authenticated encryption block. The genuine camera communicates the authenticated encrypted image data together with the nonce, so that the genuine receiver is able to decipher the information and verify the integrity of the data and the authenticity of the camera because no other camera is able to reconstruct the shared key even with the public data provided by the server. Figure 2 (a) and (b) illustrate, respectively, the registration and normal mode phases. In the example, an ECC based on the repetition of 5 bits is employed.

The secret key shared between the camera and the receiver should change to increase security. Hence, after several times, a new secret key should be derived from the former one using a Key Derivation Function (KDF) that follows NIST recommendations. Details of this procedure as well as details of how to update the firmware of the camera in a trustworthy way can be seen in [13].

The quality of a PUF response is evaluated with two figures of merit [19]. One of them is reliability, that is, two responses from the same PUF (in this case the start-up values of the same SRAM cells) should be very similar. The other one is uniqueness, that is, two responses from different PUFs should be very different. The responses from PUFs can be compared through the Hamming Distance (HD). IntraHD values are

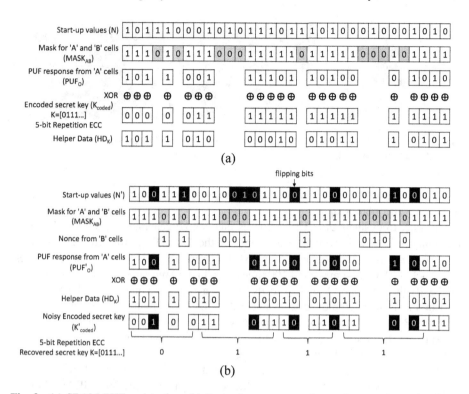

Fig. 2. (a) SRAM PUF registration. (b) Secret key reconstruction and nonce generation from SRAM PUF (a 5-bit repetition ECC is used in the example).

obtained by comparing the responses from the same SRAM and InterHD values are obtained by comparing the responses from different SRAMs. Ideally, the IntraHD values should tend to zero (that is, start-up values from several power-ups of the same SRAM are reliable) and the InterHD values should be around 0.5 (that is, the responses are unique of each device and have no bias). Thus, the distribution of the IntraHD values is well separated from the distribution of the InterHD values.

4   Experimental Results of the Proof of Concept

As a proof of concept, a low-cost IoT camera based on Raspberry Pi 2 model B was considered. It employs a Raspberry Pi Camera Module v2 which has an 8-megapixel sensor and can provide video as well as still photographs. The AS6C1008 CMOS SRAM which can be connected to the GPIOs of the Raspberry was employed as SRAM PUF. The Picamera library for Python was used to work with the camera module and the RPi.GPIO library allows working easily with the GPIO and, hence, the SRAM PUF. The PyCrypto library was used to manage the AES encryption algorithm and the Tkinter library was employed to program a Graphical User Interface to

Fig. 3. The IoT camera (on the left), the authenticated encrypted image (in the center), and the original image (on the right).

visualize the results. Figure 3 shows a photograph of the IoT camera and the processing result on a still photograph.

In order to evaluate the PUF responses that can be generated by the SRAM PUF, the analysis was done with measurements of the first 512 words from 20 different SRAMs (each SRAM is organized as 131,072 words by 8 bits). The start-up values from each SRAM were measured 100 times. The first 30 measurements were employed to classify the cells into 'A' and 'B' cells (thus generating the masks) and the rest of the measurements were employed to evaluate the PUF performance. After obtaining the 'A' and 'B' cells, the associated sequences were truncated to 2,537 and 1,126 bits, respectively, in order to generate sequences with the same length in all the SRAMs (those sizes were fixed by the smallest masks).

The PUF reliability was evaluated by computing the Hamming Distance between sequences composed of 2,537 start-up values of 'A' cells from the same SRAM. For 20 SRAMs and 70 sequences for each one, the total number of comparisons is 48,300 ($20 \times 70 \times 69/2$). The mean of the Hamming Distance values is 0.51%, which is a value close to the ideal value of 0%. For the evaluation of the PUF uniqueness, all the sequences of one SRAM were compared to all the sequences of the rest of the SRAMs. For 20 SRAMs and 70 sequences obtained for each one, the total number of comparisons is 931,000 ($70 \times 70 \times 20 \times 19/2$). In this case, most of the comparisons are located around 49.95%, which is close to the ideal value of 50%. Thus, the sequences have the same number of 1's and 0's and there is no bias. These results are illustrated through the IntraHD and InterHD distributions in Fig. 4(a). The SRAMs considered are suitable for obfuscating secret keys: the PUF responses of different SRAMs are quite different so that the helper data do not reveal information about the secret key and only the camera with the genuine SRAM is able to reconstruct the secret key.

A similar evaluation was performed for the generation of nonces from the SRAMs. The nonces were obtained from sequences composed of 1,126 start-up values of 'B' cells. The comparisons were 48,300 for the intraHD. The resulting distribution is shown in Fig. 4(b). Most of the intraHD values are around 12%. However, there are intraHD values distributed from 8.61% (minimum intraHD value) to 70.69% (maximum intraHD value). Therefore, sequences obtained from successive start-up values of 'B' cells of the same SRAM are sufficiently different to generate nonces.

The schemes for the enrollment and reconstruction of the secret key (described in Sect. 3) can be implemented as firmware in the IoT camera. The only hardware

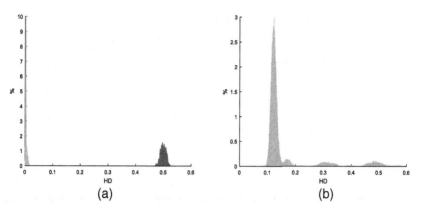

Fig. 4. (a) IntraHD (on the left) and InterHD (on the right) distributions for sequences composed of 'A'-cell start-up values. (b) IntraHD distributions for sequences composed of 'B'-cell start-up values.

requirement is that the camera has a SRAM that could be powered down (which is usual to reduce power consumption). At the enrollment phase, the $MASK_{AB}$ is created and saved, the camera user (or central server) establishes the master secret key to be used in the communication in a controlled environment (previously, for instance, to place the camera in its final location) and the helper data are created and saved. To cope with the maximum intraHD value measured for the 'A' cells (13.32%), the codeword (K_{coded}) is generated from the secret key by a 25-bit Repetition Error Correction Code. If the intraHD distribution is modeled as a binomial cumulative distribution and 13.32% is taken as the probability of bit flipping, the probability of a string of 25 bits with more than 12 flipping bits (the probability of reconstructing the key with an error in a bit) is as low as $4.5 \cdot 10^{-6}$. Since secret keys of 128 bits are considered as commented in Sect. 3, 3,200 start-up values from 'A' cells are needed. Since the minimum percentage of 'A' cells measured in the SRAMs was 56.91%, 703 words are read from the SRAM. The start-up values from 'A' cells are selected from the 703 words using the $MASK_{AB}$ created and they are truncated to 3,200 bits to form the PUF response (PUF_O). The codeword (K_{coded}) is combined with the PUF response (PUF_O) by a XOR operation to result the Helper Data (HD_K). $MASK_{AB}$ and the HD_K are the only data stored. In the normal mode of operation, the 703 words are read again from the SRAM and processed to reconstruct the 128-bit secret key required by the integrated authenticated encryption algorithm, using the $MASK_{AB}$ and the HD_K stored. The $MASK_{AB}$ is also employed to select the start-up values from 'B' cells (128 bits) to obtain the nonce/IV required by the AES-CBC encryption algorithm.

Table 1 shows a comparison with other proposals in the literature also aimed at including PUF-based security into cameras [11, 12]. Our proposal is preferred whenever the hardware of the camera cannot be designed to integrate the PUF into the image sensor [11] or into the controller of the virtual sensor node [12].

Table 1. Comparison with other proposals.

Proposal	Average intra HD	Average inter HD	No. devices	Specific hardware
Image sensor PUF [11]	0.20%	49.37%	5	Required
Trusted visual sensor node [12]	1.40%	49.0%	9	Required
This work	0.51%	49.95%	20	Not required

5   Conclusions

This work proposes a low-cost security solution to provide authentication, integrity and confidentiality to the image data obtained from IoT cameras. The solution is based on the use of standard cryptographic modules usually available in the hardware of the cameras (AES module). The 128 bits required for the secret key and the 128 bits needed for the nonce/IV of AES-CBC are generated from the start-up values of a SRAM of the camera acting as a PUF. Experimental results of the intraHD and interHD distributions prove that the PUF responses of standard off-the-shelf SRAMs satisfy reliability and uniqueness requirements for the secret keys and variability requirements for the nonces/IVs. A simple repetition Error Correction Code is enough to correct the low bit flipping of the memory. An IoT camera with a SRAM that could be powered down and up can be registered and updated with a trustworthy firmware that implements the proposed solution. Since SRAMs are available in many sensors and actuators, the proposed solution can be applied to ensure the authentication, integrity and confidentiality of the data generated in many other IoT scenarios.

Acknowledgments. This work was supported in part by TEC2014-57971-R project from Ministerio de Economía y Competitividad of the Spanish Government (with support from the PO FEDER-FSE) and 201750E010 (HW-SEEDS) project from CSIC. The work of Miguel A. Prada-Delgado was supported by V Plan Propio de Investigación through the University of Seville, Seville, Spain.

References

1. Kolias, C., Kambourakis, G., Stavrou, A., Voas, J.: DDoS in the IoT: Mirai and other botnets. IEEE Comput. **50**(7), 80–84 (2017)
2. Chen, S., Pande, A., Mohapatra, P.: Sensor-assisted facial recognition: an enhanced biometric authentication system for smartphones. In: Proceedings of the 12th Annual International Conference on Mobile Systems, Applications and Services, pp. 109–122 (2014)
3. Li, C.-T.: Multimedia Forensics and Security. Information Science Reference, Hershey (2009)
4. Lian, S.: Multimedia Content Encryption: Techniques and Applications. CRC Press, Boca Raton (2008)

5. Winkler, T., Rinner, B.: Privacy and security in video surveillance. In: Atrey, P., Kankanhalli, M., Cavallaro, A. (eds.) Intelligent Multimedia Surveillance: Current Trends and Research, pp. 37–66. Springer, Heidelberg (2013). https://doi.org/10.1007/978-3-642-41512-8_3
6. Lukas, J., Fridrich, J., Goljan, M.: Digital camera identification from sensor pattern noise. IEEE Trans. Inf. Forensics Secur. 1(2), 205–214 (2006)
7. Sanlyde, D., Skorobogatov, S., Anderson, R., Quisquater, J.-J.: On a new way to read data from memory. In: Proceedings of the First International IEEE Security in Storage Workshop, pp. 65–69 (2002)
8. Choi, P., Kim, D.K.: Design of security enhanced TPM chip against invasive physical attacks. In: IEEE International Symposium on Circuits and Systems (ISCAS), pp. 1787–1790 (2012)
9. Herder, C., Yu, M.-D., Koushanfar, F., Devadas, S.: Physical unclonable functions and applications: a tutorial. Proc. IEEE 102(8), 1126–1141 (2014)
10. Shokrollahi, J., Martin, C.: Method for Authenticating a Charge-Coupled Device (CCD). Patent No. 8817123 (2014)
11. Cao, Y., Zhang, L., Zalivaka, S.S., Chang, C.-H., Chen, S.: CMOS image sensor based physical unclonable function for coherent sensor-level authentication. IEEE Trans. Circ. Syst. I Regul. Pap. 62(11), 2629–2640 (2015)
12. Haider, I., Höberl, M. Rinner, B.: Trusted sensors for participatory sensing and IoT applications based on physically unclonable functions. In: Proceedings of the 2nd ACM International Workshop on IoT Privacy, Trust, and Security (IoTPTS), pp. 14–21 (2016)
13. Prada-Delgado, M.A., Vázquez-Reyes, A., Baturone, I.: Trustworthy firmware update for Internet-of-Thing devices using physical unclonable functions. In: Global IoT Summit, (2017)
14. Massoudi, A., Lefebvre, F., De Vleeschouwer, C., Macq, B., Quisquater, J.-J.: Overview on selective encryption of image and video: challenges and perspectives. EURASIP J. Inf. Secur. 2008, 1–18 (2008)
15. Jeon, Y., Kim, Y., Kim, J.: Implementation of a video streaming security system for smart device. In: IEEE International Conference on Consumer Electronics (ICCE), pp. 97–100 (2014)
16. National Institute of Standards and Technology: Recommendations for Block Cipher Modes of Operation. NIST Special Publication 800-38A (2001)
17. Souyah, A., Faraoun, K.M.: A review on different image encryption approaches. In: Chikhi, S., Amine, A., Chaoui, A., Kholladi, M.K., Saidouni, D.E. (eds.) Modelling and Implementation of Complex Systems. LNNS, vol. 1, pp. 3–18. Springer, Cham (2016). https://doi.org/10.1007/978-3-319-33410-3_1
18. Caragata, D., Mucarquer, J.A., Koscina, M., El Assad, S.: Cryptanalysis of an improved fragile watermarking scheme. AEU Int. J. Electron. Commun. 70(6), 777–785 (2016)
19. Baturone, I., Prada-Delgado, M.A., Eiroa, S.: Improved generation of identifiers, secret keys, and random numbers from SRAMs. IEEE Trans. Inf. Forensics Secur. 10(12), 2653–2668 (2015)
20. Dodis, Y., Ostrovsky, R., Reyzin, L., Smith, A.: Fuzzy extractors: how to generate strong keys from biometrics and other noisy data. SIAM J. Comput. 38(1), 97–139 (2008)
21. Prada-Delgado, M.A., Vázquez-Reyes, A., Baturone, I.: Physical unclonable keys for smart lock systems using bluetooth low energy. In: 42nd Annual Conference of the IEEE Industrial Electronics Society (IECON), pp. 4808–4813 (2016)

Smart Wearable System for Safety-Related Industrial IoT Applications

Ali Hayek[1]([✉]), Samer Telawi[1,2], Johannes Klos[1,2], Josef Börcsök[1,2], and Roy Abi Zeid Daou[2]

[1] Institute for Computer Architecture and System Programming, University of Kassel, Wilhelmshoeher Allee 71, 34121 Kassel, Germany
{ali.hayek, samer.telawi, johannes.klos, j.boercsoek}@uni-kassel.de
[2] Department of Biomedical Engineering, Lebanese German University, Sahel Alma, Lebanon
r.abizeiddaou@lgu.edu.lb

Abstract. The Industrial Internet of Things enables the realization of modular, flexible and efficient production processes. Machines and production plants are networked over various communication channels and organize themselves in an intelligent way to create products tailored to the customer's specific needs. Highly networked system structures will evolve including the interference of humans as well as of machines. Apart from security, functional safety plays an increasingly important role in the networking of humans and machines. Especially in environments where humans interact with dangerous systems or moving in the same area as autonomous driving robots, it is very important to provide a maximum of safety. In this paper, a system solution is introduced, which detects the movement of persons, prevents collisions between autonomous driving machines and humans, and decreases the probability of potential hazards in the interaction between humans and machines, while the movement of all participants should not be restricted.

Keywords: Industrial Internet-of-Things · Safety systems · Motion detection
Smart wearables

1 Introduction

According to the ideas of the industrial Internet of Things (IIoT) a factory should be based on intelligent and modular units that cooperate closely together. Production plants are able to coordinate their manufacturing process independently, while communicating with production robots at the same time, and furthermore, they are able to organize their maintenance independently and to work on logistics tasks in terms of transport vehicles. Depending on their tasks, all elements of the production are equipped with sensors and actuators and they are networked over a sophisticated IT infrastructure. More and more parts of the workflow are performed by independently acting and autonomously moving robots. Therefore the interaction between human and machine is becoming increasingly important in such production plants.

© ICST Institute for Computer Sciences, Social Informatics and Telecommunications Engineering 2018
G. Fortino et al. (Eds.): InterIoT 2017/SaSeIoT 2017, LNICST 242, pp. 154–164, 2018.
https://doi.org/10.1007/978-3-319-93797-7_17

Particularly in the area of IIoT applications, where serious accidents can happen, the focus has to be put on the safety and reliability of a plant. Potential sources of failures have to be avoided and considered and corresponding safety measures have to be taken already in the developing stage, so that such failures become controllable. The safety of human beings and environment has to be guaranteed during the entire lifespan of a plant. To minimize the risk to human beings and environment, potential hazards and dangers have to be taken into consideration and analyzed. Production processes have to be monitored and controlled by a corresponding safety system. Such safety system has to meet strict requirements in context of functional safety as they are defined, for example, in the standard IEC 61508. An introduction to safety systems, referring in particular to safety-related system-on-chips (SOC), will be given in the Sects. 2 and 3.1.

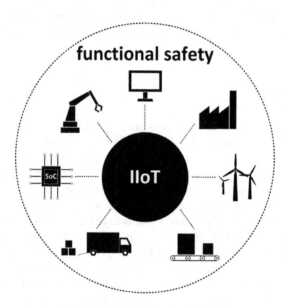

Fig. 1. IIoT and functional safety

In IIoT applications, human workers strongly interact with robots and machines. All of them take an active part in an industrial process, for example, in the same industrial hall or production line. Thereby the risk of incidents between the participants increases. To minimize this risk it is of high relevance that the robots and machines can react on human actions, for example, by detecting the motions of the human workers as early as possible and act in an appropriate and primarily safe way. In this context, several research groups and also companies around the world are currently working on robots and machines capable of interacting with humans as naturally as humans interact with each other.

However, the main focus of our research work is led on the exploration of miniaturized and safety-related systems, which can be used for smart wearables within a manufacturing plant for example. Inspired by the idea, this work presents the idea of having shoes equipped with a miniaturized and safety-related motion detection system, which can be worn by workers in an industrial environment. Such an apparently simple system requires a broad set of technical and safety-related capabilities like, safe and accurate motion detection, safe and secure wireless communication and compact size, which motivates the approach presented in this paper. To achieve this, smart shoes equipped with different kinds of sensors should capture the human walk, recognize patterns and calculate walking routes. Safe acquisition and processing of data as well as safe transmission of data and orders to the interacting robots is essential.

The main objective of this paper is a system design that provides the sensors required to analyze the position, velocity and motion data, evaluates these data and sends them to involved robots in a functional safe way. Furthermore is it able to drive the robots into a safe state in case of dangerous failure. The system size is compact and does not need any external physical connections so that it can be included into working shoes and so does not restrict the motion of the carrier but enables a maximum of flexibility to him (Fig. 1).

2 Safety Systems

Electronic safety systems should be designed and certified conforming to safety standards such as the standard IEC 61508 [2]. Therefore, several requirements on development process, and system architecture and design should be met by employing different methodologies. In this context, functional safety is playing an increasingly important role for IIoT applications, especially due to two aspects: On the one hand, processes have further been automated, machines acting autonomously, and on the other hand, the networking of plants and machinery is increasing and does not stop at factory gates. In order to reduce the risks for humans, environment and economics to an acceptable level measures have to be taken to avoid systematic errors, detect and control random failures and to reduce the risk of dangerous failures to a minimum. Therefore, a safety concept has to be created including the hazards that can be implied in a system and the hazards have to be detected by hazard and risk analyses. In order to classify the safety risk so-called Safety Integrity Levels (SILs) are used according to IEC 61508 - from SIL 1 (low) to SIL 4 (high). Depending on the risk particular measures have to be taken that serve to reduce the probability of default of the system so that the required SIL can be reached.

All the mechanisms, which are implemented for the risk reduction of a system, are together to be regarded as safety architecture of the system. The safety architecture is defined by the number of independent channels and the minimum number of properly functioning channels for error-free operation. For example, the 1oo2 architecture (one out of two) consists of two independent channels. To perform safety functions correctly, the channels are connected in such a way that one of them is sufficient for triggering the safety function [1].

The 1oo2 architecture is used for critical systems or systems with a high safety. Several specific parameters as, for example, the Probability of Failure on Demand (PFD), Hardware Fault Tolerance (HFT), Safe Failure Fraction (SFF) etc. [2] have to be met so that a high safety integrity level can be reached by safety architecture. For example, for a SIL 3 classification test coverage of 99% has to be reached. This high level of test coverage is often hard to reach when the hardware is not suitable for safety applications. In this case, integrated self-tests are used very often to reach the required test coverage. The required coverage can be reduced through the use of redundancy. If, for example, a system allows fault tolerance a fault detection of a SIL 3 system of only 90% has to be reached. A very common concept for fault tolerance is represented by the usage of 1oo2D (one out of two with diagnosis) architecture. The entire hardware - including the sensors - is provided in duplicate implying two systems that are independent of each other. The safety concept used in this work is based on a miniaturized safety system, which is developed in accordance the second edition of the standard IEC 61508. This edition was published in 2010 and introduced the term "on-chip redundancy" allowing the design of safety-related digital systems on a single silicon chip up to SIL 3. Systems which are relevant to safety-related functionality have to undergo a certification process.

Furthermore, inserting security aspects to safety architectures used in IIoT applications is of great relevance [3]. However, security is not in the focus of the present work, and will be part of future work.

3   Concept

The main idea behind the proposed approach is the design of a compact safety system, which is suitable for an implementation and use in IIoT applications in the field of functional safety. The system should be composed of an on-chip safety system and a system of different sensors. The on-chip safety system was particularly chosen because of its small size, high performance capacity and its wide range of interface. Moreover, the on-chip safety system does consist of an entire, safety-related programmable logic controller (PLC) and a communication processor on one single, compact chip. The sensor system consists of three vibration sensors to detect the motion of the carrier and a GPS sensor to measure the absolute position and the movement. Due to the integration of safety system and sensor system in one board, the whole system is very small and thus it could be used for wearable systems. Since the power supply can be provided by a battery and the communication is carried out using wireless interface (WiFi), there is no need of any physical connection between carrier and other systems.

Furthermore, due to the on-chip safety system it is possible to collect and process sensor data and operate connected actuators in a safety-related way. The connection to other systems and robots will be via WiFi. The user will be in the position to retrieve status data and he will be able to operate the connected periphery as well (Fig. 2).

The safety system complies with 1oo2D architecture as it is described in IEC 61508 [2]. This means that the safety system consists of two identical subsystems (channels) with diagnostic units. The diagnostic units continuously monitor the states of both channels and instruct them in a case of errors, in a way that the system is transferred into a pre-defined safe state. Apart from the redundant safety component, the on-chip safety system has to consist of an additional processor, which is coupled in a non-

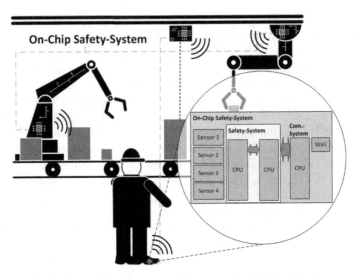

Fig. 2. Concept for smart wearable system for IIoT applications

interacting way to the 1oo2D system and serves for communication and monitoring processes.

The on-chip safety system and its architecture are described in more detail in Sect. 3.1. A description of the used sensors is given in Sect. 3.2. Furthermore, Fig. 3 shows the PCB-prototype of the implemented circuit design in this work with its main components. The size of the board is 130 mm × 75 mm, and it is supplied with 24 V which is transformed to 3.3 V and 1.8 V via the voltage regulator. Furthermore, redundant power monitoring elements are integrated in the circuit. If a voltage reduction is detected the safety chip will be reset in order to go the safe state.

Fig. 3. Embedded safety platform

The JTAG interfaces are required for programming the chip. Further battery-operated more compact design will be part of a future work.

3.1 On-Chip Safety System

The on-chip safety system consists essentially of two main components: a safety system and a communication system. While the safety system is based on a fully redundant safety-related 1oo2D-architecture with an on-chip-diagnosis unit, the communication system is composed of a simple processor serving as a black communication channel. All three processor systems are based on 8-bit processor. Both systems are decoupled from each other to achieve a freedom of interference. Each system has own interfaces for communicating with the outside world [4].

As a safety integrity level, SIL 3 is targeted as the maximum possible SIL according to the standard IEC 61508 [2]. In order to meet SIL 3 requirements, several measures and methods are realized at coding and implementation level, such as physical placement and routing.

Safety System: The target safety system consists of two identical processor units. Each of them possesses the same technical characteristics, parameters and its own memory, and communication interfaces. The communication interfaces can be served by one of the processor units. In the following the main feature of the safety system are listed:

- on-chip SRAM data and on-chip flash program memory, for each channel
- Timers, interrupt controller and on-chip debugger
- Digital inputs, digital outputs, PWM outputs and frequency inputs
- Serial communication interfaces

Communication System: The communication processor has the same technical characteristics and parameters as the safety system. Additionally, other communication interfaces are used. The main features of the communication system are the following:

- on-chip SRAM data and on-chip flash program memory
- Digital inputs and outputs
- Timers, interrupt controller and on-chip debugger
- Extended Serial communication interfaces

Safety Measures: In the following, special architectural and safety-related features of the presented chip are summarized:

- Safety-related subsystem based on 1oo2D-architecture with on-chip diagnosis: On-chip diagnosis unit and clock monitoring unit
- Memory Protection Unit
- Watchdog and power supply monitoring interfaces
- Hardware mechanisms for decoupling both systems

3.2 Sensors

Vibration as a definition is a dynamic mechanical phenomenon in which a periodic oscillatory motion is involved around a reference point [5]. Generally, the ability of a system to withstand vibration and shock depends upon "g" level the system can withstand. In that, a sensor-accelerometer is used to measure these "g" levels.

An accelerometer is a sensor that reflects and measures the physical acceleration experienced by a movable object due to inertial forces or due to mechanical stimulation. It is comprised of a mechanic sensing element engaged with a mechanism which converts its sensed motion into an electrical output signal [6].

The mono-axial accelerometer is based on the Newtonian mechanics. A mass "M" is moving periodical attached to a spring and damped by a viscosity damping element. The stiffness of the spring is given by "k"; the coefficient of the damping element is given by "b". The acceleration "a" is then a function of mass, stiffness, viscosity and deflection x:

$$a = -\left(\frac{b}{M}\right) * \dot{x} - \left(\frac{k}{M}\right) * x \tag{1}$$

In this model the acceleration is measured just by well-known parameters and the measured deflection. So there is no need of any external references, which could otherwise be a problem for the usage in safety-related applications (Fig. 4).

In this research work three "BMA180" acceleration sensors are used, which are manufactured by Bosch Sensortec. The "BMA180" is a digital sensor for the tri-axial

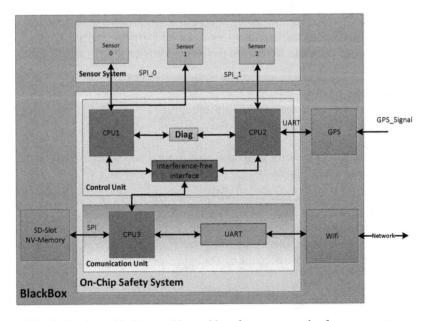

Fig. 4. Hardware black box with on-chip-safety-system and safe sensor system

measurement of static acceleration as well as dynamic acceleration. It provides a measurement range up to 16 g and can be configured in seven different measurement ranges. In addition there it provides measurement of the absolute orientation in a gravity field. The sensor is based on a two-chip assembly and the output acceleration signal is provided via 4-wire serial peripheral interface (SPI) as a digital full 14-bit.

The sensor system is based on 1oo3 safety-related architecture. Each of the three "BMA180" acceleration sensors transmits the data synchronously via SPI to the SIL3 chip, where two sensors are connected to CPU1 via SPI 0 and the third sensor is connected via SPI 1 to CPU2. Between the sensors and CPU the communication is based on master-slave principle whereby the CPU works as the master and the sensors as slaves.

For this work the 2-g mode is used for all three sensors. So the sensors have a resolution of 0.5 mg. The tilt sensing has an accuracy of 0.25°. In standard mode, the current consumption is 650 μA, and a supply voltage of 2.4 V is required [7].

The GPS module is connected via Universal Asynchronous Receiver Transmitter (UART) interface to provide the position and velocity of the carrier. This communication is not safety-related.

4 State-of-the-Art Techniques

The existing concepts of motion detection for wearable systems (shoes) by sensors are settled in the field of sports or for medical or therapeutical purpose so far.

For example R.E. Morley et al. presented in 2001 a system consisting of four pressure sensors, two temperature sensors and two humidity sensors to detect the motion of diabetes patients [8].

In the year 2004 I.P.I. Pappas et al. built a system that detects the different stages of walk by three force sensors and one gyroscope. Aim of this project is to find the best point to give an electrical stimulation and thus facilitate to walk for persons with steppage gait [9].

In 2008 Stacy Morris Bamberg et al. developed a system containing of many sensors. Amongst others velocity sensors measure the speed, gyroscope the direction, force sensors the force distribution under the foot sole and an electrical field sensor the height of the foot over the ground. However this system is not accurate enough to use it in an industrial environment. Furthermore the measurements are not functional safe in terms of IEC 61508 [10].

In the following years Stacy Morris Bamberg and her team improved this system for special application as e.g. for stroke patients [11] or to reduce the costs [12] but not for the use in industrial environments.

For the use in industrial environments safety mats equipped with pressure sensors are available [13]. These mats detect the presence of people on the sensing surface. So they can communicate with machines in order to avoid dangerous interactions between humans and machines. However, the persons can only move on predefined routes and not free in the whole industrial plant. Furthermore these mats are a barrier for some kinds of robots and the usage of heavy vehicles could damage these mats and thus lead to a malfunction of the safety system.

5   Results

First measurements were made with this system only in the right shoe. There was tried to detect different velocities and turning of the carrier in different directions. Just the x value of the vibration sensors was used to analyze the motion, because it was sufficient to detect these motions. For motions in all three dimensions as climbing stairs it is necessary to analyze the other values as well.

Figure 5 shows a comparison between walking and running. It is easy to see the different time between single steps (green lines). Also the time a step needs is shorter while the carrier is running. Combining these two parameters it is possible to determine the velocity and especially changings in the velocity of the carrier.

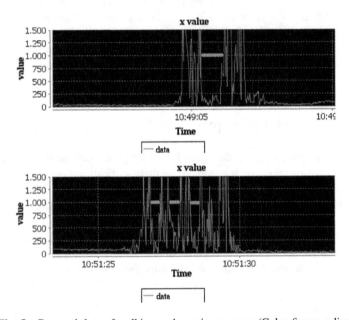

Fig. 5. Captured data of walking and running process (Color figure online)

Figure 6 shows a turn to the right in comparison to a turn to the left. The moving leads to an edge in the data while the step. The direction of this edge depends on the moving direction. A turn to the right results in a rising edge, while a turn to the left results in a falling edge. There is an edge in only one step in each data set because the system was just integrated in one shoe.

Both measurements show that it is possible to detect the most important motion patterns by this system. Due to the fact that it is possible to identify a changing in velocity and direction in real time, it is possible to predict the walking route of the carrier. This will allow avoiding collisions with autonomously driving robots and shutting down of potential source of danger for human workers.

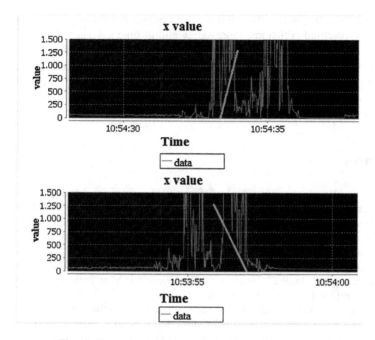

Fig. 6. Captured data of turn left and turn left process

6 Conclusion and Future Work

A compact system for detecting motion, processing data and control robots is formed. The whole system is integrated into one single board and is capable to be integrated in a normal working shoe. The system is able to meet the requirements of functional safety because of the on-chip safety system. The 1oo2 architecture and a reactionless decoupled system created by the safety and the communication system form the basis for the on-chip safety system. The sensors can detect very accurate the position, velocity and motion of the carrier and thus avoid collisions with robots or potential dangerous interactions. Furthermore, the system is capable to shut down interacting machines and so offers safety to persons working together with robots in the same industry hall or production line. The entire system is very compact. Because of its low power consumption it is possible to power it by a battery. Linked to the data transmission via WiFi, the system is mobile and thus provides a maximum flexibility to the carrier. Both parties, humans and robots, can move flexible in the whole area and are not limited by predefined routes.

Based on the flexibility and safety, there are many possible environments to use it. It is viable in all settings where people and robots move in the same area without fixed routes or processes. Another application is in the interaction between humans and potential dangerous systems such as laser or welding units. These systems could shut down autonomously if human workers enter a safety-critical area. Also it is thinkable to use it to optimize the pathways of all interacting robots dynamically in real time, which leads to less potential collisions, more safety and to time savings.

For future work the identifying of motion patterns could be improved and automated. Software could be developed that predicts the walking routes based on the recognized patterns and so guides robots on safe routes. Furthermore the system could be downsized in order to make it more comfortable to wear it the whole working day. Also the communication between several systems could be tested.

References

1. Telawi, S., Hayek, A., Börcsök, J.: Safety-related system for detecting and controlling vehicles motion. In: Third IEEE International Conference on Technological Advances in Electrical, Electronics and Computer Engineering, Beirut, pp. 80–84 (2015)
2. International Electrotechnical Commission IEC/EN 61508: International standard 61508 functional safety: Safety Related systems: Second Edition, Geneva (2010)
3. Preschern, C., Kajtazovic, N., Kreiner, C.: Built-in security enhancements for the 1oo2 safety architecture. In: IEEE International Conference on Cyber Technology in Automation, Control, and Intelligent Systems, Bangkok (2012)
4. Hayek, A., Machmur, B., Schreiber, M., Börcsök, J., Gölz, S., Epp, M.: HICore1: "Safety on a chip" turnkey solution for industrial control. In: 25th IEEE International Conference on Application-Specific Systems, Architectures and Processors, Zurich, pp. 74–75 (2014)
5. Fraden, J.: Handbook of Modern Sensors: Physics, Designs, and Applications, 4th edn. Springer, New York (2010). https://doi.org/10.1007/978-1-4419-6466-3
6. National Center for Biotechnology Information. http://www.ncbi.nlm.nih.gov
7. Telawi, S., Machmur, B., Suna, Y., Hayek, A., Börcsök, J., Pinders, U., Schreiber, W.: Network-based safety-related vibration and position analysis for railway vehicles: In: IEEE International Conference on Connected Vehicles and Expo (ICCVE), Vienna, pp. 155–161 (2014)
8. Morley, R.E., Richter, E.J., Klaesner, J.W., Maluf, K.S., Mueller, M.J.: In-shoe multisensory data acquisition system. IEEE Trans. Biomed. Eng. 48(7), 815–820 (2001)
9. Pappas, I.P.I., Keller, T., Mangold, S.: A reliable, gyroscope based gait phase detection sensor embedded in a shoe insole. Proc. IEEE Sens. 2, 1085–1088 (2002)
10. Bamberg, S.J.M., Benbasat, A.Y., Scarborough, D.M., Krebs, D.E., Paradiso, J.A.: Gait analysis using a shoe-integrated wireless sensor system. IEEE Trans. Inf. Technol. Biomed. 12(4), 413–423 (2008)
11. Howell, A.M., Kobayashi, T., Chou, T.R., Daly, W., Orendurff, M., Bamberg, S.J.M.: A laboratory insole for analysis of sensor placement to determine ground reaction force and ankle moment in patients with stroke. In: 2012 Annual International Conference of the IEEE Engineering in Medicine and Biology Society, San Diego, CA, pp. 6394–6397 (2012)
12. Howell, A.M., Kobayashi, T., Hayes, H.A., Foreman, K.B., Bamberg, S.J.M.: Kinetic gait analysis using a low-cost insole. IEEE Trans. Biomed. Eng. 60(12), 3284–3290 (2013)
13. http://literature.rockwellautomation.com/idc/groups/literature/documents/um/440f-um001_-en-p.pdf

Author Index

Printed in the United States
By Bookmasters